ASSESSING EDUCATIONAL PRACTICES

ASSESSING EDUCATIONAL PRACTICES: THE CONTRIBUTION OF ECONOMICS

Edited by William E. Becker and William J. Baumol

The MIT Press
Cambridge, Massachusetts
London, England

Russell Sage Foundation
New York

Printed and bound in the United States of America.

Library of Congress Cataloging-in-Publication Data

Assessing educational practices: the contribution of economics / edited by William E. Becker, William J. Baumol.
    p.   cm.
Includes bibliographical references and index.
ISBN 0-262-02398-9 (hc: alk. paper)
  1. Educational evaluation—United States. 2. Education—Economic aspects—United States.
  3. Educational productivity—United States. 4. Human capital—United States. 5. Teachers—Salaries, etc.—United States. 6. Econometrics. I. Becker, William E. II. Baumol, William J.
LB2822.75.S86   1995
338.4′561370′973—dc20   95-19803
                                                CIP

CONTENTS

FIGURES AND TABLES

PREFACE

The 1983 report *A Nation at Risk,* by the National Commission on Excellence in Education spawned many studies and proposals for reform of the nation's school systems. Despite the evident quality of many of these studies, we believe that they have not yet taken full advantage of the added insights that can be contributed by the economist's approaches to the study of educational issues.

This volume discusses several such issues for which the tools of economics seem to offer illumination. We have brought together a group of recognized scholars in economics who themselves have made significant contributions to the study of the economics of education, to describe the pertinent analysis and explain the methods of investigation. Unlike the writings they have produced for their fellow economists, however, here they have undertaken to write for the noneconomist, in an attempt to serve practitioners and researchers in education who are not familiar with the theories and empirical tools that an economist brings to an analysis of educational topics. They introduce theoretical and statistical methods suitable for the analysis of educational process and its consequences for students, teachers and society. They demonstrate a way of thinking that yields no dogmatic conclusions but, rather, focuses upon what is gained and what is lost from any proposed solution to an educational problem.

The thirteen economists who have contributed to this volume draw heavily from their own research in demonstrating pertinent current techniques of analysis. We are grateful to all of them for their contributions.

The manuscript layout and editing were done by Suzanne Becker, who is assistant editor of the *Journal of Economic Education.* As always, her patience, eye for detail and skill in the English language call for enthusiastic acknowledgment and appreciation. Word processing and manuscript expediting were done by Julie Marker of the Department of Economics at Indiana University. We are also indebted to her for keeping us all on schedule. Final art work was prepared by Graphic Services at Indiana University under the direction of Susie Hull to whom we are also grateful.

Finally, we must acknowledge the grants and support that were vital to completion of this project. The Russell Sage Foundation granted us indispensable funding supplemented by the support of the National Council on Economic Education via the *Journal of Economic Education.* Both the C.V. Starr Center for Applied Economics at New York University and the Office of the Dean at Indiana University must also be thanked for the resources they provided. To all of them we are delighted to express our deep appreciation.

William E. Becker
William J. Baumol

ASSESSING EDUCATIONAL PRACTICES

CHAPTER 1

THE ECONOMIST'S APPROACHES

William J. Baumol

William E. Becker

Those who are interested in education are not necessarily familiar with many of the research methods that have been designed or improved by economists for use in studies of educational practices and the institutions and markets in which education takes place. Economists clearly can have no claim to generally superior insights on educational issues. Yet there are several characteristics of this subject for which the tools of economists may offer some special illumination. Most obviously, the economist's training provides understanding of the financial side of education from which investigators trained in other disciplines may conceivably profit. Today colleges of education have courses devoted to the financing of schools, with many specialized books and articles describing the application of economics in its analysis. Economists have also learned a lot about market structures, which can be applied directly to education; yet, these tools of market analysis are unfamiliar to many practitioners in education. In addition, and perhaps even less recognized in education research, is the empirical economist's ability to cope with data that are incomplete and messy, using tools that were designed as substitutes for controlled experiments that are so difficult to carry out in the economic arena. This book is intended for the nonspecialist in economics and seeks to provide the education practitioner and education researcher with demonstrations of the tools of analysis employed by economists in educational areas other than school finance. It introduces the tools used in the economics of education to analyze the educational process, its consequences for students, and teacher inputs.

I. ECONOMISTS' TRADITION OF INTEREST IN EDUCATION

Economists have long applied their way of thinking and the instruments of their discipline to the study of education. In *The Theory of Moral Sentiments* (1759), for example, Adam Smith provided what may be the first published attempt at a discussion of education in terms of cost-benefit analysis:

> The education of boys at distant great schools, of young men at distant colleges, of young ladies in distant nunneries and boarding-schools, seems in the higher ranks of life to have hurt most essentially the domestic morals, and consequently the domestic happiness, both of France and England ... Surely no acquirement which can possibly be derived from what is called a public education can make any sort of compensation for what is almost certainly and necessarily lost by it. (Smith, 1759/1976; 363-4)

Smith's analysis clearly suffered from failure to seek any pertinent data but his comparison of costs and benefits indicates the thought process of much of subsequent economic theory. As the analytic tools used by economists grew in sophistication, and requisite data became available, it became clear that Smith's skeptical conclusion does not stand up in the relevant microeconomic models and the statistical tests commonly used by empirical economics to give quantitative substance to those models. By the 1960s the available data, in the hands of Schultz (1961), Mincer (1962), Gary Becker (1964) and other economists after them, showed that in economic terms alone the value of the knowledge and skills students acquire in school greatly exceeds the cost of their acquisition.

Surprisingly, as Gary Becker (1989) reports, educators resisted this work on the economic effects of education: a focus on jobs and earnings was considered too narrow to begin to encompass the many contributions of education to the student and to society more broadly. This is undoubtedly true, but surely the economic returns to education can hardly be considered totally devoid of interest, particularly in a world in which those who are poorly educated arguably face handicaps affecting every element of their existence, handicaps whose immediate source is to be traced in good part to the economic disadvantages to which inadequate education condemns them. In any event, if it can indeed be demonstrated that the economic benefits of education alone are more than sufficient to compensate for its costs, it must surely follow *a fortiori* that the full set of educational benefits cannot fail a cost-benefit test.

II. ON THE CONTENTS OF THIS BOOK: GENERAL OBSERVATIONS

Of course, evaluation of the costs and benefits of education is hardly the only educational topic to which economists have devoted themselves. The essays that follow, all of them especially commissioned for this volume, will serve to suggest the range of subjects that practitioners of our discipline have pursued.

Thus, these papers will introduce the reader not only to the methods economists use for the purpose, but also to the sorts of educational issues that attract their attention.

Still, as already noted, the central focus of the volume is research methods, and it will be noted that these fall into two broad categories. The first is made up of theoretical procedures: analytic methods based on logic and mathematics to investigate such matters as the efficacy of different tools for the stimulation of educational quality. In particular, the theoretical studies in the educational arena have centered about the prospective role of the market mechanism, and the contribution, if any, that it may be able to make to stimulate quality or contain costs. The second is composed of statistical (econometric) approaches: the methods that have been adopted or specially designed for the analysis of pertinent quantitative data. Ideally these two approaches go hand in hand, as demonstrated by the chapters in this book.

The nine chapters of this edited volume focus on what economists have learned about the assessment and practice of education at the precollege level. Both economic theory and econometrics are brought to bear on issues such as the best organizational structure for schools, class size, teacher turnover, merit pay, and similar subjects of importance both to educators and to policy makers.

III. ECONOMIC THEORY IN EDUCATIONAL RESEARCH

Educators, like engineers, physicians, and members of other highly skilled disciplines, tend to think of quality in terms of certification and standards. The idea behind competency-based education, for example, is that a student either has acquired a desired skill or he or she has not. Teachers and students are to keep working until the standard of compliance is met. Schools are to be structured for the smooth transition of students from one task to another in the sequential acquisition of skills needed to fulfill the competency requirement. The tasks, skills, and competencies requirement desired may be determined by the teacher, administrator, school board, and the state, with input from parents and community groups.

Competition among students or schools and relative comparisons have little or no role in the egalitarian funding formulas of public education. Typically, different degrees of achievement of a goal, the market value of skills learned, and the cost of achieving and demonstrating competency are not part of the rhetoric of competency-based education. The tenets of classical economic theory (in which resources are employed in the production of an output, and competition ensures that the allocation of resources among products best serves the public interest) appear to stand in stark contrast to this educational mindset.

The four chapters by Frederick Flyer and Sherwin Rosen; Rendigs Fels; Masato Aoki and Susan Feiner; and John Bishop illustrate the use of economic analysis in assessing the costs and benefits of alternative organizational forms for the delivery of education. These chapters give explicit attention to the role of competition and the possibility that it will promote the public interest. They point out that competition offers choice to consumers and requires a multiplicity of suppliers. They show that competition can only lead to "the best" allocation of resources if consumers are informed, the results of their choices are known with little delay, and independent suppliers succeed or fail in accordance with their performance in fulfilling consumers' choices. Each of the four chapters provides an analysis of the extent to which these characteristics apply in education.

Production Function Analysis

Schools are generally intended to accomplish more than mere sorting of students. They are expected to impart skills and knowledge. Economists refer to the skills and knowledge possessed by individuals as "human capital." This term is intended to draw attention to the fact that the time, effort and money spent directly or indirectly on education constitutes an investment -- a tying up of resources, in the hope and, indeed, the expectation, that it will yield valuable returns in the future, not just in financial yields, but also in the form of appreciation of such things as art, music and history, in contributions to health and safety and to accumulation of knowledge generally. As with physical capital (tools and machines), human capital is created by a production process that economists describe mathematically as "a production function." Such relationships for the education process have been studied empirically by economists. The nature of educationally-produced human capital, the production function describing how it is created, and the manner in which these relationships have changed over time are important considerations in planning for efficient use of school resources.

A representative production function relationship for classroom instruction may, for example, assume that the learning performance of a representative student depends on the student's aptitude, the student's study time, the educational attainment of the student's mother, the teacher's experience, the "treatment" undergone by the student (e.g., class time devoted to individual drill, class time devoted to group activities, the school environment, class size, peer grouping, and the like). In other words, the educational production function can be described as a listing of the set of variables that are assumed to be the prime determinants of the amount of human capital the student acquires as the result of schooling.

Flyer and Rosen, in Chapter 2, discuss economic efficiency in education, defining it, as it usually is in economics, as the ability of an organization to get the most out of its limited resources, implicitly using a production function framework for the analysis. In their chapter they argue that technology, not the organization *per se*, defines the outer limits of what is possible. The production function that we just described indicates that educational output depends on the joint efforts and abilities of teachers, students, and parents and, implicitly, on the ways in which these efforts complement each other. Flyer and Rosen argue that there is no reason to believe *a priori* that schools financed through the government sector will have access to or use production functions different from those operated by the private sector. But the way in which the components of an education are put together, the extent to which all participants have a stake in the outcome of the educational process, and the manner in which their interests harmonize with one another all have an important bearing on the final results.

Virtues and Shortcomings of Competition in Education

Debate on proposals such as school vouchers has led to reexamination of the conclusions of the economist's standard models about the virtues and shortcomings of the competitive mechanism. One of the most enduring products of economic theory is that in suitable circumstances a free competitive market for any good or service that is desired by consumers will ensure that those products are supplied to consumers as efficiently and effectively as possible. The theory is, however, far more evenhanded in its judgment than this conclusion may at first suggest.

The economic literature is replete with discussions of what is referred to as "market failure" -- circumstances in which the performance of the market is far from ideal. For example, it is pointed out that such unfortunate results can occur as a result of monopoly in product supply, ill-informed demanders, or effects external to the interaction of supply and demand. These "externalities" are the incidental side effects of some economic activity that can be damaging or beneficial to others, as when the production of electricity also generates smoke that leads to environmental deterioration in a neighborhood, or where the education of the bulk of a nation's population benefits even those who are not educated themselves. In short, the economic model of a market offers weapons both to those who favor policies designed to stimulate competition among the institutions that supply pre-college education and those who oppose it.

The chapters by Rendigs Fels, Chapter 3, and by Masato Aoki and Susan Feiner, Chapter 4, illustrate such different views and the use of economic analysis in assessing the benefits and shortcomings of competition in terms of the public interest in education. Despite the difference in their orientation, the chapters demonstrate that economic theory offers common grounds on which the debate can be joined responsively, in contrast with discussions in which the participants miss the substance in one another's observations altogether. Thus, both of these articles emphasize that competition can only lead to an efficient allocation of resources if consumers are informed, the results of their choices are foreseeable at the time when decisions are made, and independent suppliers succeed or fail on the basis of their performance in satisfying consumer choices. Both chapters provide an analysis of the extent to which these characteristics apply to education.

Fels considers the optimal mix of courses to be offered by schools of differing size. He observes that an important difference between firms operating in the private sector and public schools is that the latter are not subject to financial failure and are not driven out of business for using inappropriate technology or for producing the wrong product mix. He argues that in the absence of this penalty for poor performance it is difficult to determine which if any schools are doing the right thing.

Aoki and Feiner focus on the implications of school choice and voucher systems for students at risk; they are skeptical about the panacea that choice is supposed to provide. Families may be willing to trade off one school attribute for another, and schools may be able to capitalize on the fact that families buy a "bundle" of school goods. The families of students may be resigned to an inadequate local school, as measured by its students' test scores, for reduced travel time, after school programs, or ignorance of the exact nature of the tradeoffs.

A private business can reasonably be assumed to have one dominating objective: profit. Public schools have many objectives, one of which is the grading or screening of students on the basis of their performance. Economic theory suggests that employers should be willing to pay for the skill (human capital) embedded in their employees with the aid of the education process but the analysis by John Bishop, in Chapter 5, suggests that employers are not interested in precollege records. He argues that schools are not even equipped to provide those records when prospective employers ask for them.

Bishop argues that, because of collusion among students in the classroom, competition among students for grades cannot be expected to ensure commendable student performance. In addition, as long as potential employers show little interest in high school classroom performance, and schools are unwilling (and legally unable) to share relative performance records, there may be no vehicle other than standardized testing to stimulate student learning. Bishop's work does not rule out the role of competition in classroom testing and grading; rather, it emphasizes the missing ingredients whose absence prevents competition from providing effective incentives for student learning.

Outcomes for Students, and School Expenditures

A fundamental tenet of economic theory is the proposition that individuals respond to incentives. Yet some studies of student performance and other attributes of schooling appear to cast doubt on the applicability of this premise to the learning process. Studies investigating the social return to increased expenditure to education, that is, the benefit to be expected from an increase in expenditure per student, have preponderantly relied on standardized student test scores as their measure of the student's educational accomplishments. These investigations have generally yielded the disappointing result that increased funding provides little consistent and material educational yield.

Hanushek (1989, 1991), after reviewing 38 studies involving 187 test score equations, popularized the notion that per pupil expenditures, and key instructional variables represented by teacher/pupil ratios, teacher experience, adding material and supplies, and the like were unimportant in explaining student performance. Recently in an exchange with Hanushek (1994), Hedges, Lane, and Greenwald (1994a and 1994b) cast doubt on Hanushek's assertion regarding the irrelevance of per pupil expenditures. Their presentation of Hanushek's data, however, still suggests that the focal point of much discussion in education, the teacher/pupil ratio, is irrelevant in explaining student performance when measured by test scores.[1]

Using another indicator of student achievement, however, David Card and Alan Krueger, in Chapter 6, obtain dramatically different results. Instead of focusing on standardized test scores, Card and Krueger employ the earnings of students after they have left school. In addition to their own work, they have assembled a substantial number of other studies that also use subsequent earnings as their measure of the success of the educational process. Their review reveals a high degree of consistency among the studies in their estimates of the returns to an increase in the funding of a school. They find that a 10 percent increase in school expenditures (on teachers' salaries, reduction in pupil/teacher ratios, increased availability of teaching materials, and the like) is associated with a one to two percent increase in *annual* earnings for the student in later life. The fact that these increased earnings accrue to the recipients year after year means that the income gain to the students easily makes up for the earlier increase in teaching costs with which the financial gains are associated.

The time interval required to measure the earnings effects of various school programs is a serious complication besetting this approach. The clear advantage of test scores is that they can be obtained quickly and cheaply. Tests can be administered periodically to a cohort of students as it moves through grades one to twelve and then analyzed as a time dependent production function relationship, as demonstrated by Charles Link and James Mulligan in Chapter 7. The very low association between school expenditures on the educational environment and test results, however, raises the suspicion that those scores provide relatively limited information on the effects of education upon the student. As an alternative to test scores, Card and Krueger suggest that indicators such as course completion rates, graduation rates, college matriculation rates, and other such indicators of participation in the educational process, which are known to be associated with higher postschool earnings, can serve as relatively undelayed indicators of the economic returns to higher spending levels.

Card and Krueger's work suggests that teachers' salaries (which are directly affected by educational levels and experience) are related to future student earnings. The incentive effects of merit pay for teachers and administrators are considered further by Elchanan Cohn in Chapter 8. Merit pay may be a way to beat the problem caused by differences between the objectives of the parents and those of administrators and teachers. Merit pay can, in principle, provide an inducement for teachers' activities to conform more closely to the goals of the parents. To succeed in this purpose, however, merit pay requires a well-defined measure of the desired results. Schools produce many outcomes, only some of which are measurable. Even if a school's performance in terms of each of its goals could be measured, it might not be feasible to combine these measures into a single index, particularly because of the influence of the local political arena on the choice of goals.

Regardless of whether a pay system is based on merit, seniority, or some other measure, labor economists have long emphasized the importance of the rate of remuneration on an individual's willingness to work. The work of Peter Dolton and Wilbert van der Klaauw, in Chapter 9, serves to confirm this and to strengthen the case for the hypothesis that increased expenditures on schools can indeed improve education, contrary to the implications of many earlier studies. These authors provide strong empirical evidence that the higher the compensation levels offered in other occupations and the lower the salaries obtainable by teaching, the more likely it is that teachers will leave teaching and not return. Moreover, in these circumstances it is the best educated teachers who are most likely to leave, and the lower the teachers' earnings the sooner their departure from the profession occurs.

IV. STATISTICAL METHODS AND EDUCATION RESEARCH

Sir Ronald A. Fisher drew the attention of the research community to the importance of "random arrangements" in experimental design.[2] For many years Fisher was associated with an experimental agriculture station in England. A typical issue examined there was whether different types of fertilizers provide different yields. Fisher designed experiments in which plots of land were randomly assigned to different fertilizer treatments. By measuring the mean yield on each of several different randomly assigned plots of land, Fisher eliminated or "averaged out" the effects of nontreatment influences (such as weather and soil content) so that only the effect of the choice of fertilizer was reflected in differences among the mean yields. In many branches of educational research Fisher's random experiment concept assumed the role of the ideal. In textbooks on tests and measurements, for example, hypothetical classrooms (or students) were treated as if they could be assigned randomly to different instructional procedures.

Unfortunately, in many real applications strict adherence to the principles of Fisherian experimental design is impossible. In education research the data available are usually not generated by well-defined experiments employing simple random sampling procedures. Econometricians have learned that the difference between the handling of experimental data and data obtained wherever the opportunity arises is often a difference in degree, but not in kind. The proper computations for an analysis of variance, for example, are the same regardless of the manner in which the data were collected. Our ability to extract causal inferences from an analysis, however, is not unaffected by sample selection procedures. Unknown influences may well bias the results when an experiment does not employ random sampling. But, as stated by econometrician Edward Leamer, "No one has ever designed an experiment that is free of bias, and no one ever can."(1983, 33) We typically have to work with the data at hand.[3]

V. IMPERFECTIONS IN EDUCATIONAL EXPERIMENTS

Although dirty data problems can never be eliminated altogether, economists generally would prefer to have the benefits of random sampling in controlled experiments. It is clear that experimentation is, at least prospectively, a very powerful tool for education research, and it is entirely feasible in theory and in some applications, as persuasively argued by Orley Ashenfelter (1987). There is every reason to encourage education researchers to employ this tool as extensively as they can, making whatever use they can of the teachings on experimental design, and systematically building the appropriate collection of data into their procedure before any experiment is actually launched. Yet, there are at least four general reasons why one cannot count on obtaining the clean statistics derivable from perfectly controlled experiments and random assignment.

First, there really does remain a problem of public acceptability, particularly of experiments using a control group. As we have learned when trying to carry out some education experiments of our own, there are sure to be objections from both the students (or the parents of the students) who are assigned to the control group, as well as from those who are assigned to the treatment group.

Experiments in education are constrained by the ethical requirement that the subjects be informed that they are to participate in an experiment, and it is probably neither feasible nor moral to keep from them the character of the group to which they are assigned, if even on a random basis. It is to be expected that at least some of those who are sent to the control group will feel that they are deprived of the chance to profit from new and promising teaching techniques, while some of those assigned to the treatment group are sure to fear that they are about to be subjected to untried and perhaps even hare-brained teaching innovations, and that their learning will suffer as a result. The sad fact is that many of the deviations from traditional teaching practice that have passed for real teaching experiments have purchased their public acceptance at the expense of good experimental design, holding out, with little evidence, the promise that the participants will benefit.

Second, although not always acknowledged, virtually any education experiment, no matter how inadequately thought out, is likely to confer some benefits upon the participants. There are at least two reasons. Such experiments are apt to attract teachers of superior ability and to stimulate their enthusiasm. There also is the Hawthorne effect (sometimes called "the placebo effect"). It is now well documented that in social experiments, mere participation is virtually certain to elicit improvement in the performance of the participants. The fact that they know they are experimental subjects, or that they can observe that there has been some change in the way in which they are being treated, elicits changes in attitude and behavior that are generally considered beneficial. This phenomenon alone is enough to show that there are limits to the accuracy of the information one can hope to derive from social experiments. Control groups help, but the Hawthorne effect ensures that the behavior and performance observed in an experimental class will be different from those elicited by the identical educational procedures if they are later instituted in a routine manner. We can be fairly sure that their subsequent benefits to the students will be more moderate than those contributed by the earlier experiment, but we cannot be sure of the likely magnitude of the difference.

Third, the feasibility of controlled and randomized experiments is circumscribed by the environment in which we live, that simply does not allow all other things to be held constant, as required in a controlled experiment. What if a recession unexpectedly occurs during an experiment and some students' parents lose their jobs? Or consider, as another example, an experiment to determine the influence of family structure on student learning. Suppose an experimental class consists exclusively of students from traditional two-parent families. What is to be done with pupils whose parents unexpectedly separate during the experiment? How does one allow for any effect of the presence of these pupils upon the performance of their classmates? Or is one forced to do nothing and to continue to collect data on the performance of the class, knowing that the data have become slightly sullied?

Finally, experimental purity is inhibited by the fact that people respond to incentives. In the rare case in which data collection is designed in advance and treatment groups are randomly assigned, the experiment still cannot be deemed "controlled" or "purely random" because human subjects are apt to refuse to be treated like laboratory animals or inanimate objects. As discussed by Becker and Rosen (1993), inanimate objects, like shirts, can be assigned to one bin, which can be associated with a given process and expected failure rate, and can be compared with the contents of another bin, representing a different process and failure rate, with no feedback to the object itself. In the case of students, however, they may not just go passively to one "bin" rather than another. Attempts to control for such incentive effects cannot be handled easily even in supposedly randomized experiments.

Students may be assigned randomly to one treatment group or another but there is nothing to prevent them from physically dropping out or reducing their involvement as the result of their assignment or some other incentive to quit. Those who drop out after a program is under way can completely destroy random assignment at the start of the program. The simple notion that "value added" can be measured by the change in test scores from pretest to posttest can be undermined by dropouts between the posttest and pretest if the factors influencing the identity of those who drop out are also related to performance on the tests.

In sum, in education experiments other things are sure to change in a variety of ways, some of them simply unobservable to the experimenter. And this brings back to the education researcher the sorts of unclean data, which are subject simultaneously to a multitude of substantial influences and random shocks, with which the econometrician has had to work.

VI. ON ECONOMETRIC APPROACHES

Empirical economics has over the years arguably benefitted from its prime handicap: the unavailability of randomized experiments. The absence of experimental data has undoubtedly provided the incentive for the econometricians to exert their considerable ingenuity to devise powerful methods to identify, separate out, and evaluate the magnitude of the influence exercised by each of the many variables that determine the shape of any economic phenomenon. They have also been led to pioneer in the design of techniques to deal with the simultaneous relationships that often underlie economic data. In short, they have found it useful to design an armory of analytic weapons to deal with the messy and dirty statistics thrown off by real economic activities, seeking to extract from them the *ceteris paribus* relationships that empirical work in the natural sciences is able to "average out" with the aid of randomized experiments. At its most basic level the tools economists have exploited to extract the influence of uncontrolled variables begin with the disaggregation of descriptive statistics, as shown by Flyer and Rosen in Chapter 2, and then move into multiple regression, as designed by George Yule at the turn of the twentieth century, and introduced here by Fels in the Chapter 3 Appendix.[4]

Historically, regression studies have generally employed two types of data: cross-section data and time-series data. The term "cross-section data" refers to statistics for each in a broad set of entities in a given time period, for example the fifty numbers indicating how many tenth grade students were studying French in each of the fifty States in 1992. Time-series data, in contrast, are figures for a given entity in a series of different time periods, i.e., the total number of U.S. students who completed high school in each year from 1970 through 1991. Cross-section data sets have typically consisted of observations of different individuals all collected at a point in time. Time-series data sets have been primarily restricted to institutional data collected over particular intervals of time. More recently empirical work within labor economics has emphasized panel data, which are a combination of cross-section and time-series data. In panel analysis, the same group of individuals (a cohort) is followed over time. In a cross-section analysis things that vary among individuals, such as sex, race and ability, must either be "averaged out" by randomization or controlled for. But for a group such things tend to be constant from one time period to another and thus need not distort a panel study even though the assignment of individuals among treatment/control groups is not random.

Cohorts may decay over time. For example, a cohort of working teachers will not remain the same size over time because some will leave the profession and never return; others may leave and then return. The study of such time processes is known as hazard analysis, which has been described by Kiefer (1988).

There are many other econometric approaches with which this book does not begin to deal. Yet, the chapters in this volume do provide an introductory sample of those techniques, and an illustration of the insights that can be obtained with their aid.

Most of the studies in this volume employ or refer to multivariate analysis and multiple regression in at least one of its many forms. Sample selection problems from the pretest to the posttest are dealt with by Becker and Walstad (1990) and Peterson (1992). Such problems have been studied extensively by econometricians in their relation to multiple regression and this issue arises in several chapters in this book. For example, Card and Krueger, Chapter 6, discuss the selection problems that arise in assessing the earning effects of high school expenditure levels when some students do not finish high school and some do not go to work or to college. The concept of a hazard function that describes the proportion of individuals for whom there is the risk of change in status also has been used in the study of teacher turnover, as discussed here in the chapter by Dolton and van der Klaauw, Chapter 9. Link and Mulligan, Chapter 7, present an example of a panel data analysis involving reading test scores. They show how statistical problems caused by many variables that are difficult to control and measure in nonrandom, cross-sectional studies largely disappear in panel studies.

The essays in this book that make substantial use of statistical analysis all illustrate the ways in which economists have learned to adapt to the handicap of imperfect data far removed from those that would emerge from controlled experiments. It is from this adaptation and the analytic tools invented to deal with nonexperimental data that educational research can perhaps profit most.

VII. CONCLUSION

This brief survey of the contents of this book was intended primarily to identify the broad range of the methods that economists have applied in their work in general, and in their examination of educational issues in particular. It is this diversity of tools and their analytic power, rather than any particular conclusions about education that this book is about. Thus, readers who may disagree with the conclusions of some of the essays, or even those who reject them all, will, we hope, be able to profit from reading this volume.

NOTES

1. As observed by Hanushek (1994, 7), Hedges, Lane, and Greenwald report 152 estimates of the effect of the teacher/pupil ratios on student performance: 14 are positive and statistically significant; 13 are negative and statistically different from zero; 34 are positive and statistically insignificant; 46 are negative and statistically insignificant; and 45 are statistically insignificant but with no reported sign.

2. In what is possibly the most influential book in statistics, *Statistical Methods for Research Workers*, Fisher wrote:

> The science of statistics is essentially a branch of Applied Mathematics, and may be regarded as mathematics applied to observational data. (p. 1)
> Statistical methods are essential to social studies, and it is principally by the aid of such methods that these studies may be raised to the rank of sciences. This particular dependence of social studies upon statistical methods has led to the unfortunate misapprehension that statistics is to be regarded as a branch of economics, whereas in truth methods adequate to the treatment of economic data, in so far as these exist, have mostly been developed in biology and the other sciences. (1970, p. 2)

Fisher's view, traceable to the first version of his book in 1925, is still held today by many scholars in the natural sciences and departments of mathematics. Econometricians (economists who apply statistical methods to economics), psycho-metricians, cliometricians, and other "metricians" in the social sciences have different views of the process by which statistical methods have developed. Given that Fisher's numerous and great contributions to statistics were in applications within biology, genetics, and agriculture, his view is understandable although it is disputed by sociologist Clifford Clogg and the numerous commenters on his article "The Impact of Sociological Methodology on Statistical Methodology," *Statistical Science*, (May, 1992). Econometricians certainly have contributed a great deal to the tool box, ranging from simultaneous equation estimation techniques to a variety of important tests of the validity of a statistical inference, and economists such as Koopmans, Haavelmo, Chow, Goldfeld and Quandt have made fundamental contributions now in widespread use.

3. It is true that in recent decades there have been a few approximations to controlled economic experiments, such as the huge study of the negative income tax. Moreover, there is the ingenious and fruitful work using simulated experimental markets usually populated by graduate student subjects. Nevertheless, it remains true that projects like that on the negative income tax are far from perfectly controlled or controllable, and they are, in any event, much too costly and difficult to carry out to become widespread. And, surely, no one claims that the simulated markets of experimental economics are anything like clones of the markets of reality.

4. As discussed in Becker (1995), George Yule (1871-1951) designed "net or partial regression" to represent the influence of one variable on another, holding other variables constant. He invented the multiple correlation coefficient R for the correlation of y with many x's. Yule's regressions looked much like those of today. In 1899, for

instance, he published a study in which changes in the percentage of persons in poverty in England between 1871 and 1881 were explained by the change in the percentage of disabled relief recipients to total relief recipients (called the "out-relief ratio"), the percentage change in the proportion of old people, and the percentage change in the population. He obtained the statistically-estimated equation

Predicted change percent in pauperism $= -27.07$ percent
$+ 0.299$(change percentage in out-relief ratio)
$+ 0.271$(change percentage in proportion of old)
$+ 0.064$(change percentage in population).

Stephen Stigler (1986, 356-7) reports that although Yule's regression analysis of poverty was well known at the time, it did not have an immediate effect on social policy or statistical practices. In part this meager response was the result of the harsh criticism it received from the leading English economist, A.C. Pigou. In 1908, Pigou wrote that statistical reasoning can not legitimately be used to establish the relationship between poverty and out-relief because even in a multiple regression (which Pigou called "triple correlation") the most important influences, superior program management and restrictive practices, cannot be measured quantitatively.

Pigou thereby offered the most enduring criticism of regression analysis; the possibility that an unmeasured but relevant variable has been omitted from the regression and that it is this variable that is really responsible for the appearance of a causal relationship between the dependent variable and the included regressors. Both Yule and Pigou recognized the difference between marginal and partial association.

Today some statisticians assign credit for this identification to E. H. Simpson (1951); the proposition referred to as "Simpson's paradox" points out that marginal and partial association can differ even in direction so that what is true for parts of a sample need not be true for the entire sample. This is represented in the following figure where the two separate regressions of y on the high values of x and the low values of x have positive slopes but a single regression fit to all the data shows a negative slope. As in Pigou's criticism of Yule 90 years ago, this "paradox" may be caused by an omitted but relevant explanatory variable for y that is also related to x. It may be better named the "Yule-Pigou paradox" or "Yule-Pigou effect." Much of modern day econometrics has been devoted to this problem.

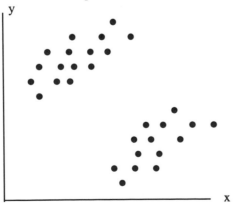

REFERENCES

Ashenfelter, O. 1987. The case for evaluating training programs with randomized trials. *Economics of Education Review,* 6 (4), 1987: 333-338.

Becker, G. 1964. *Human capital: A theoretical and empirical analysis, with special reference to education.* New York: Columbia University Press.

_____. 1989. A note on this issue. *Educational Researcher, 18*(4): 4.

Becker, W. 1995. *Statistics for business and economics.* Cincinnati: South Western Publishing.

_____, and Rosen, S. 1992. The learning effects of measurement and evaluation in high school. *Economics of Education Review.* 11(2): 107-18.

_____, and Walstad, W. 1990. Data loss from pretest to posttest as a sample selection problem. *Review of Economics and Statistics,* (February): 184-188.

Clogg, C. 1992. The impact of sociological methodology on statistical methodology. *Statistical Science,* (May): 183-196.

Fisher, R. 1970. *Statistical methods for research workers.* 14th ed. New York: Hafner Press.

Hanushek, E. 1989. The impact of differential expenditures on school performance. *Educational Researcher* (May): 45-51.

_____. 1991.When school finance 'reform' may not be a good policy. *Harvard Journal of Legislation.* 28: 423-456.

_____. 1994. Money might matter somewhat: a response to Hedges, Lane, and Greenwald. *Educational Researcher,* (May): 5-8.

Hedges, L., Lane, R., and Greenwald, R. 1994a. Does money matter? A meta-analysis of studies of the effects of differential school inputs on student outcomes. *Educational Researcher,* (April): 5-14

_____. 1994b. Money does matter somewhat: A reply to Hanushek. *Educational Researcher,* (May): 9-10.

Kiefer, N. 1988. Economic duration data and hazard functions. *Journal of Economic Literature.* (June): 646-722.

Leamer, E. 1983. Let's take the con out of econometrics. *American Economic Review,* (March): 31 -43.

Mincer, J. 1962. On the job training: Costs, returns, and some implications. *Journal of Political Economy, 70,* 50-79.

_____. 1974. *Schooling, experience, and earnings.* National Bureau of Economic Research, Columbia University Press.

Peterson, N. 1992. The high school economics course and its impact on economic knowledge. *Journal of Economic Education.* (Winter): 5-17.

Schultz, T. W. 1961. Education and economic growth. In N. B. Henry (Ed.), *Social forces influencing american education.* Chicago: National Society for the Study of Education.

Simpson, E. H. 1951. The interpretation of interaction in contingency tables. *Journal of the Royal Statistical Society,* (B 13): 238-241.

Smith, A. [1759]1976. *The theory of moral sentiments.* Reprint. Indianapolis: Liberty Classics.

Stigler, S. 1986. *The history of statistics: The measurement of uncertainty before 1900.* Cambridge, Massachusetts: The Belknap Press of Harvard University Press.

CHAPTER 2

SOME ECONOMIES OF PRECOLLEGE TEACHING

Fredrick Flyer

Sherwin Rosen

Economists have analyzed how education affects living standards. Education is an investment that creates economic value by increasing students' skills and future earning power. Impressive empirical evidence supports this point (Rosen, 1987b). Virtually every high income country in the world uses advanced technology and devotes large amounts of national income to develop and maintain a skilled, well-educated labor force. Low income, undeveloped economies invest much less in their human resources and are locked into more backward, less productive technologies. And within countries, persons with greater skills and education have larger earnings. Wage differences between more and less educated workers reflect personal productivity differences. They represent the financial return to educational investments and influence the incentives for parents and their children to acquire further education.

No one today seriously doubts the strong connection between the quality of a nation's human resources and its economic well-being. Yet the slowing down of U.S. economic growth in recent years and the demonstrated ability of other countries to catch up with us have raised fears that the productivity of our educational system is less than it should be. These concerns are manifest in the amount of public attention paid to declining test scores of college applicants in the 1970s and 1980s, current debates about the merits of national standards for schools, and the disappearance of the job base from the cores of major urban areas.

In some large sense, these fears raise fundamental questions about the efficient organization of schools. Are there alternative ways of allocating educational resources? The education of young children in America (and elsewhere) largely has been organized through the state and local government sector for well over one hundred years. But alternatives are presented to us all the time. There are significant differences in size, quality, and comprehensiveness among public school districts and systems, and there is extensive participation by religious and other private organizations in the education sector. Along with the worldwide trends toward privatization currently, there are parallel discussions of wholesale changes in the organization of education, especially in moving toward more decentralized organizational forms and methods for simulating a competitive market environment. For example, in Sweden concerns about technological competency and economic backwardness recently have led to radical reforms to decentralize public schools and stimulate development of a private educational sector.

Certainly the manner in which the provision of education is organized affects social outcomes. But the fact is that the economic problem to be solved is the same in all cases. Different forms of organization primarily relate to how the component elements of an education are packaged and assembled, because the set of alternative technologies available to produce educational services is more-or-less universal. The overriding fact is that education is a very labor-intensive business. This serves as the principle social constraint on its cost and social effectiveness, however it is provided. Education is labor intensive because students and their parents must devote large inputs of their own time and effort to produce it, and because substantial teacher inputs are essential for the educational process. If there is one key to understanding the economics of the educational sector, surely this is it.

Variations on this theme are developed in what follows. We begin with a brief discussion of some general aspects of economic organization. How do prices and consumer choices interact with technology and self-interest to produce different outcomes? Next we track how the real costs of elementary and secondary education in the United States have evolved over the past three decades or so, and show how this is related to changing teachers' salaries and other costs, as well as to changes in the student-teacher ratio.

To anticipate our major findings, the relative costs of elementary and secondary education in the United States have increased substantially over the past thirty years. Much of this is attributable to the huge growth in enrollments associated with changing demographic conditions. However, the per-student cost also has increased substantially, independent of scale. The major contributory factor here is that the pupil-teacher ratio has fallen dramatically (by one-third) since 1960. Declining relative wages of teachers have worked against this trend, but have been more than offset by substantial growth in specialized skills, teacher training, and certification. An increasing share of our primary and secondary educational resources apparently has been devoted to accommodating and improving the performance of students who are inherently more difficult and more costly to teach. These system-wide changes add noise for assessing the causes and consequences of changes in gross value measures of educational productivity, such as test scores.

I. THE ECONOMIC ORGANIZATION OF SCHOOLS

Economic efficiency refers to the ability of an organization to get the most out of its limited resources. Technology, not organization per se, defines the outer limits of what is possible. For instance, educational output always depends on the joint efforts and abilities of teachers, students, and parents, and how these efforts complement each other, irrespective of whether the school is financed through the government or the private sector, or whether it is conducted in a one-room school or in a big city system. The way in which the components of an education are put together, the extent to which all participants have a stake in system outcomes, and how their interests harmonize with each other have important bearings on final results. Here is where organization makes a real difference.

Organizational forms are constantly evolving in a decentralized economic system, something like a Darwinian natural selection process. Experimentation by individuals motivated to gain advantage over competitors occasionally results in finding better ways of doing things. These innovations improve social performance by eliminating less efficient competitors. They provoke survivors and new entrants to adopt the new, more efficient methods. This may be one of the most important efficiency aspects of decentralized, market-like economic activity.

An example not too far from home illustrates this point. It is widely thought that the American college and university system is the world's best right now. It is also one of the world's most decentralized systems. In other countries, central governments play the major role in financing and directing resources in institutions of higher learning. In the United States, state and local government institutions compete with each other and with an extensive private sector for both students and faculty. It is no coincidence that these differences in organization produce much different outcomes.

II. COMPENSATION AND ORGANIZATION

The first economist to comment seriously on the social organization of education was Adam Smith, who in *The Wealth of Nations* critically discussed the nature of education during his own student days at Oxford and Cambridge in the eighteenth century. Smith had few, if any, positive things to say about those institutions. He left for the University of Glasgow as soon as possible, where he spent his most productive years as teacher and scholar. Many of the things that one can read in Smith periodically reappear in modern critiques of education at all levels, in books with such titles as *Profscam* and *Imposters in the Temple*, and in Congressional Testimony every now and again.

Oxford and Cambridge in Smith's day were rather sorry institutions, with few of the outstanding characteristics for which they are so well known today. Smith attributed the poor results to administrative and organizational inadequacies arising from the privileged status of these institutions. Internal governance and outside oversight did not effectively substitute for the absence of external competition from other universities in Great Britain. Smith observed that the teachers in those institutions were insufficiently motivated by the needs of students and that University administration worked to the advantage of teachers at the expense of students. It insulated teachers from outside evaluation and encouraged them to pander to each other in socially unproductive ways. It is amusing to note that the historical inspiration for a theme that has been repeated countlessly originated in 1776. It was a very good year.

Extraordinary thinker that he was, Smith did not rest content with mere criticism of the status quo. He had a concrete, revolutionary proposal for improving the situation. He felt that the insularity and lack of interest of his own professors in their students was caused by the absence of formal, explicit connections between teachers' financial positions and their customers' (students) assessments of their job performance. He made one of the earliest economic arguments for payment by piece-rates. Teachers would be motivated to give better service if they were paid directly by students. Then the instructor's income would increase with the number of students he could attract, and the interests of teachers and students would be better harmonized. This system was in place at the University of Glasgow and was an important consideration inducing him to take a position there.

In those days (and into the early twentieth century at Glasgow and a few other places), the custom was for professors to collect fees, usually in gold coin, directly from students who enrolled in a course on the first day of class. These payments are akin to an author's royalty on the sales of a book: Few would buy it if they already had read it. Books and educational services have marketable value only in prospect and before the fact. Every society evolves elaborate information systems to evaluate those prospects. In Smith's scheme, teachers would be motivated to build up the reputation of their courses to attract future students. It should be pointed out that Smith's high reputation allowed him to fare quite well in popularity and class size.

We know that modern universities, born in Paris and Bologna of the Middle Ages, originated as private transactions (Rashdall, 1895). Groups of students with common interests would collectively contract for a teacher's services and lectures. Fees were privately negotiated and often went through agents and other intermediaries. The "school" itself was a kind of loose confederation that served as a clearing house for these transactions. It was something like a stock exchange or a shopping mall. It provided a wide menu of alternative choices for all concerned. As time went on, more formal administrative arrangements were set up and more uniform fees were established. The "shopping mall school" gradually gave way to the "amusement park school," where students were charged a single admission fee (tuition) and allowed to line up free of additional charge at the individual "amusements."

Some historians think that entry of the Church into the education business in the Middle Ages undermined the private teacher-student fee system and caused it, through the forces of competition, to vanish (Post, 1932). Church doctrine held it immoral to charge students. On some interpretations it also held that payment of teachers was immoral because their services and talents were thought to be gifts of God. Education was provided free to students in Church schools, and the quality was high enough to divert students away from other institutions.

Elements of the same argument sometimes are addressed to private and public education today. Without debating this point, we only note that piece-rates are far less common in modern industry than was true even fifty or one hundred years ago. Payment by time input (wages or salary) dominates payment methods in the U.S. labor force right now, and the Church had nothing whatsoever to do with it. Wage and salary payments had greater survival value than piece-rates in the work-place at large, as well as in the education industry.

III. THE STUDENT-TEACHER RATIO

The provision of education is characterized by certain economies of scale: It is efficient to teach students in groups. When society was agrarian, population density was too small to organize education extensively apart from households. Rich parents could send their children away to "boarding schools." This minimized transportation costs of shuttling back and forth, but very few families could afford it.

As urbanization and population density increased, the origins of modern elementary and high schools emerged as voluntary collectives. Parents would band together to hire teachers and build school facilities for their children, often through the auspices of a religious or social organization. This brought great advantages of the division of labor that decentralized economic transactions always allow. Specialized resources, especially professional teachers, were brought to bear on more extensive formal education. Illiterate or less educated parents could educate their children by hiring someone with specialized knowledge they didn't possess themselves. The introduction of public education on a broad scale at the local level was a natural outgrowth of these forces, with important redistributive elements aimed at loosening the strong ties between parental wealth and children's future opportunities.

IV. CHOICE AND EDUCATION

Scale economies in education are not sufficiently large to support the classic economic case for its public provision, as they are, for instance, for national defense. No citizen can choose to opt out of protection of the U.S. army against foreign aggressors: protection of one basically protects all. By contrast, education is an excludable good. In spite of its public provision, substantial choice is feasible in education and is widely observed. There are important elements of competition in education between the private and public sectors, and also among public school districts.

Economists have identified a market-like mechanism even for publicly provided education of children. Choice by parents is exercised by moving to the local jurisdiction or neighborhood that provides the desired educational services for one's children. This "voting-with-your-feet" mechanism (Tiebout, 1956), as it is sometimes called, applies to all local government provided goods, such as police and fire protection, but nowhere is it more important than in elementary and secondary education. Families pay a price for their choices in the form of different school taxes and property values in different neighborhoods and juris-dictions.

Our long tradition of local government provision of education and substan-tial parental involvement in school administration, combined with high residential mobility and quality differences that are available across jurisdictions mimic certain aspects of a decentralized, competitive market. It sets up a kind of im-plicit competition between schools and jurisdictions. Jurisdictions that do not satisfy constituents' educational demands lose their tax base through declining property values and outward mobility. They become less attractive to potential new residents with children. Jurisdictions providing better services become more attractive. In this way, resources tend to flow to more efficient providers and away from the less efficient.

As stressed before, competition among suppliers is one of the strongest forces working toward efficiency and high productivity in a market economy. Though local and state governments account for the lion's share of elementary and secondary school expenditures, an important form of competition is present.

V. SPENDING ON ELEMENTARY AND SECONDARY EDUCATION

Whether changes in institutional structure have weakened these competitive forces and impeded allocative efficiency is an interesting question given the recent run-up in educational expenditures. One of the most salient changes has been the level of union penetration into teacher markets. Union coverage was essentially nonexistent before 1960. Today collective bargaining agreements cover the majority of teachers. Other changes that may have had centralizing influences on decision-making processes include shifts in relative funding burdens between local and state governments. Schools now depend more heavily on state governments for financial support, a marked shift from just a few decades ago when local governments provided over sixty percent of school funds. How these changes have affected real education costs is difficult to determine. Whatever effect was present, it had to work through declining student-teacher ratios and increased teacher specialization. This is borne out when time-series data on school costs are carefully analyzed.

VI. RECENT TRENDS

During the 1959-60 school year, total U.S. expenditure on public elementary and secondary education, including current spending, interest on school debt and capital outlays, was approximately 16.7 billion dollars. By 1989-90 it had grown to over 229.7 billion dollars.[1] This 13-fold increase far exceeded the increase in prices over those years. The price level grew four-fold, so expenditures in terms of constant purchasing power dollars increased by a factor of three during these thirty years. Table 2.1 presents some details on the rise in real and nominal expenditures. Figure 2.1 shows that growth in school expenditures exceeded growth in real national output. The percent of Gross Domestic Product (GDP) going to secondary and elementary education increased very rapidly from 3.4 percent in 1960 to 4.8 per-cent in 1971. It remained high in the early 1970s, but declined substantially by the early 1980s, before rising again toward the later 1980s.

This wave-like pattern in the fraction of national income spent on elementary and secondary education in part reflects parallel movements in total enrollment, as illustrated in Figure 2.2. Aggregate elementary school enrollment (left-scale) peaked in 1970, when there were some thirty seven million baby-boom students in kindergarten through eighth grade. By 1977 this number had shrunk to thirty three million. Enrollment in secondary schools (right-scale) hit its peak a few years later, in 1976, as these large cohorts worked their way through the system.

The patterns in Figure 2.2 reflect well-known underlying population dynamics and fertility changes over the period. Enrollment rates of very young children have been extremely high over the entire period and secondary school enrollment rates increased dramatically in the 1950s and 1960s to approximately their current level, so changing participation rates account for little of the movements in Figure 2.2.

Figure 2.3 graphs total direct expenditure per student in real (1990) dollars. Expenditures per student increased steadily, albeit with an interlude in the late 1970s. Expenditures per student flattened out after the baby-boomers left the system but resumed the previous rate of growth by the early 1980s, even though enrollment continued to decline. Per-student expenditure rose substantially relative to median family income between 1960 and 1990.

TABLE 2.1 **Elementary and Secondary School Expenditures** (in millions)

	Nominal Dollars		1990 Dollars	
Year	Current Expenditures	Total Expenditures	Current Expenditures	Total Expenditures
1960	13,307	16,713	58,756	73,797
1965	23,073	28,048	93,076	113,144
1970	36,898	43,183	124,292	145,464
1975	60,825	68,846	147,767	167,252
1980	94,092	103,162	149,246	163,632
1985	139,285	149,400	169,187	181,474
1990	206,201	229,731	206,201	229,731

[1]Current expenditures include expenditures on administration, instruction, plant operations, plant maintenance, fixed charges, and other school services.

[2] Total expenditures include, in addition, capital outlay and interest on school debt.

Sources: Department of Education, National Center for Education Statistics, *Statistics of State School Systems* and the National Education Association, *Estimates of School Statistics.*

FIGURE 2.1: Educational Expenditures as Percentage of GDP

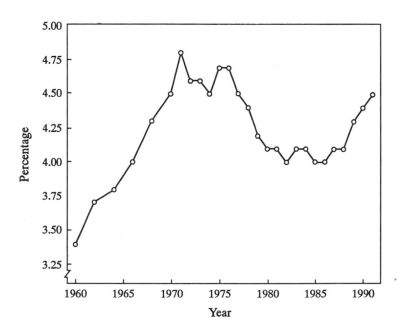

FIGURE 2.2: Elementary and Secondary Students (in thousands)

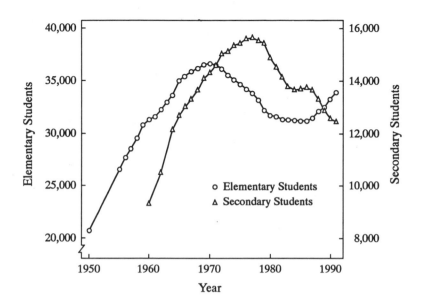

FIGURE 2.3: Real Expenditures per Pupil

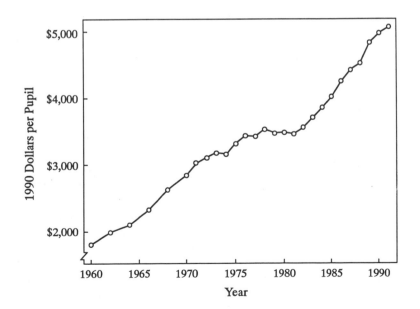

Direct expenditures differ from true economic costs. Published data on expenditures for labor, materials and services are reliable measures of the direct components of costs, but many other relevant direct expenditures and offsetting receipts are excluded. Table 2.1 does not include students' own direct expenses for books, transportation, home computers, and other goods and services. Nor does it include offsetting charitable gifts to schools, both in money and in-kind, or the value of various tax benefits (schools pay no property tax, and in some instances no sales tax). For the computation of economic costs, sizeable indirect costs of elementary and secondary education are excluded—the value of public library facilities used by students, the value of police services provided to schools, the value of volunteers' time, and numerous other services. And the capital outlays and interest on school debt included in Table 2.1 bear a tenuous connection to true capital consumption flows.

For secondary school education, the most substantial indirect cost is the value of students' time. Economic studies have found that earnings foregone by high school students are at least as large as direct costs in assessing the total costs of education to society (Schultz, 1960; Parsons, 1974). Because this conceptual issue is so well known and the problems of estimating students' foregone earnings are so complex, these (and other) indirect costs are not included in the subsequent calculations.

VII. THE DIRECT ECONOMIC COSTS OF EDUCATION

Data on current school expenditures are combined with estimated direct costs borne by students and their families, the value of school tax exemptions, capital depreciation, and foregone rent to calculate more comprehensive economic estimates of direct costs. Estimates of student-paid transportation are extrapolated from cost data on school-provided transportation in the *Digest of Education Statistics*, by assuming that students who do not use school-provided services have the same average costs as those who do.

Student expenditures on books and school supplies are estimated by assuming that secondary students purchase twelve books a year and that elementary students purchase six books a year. The yearly cost per book comes from the National Center of Education Statistics, *Statistics of Public School Libraries / Media Centers*, assuming that the average cost of a book purchased by elementary or secondary school libraries equals the average cost per book purchased by their students.

The social costs of tax exemptions, foregone rent on school real estate, and depreciation on buildings and equipment are obtained from Cohen and Geske's (1990) estimates of school property values. We assume that capital user costs are ten percent of property values. Costs are allocated to elementary and secondary schools in proportion to relative numbers of classrooms employed, calculated as aggregate enrollment at each level divided by the published student-teacher ratio.

Classrooms employed are also used to allocate costs of school administration, plant operation and maintenance, fixed charges, and other services by levels.

Real direct costs and their components for ten-year intervals appear in Table 2.2.   The near tripling of real direct costs over the three decades for both elementary and secondary schools largely was driven by growth in the costs of teachers.

The data are expressed on a per-pupil basis in Table 2.3. Between 1960 and 1990, costs per student increased by a factor of 2.5 for elementary schools, and by 2.2 for secondary schools. To put these figures in a more familiar context, the average cost of keeping a student for one year in elementary school represent- ed 6.7 percent of median family income in 1960, or about three-and-one-half weeks' salary. By 1990 it accounted for 12.5 percent of median family income,

Table 2.2: Estimated Cost of Elementary and Secondary Education (millions of 1990 dollars)

Year	Instruction Costs	Imputed Rent and Depreciation	Transportation Costs	Student Purchased Books and School Supplies	Administration, Plant Operation and Maintenance, Fixed Charges, and Other Services	Total Costs (sum of last 5 columns)
Elementary Education						
1960	24,049.8	9,861.2	5,534.0	2,164.6	10,469.1	52,078.7
1970	45,910.2	13,298.1	8,285.9	2,536.3	21,286.1	91,316.6
1980	50,009.9	13,897.7	8,909.4	2,368.9	29,403.3	104,589.2
1990	71,069.3	15,456.9	12,326.2	2,087.8	45,984.2	146,924.4
Secondary Education						
1960	15,423.2	4,144.9	1,643.6	1,637.1	4,400.0	27,248.8
1970	37,291.6	6,616.9	3,235.8	2,522.1	10,591.1	60,257.5
1980	40,801.7	7,877.2	4,187.7	2,416.1	16,665.9	71,948.6
1990	47,159.6	7,512.1	4,655.7	2,022.4	22,348.5	83,698.3

Source: See text.

so the average family spent more than 1.5 months' salary to keep a child in school for the year. For secondary students, the percentages increased from 11.8 percent (about six weeks' income) in 1960 to 18.8 percent (almost ten weeks' worth) in 1990. Instruction costs are the largest component of both elementary and secondary school costs, and necessarily account for a large portion of the rise in total costs. The other large factor contributing to increasing costs was rising administration, plant operation, and maintenance expenditures. Consisting mostly of wage costs of nonteaching school employees, administrative, operation, and maintenance expenses grew almost four-fold during the period. Changes in other direct costs contributed relatively little to the rise in education costs.

Table 2.3: Estimated per Student Annual Cost of Elementary and Secondary Education (1990 dollars)

Year	Instruction Costs	Imputed Rent and Depreciation	Transportation Costs	Student Purchased Books and School Supplies	Administration, Plant Operation and Maintenance, Fixed Charges, and Other Services	Total Costs per Student	Cost per Student as a Portion of Median Family Income
Elementary Education							
1960	768	315	176	69	334	1,662	6.7%
1970	1,251	362	226	69	580	2,488	7.5%
1980	1,576	438	281	74	927	3,296	9.9%
1990	2,133	464	370	63	1,380	4,410	12.5%
Secondary Education							
1960	1,657	445	176	176	473	2,927	11.8%
1970	2,601	461	226	176	739	4,203	12.6%
1980	2,735	528	281	162	1,117	4,823	14.5%
1990	3,748	597	370	161	1,776	6,652	18.8%

Source: See text.

VIII. COST PER CLASS

Allocating the costs of education on a per-student, per-class basis provides a back-door approach to Smith's revolutionary proposal for educational finance. How much would each student have to pay per class to cover total cost and its components under existing conditions? No doubt Smith would have objected to this calculation, because he felt that expenditures would change for the better under his scheme. Nevertheless, posing this question illuminates the importance of the student-teacher ratio as a fundamental determinant of unit costs (see Rosen, 1987a, for elaboration).

Unit costs per class are estimated by summing annual costs of instruction, foregone rent, depreciation, administration, plant operation, maintenance, fixed charges and other services, and dividing it by an estimate of the aggregate number of one-hour classes taught during the year. Expenses tied to student transportation and school supplies are ignored in this calculation.

The number of classroom hours taught by the average teacher in a day is estimated as follows: The number of physical classrooms employed is calculated by dividing aggregate enrollment by the student-teacher ratio. The number of (hourly) classes per classroom is determined by the length of the school day. The N.E.A, *Status of the American Public School Teacher, 1985-1986*, reports that the school day was fairly constant over the period, averaging 7.4 hours in 1961, and 7.3 hours in 1986. Assuming that elementary school children require supervision throughout the entire day, and that secondary students take an hour off for lunch and personal time, about seven classes are met per day by the average teacher in elementary school and about six classes are met per day by the average high school teacher. The fact that there are approximately one hundred eighty days in a school year yields classroom hours per year for the average teacher.

Table 2.4 presents the estimates. Between 1960 and 1990, the cost of a single class increased by more than seventy percent in elementary schools, and by about sixty percent in secondary schools. The contrast with per-student costs in Table 2.3 is interesting.

First, annual costs per student relative to family income increased, but costs per one-hour class as a percent of median family income was basically flat. The reason for the different paths is shown in Figure 2.4. Average class size fell by one-third over the period. Rising per-student costs per class in Table 2.4, calculated by dividing cost per class by the student-teacher ratio, was spurred by both higher production costs per class and by declining average class size.

Second, increasing real wages of school teachers accounted for slightly over half the increase in costs per class. Increasing costs of administration and plant operation accounted for the rest. Administrative and plant operation expenses were a smaller proportion of total costs in 1960 than they were in 1990, but they increased proportionately more than instruction costs. Imputed rent and depreciation costs actually fell on a per-class basis over the period.

Table 2.4: Estimated Cost of a One Hour Class--Elementary and Secondary School (1990 dollars)

Year	Instruc- tion Costs	Imputed Rent and Deprecia- tion	Administra- tion, Plant Operation and Maintenance, Fixed Charges, and Other Services	Total Costs per Class	Cost per Class as a Percent of Median Family Income	Student Direct Cost per Class
Elementary Education						
1960	17.91	7.34	7.80	33.05	0.13%	1.12
1970	24.41	7.07	11.32	42.81	0.13%	1.74
1980	25.14	6.99	14.78	46.91	0.14%	2.33
1990	31.32	6.81	20.27	58.40	0.17%	3.16
Secondary Education						
1960	32.84	8.83	9.37	51.03	0.21%	2.38
1970	46.96	8.33	13.34	68.64	0.21%	3.52
1980	42.04	8.12	17.17	67.34	0.20%	4.06
1990	49.62	7.90	23.52	81.05	0.23%	5.67

Source: See text.

IX. TEACHER SKILLS AND TRAINING

Declining class sizes have been caused primarily by changes in the composition of students and changes in educational production, related in turn to changes in family composition and working mothers. We tentatively infer this from the domination of trends in Figure 2.4. Other things equal, one might think that the baby-boom enrollment bubble in Figure 2.2 would have strained capacity and resulted in increasing class sizes for those cohorts. Then class size would gradually decrease thereafter as enrollments declined. In fact, this pattern occurred in higher education, but not at elementary and secondary levels. Figure 2.4 implies that capacity at lower levels of education continually expanded by enough to counter demographic forces.

Smaller classes imply greater direct contact between teacher and student. Teaching methods have changed to accommodate special education students as well as to serve the social needs of students in general. Greater teacher training and specialization required for these activities are clearly observed in changes in the composition of earned degrees conferred to education majors. The portion of new education graduates with degrees in specialized teaching fields has grown substantially in recent years. Table 2.5 illustrates the trend between 1967 and 1980.[2] Newly conferred general education degrees accounted for 46.3 percent of all degrees in 1967 but only for 37.8 percent by 1980, whereas degrees in special education increased from 4.3 percent of total degrees in 1967 to 11.9 percent of total degrees in 1980. The proportion of new graduates earning M.A. and Ph.D. degrees also exhibited sustained growth, accounting for 32.9 percent of total degrees conferred in 1967 and for 48.1 percent in 1980.   The overwhelming majority of teachers do not have graduate or special education degrees, but the proportion who do is increasing over time. New entrants into the teaching professions have become more specialized and more highly educated over time.

X. RELATIVE EARNINGS OF TEACHERS

The increasing age of the stock of teachers and greater educational attainment of recent entrants into the teaching profession have produced upward pressure on average teachers' earnings. Despite these tendencies, the real average salaries of teachers did not significantly increase between 1969 and 1989. Therefore the increases in real instruction costs over the past twenty years documented above are largely attributable to increases in the aggregate number of teachers required by smaller class sizes. Figure 2.5 plots average real salaries over the 1967-1989 period for employed elementary and secondary teachers, and for college graduates.[3]   Real earnings of both teachers and general college graduates declined during the 1970s and rebounded during the 1980s, but teachers' average earnings increased relative to those of college graduates during the period. Earnings of teachers were smaller than earnings of college graduates in the late 1960 s and converged toward them by the late 1980s.

Figure 2.4: Pupil-Teacher Ratios

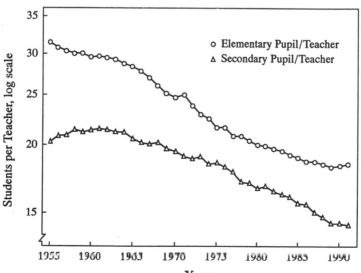

What factors caused the convergence between teachers and other college educated workers? Did returns to education and experience increase relatively more for teachers than for college graduates? Did average education levels increase more for teachers than for college graduates? What portion of the relative rise in earnings is attributable to each of these factors? Answering these questions requires examining how the economic and demographic composition of school teachers and college graduates changed over the period. We have done this by statistically analyzing the social-economic determinants of earnings of individual teachers and other college graduates in every year of the *Current Population Survey* between 1967-1989. Teachers have become much older (experienced) and more highly trained relative to college graduates over the years and this is what accounts for the convergence in Figure 2.5. Had teacher characteristics not changed, their average wage would have fallen substantially relative to college graduates.

Table 2.5: Education Degrees Conferred

	1967			1980		
	Bachelor's Degrees	Master's Degrees	Doctor's Degrees	Bachelor's Degrees	Master's Degrees	Doctor's Degrees
Education Degrees - Total	120,874	55,861	3,529	120,680	103,720	7,940
General Education Degrees (elementary, secondary, and junior high school)	67,985	15,081	398	51,370	34,723	1,731
Special Education Degrees	4,377	3,182	132	14,479	12,925	301
Other Education Degrees	48,512	37,598	2,999	54,831	56,072	5,908

Figure 2.5: Average Annual Earnings

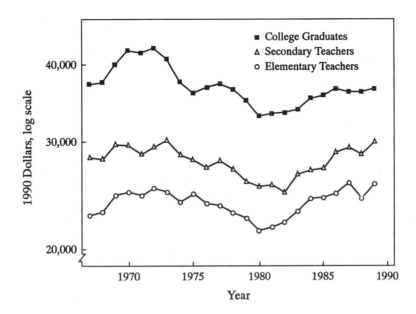

Figure 2.6 compares the *adjusted* or "standardized" earnings of college graduates to average earnings of elementary and secondary school teachers. The adjustment statistically imputes what the earnings of the average college graduate would have been if they had the same measured experience, education, and other characteristics as the average teacher in each year. These are expressed in ratio form in Figure 2.6. They indicate that if changes in demographic composition are controlled, then earnings of school teachers have been declining relative to college graduates. In 1967 elementary school teachers' average earnings were higher than what college graduates with similar characteristics would have earned. By 1989 that was reversed. College graduates with comparable characteristics were earning substantially more than elementary school teachers. A similar result is found for secondary school teachers in Figure 2.6, though the changes are smaller.

Another way of stating all this is that the returns to education and experience for teachers declined relative to other college graduates. Therefore, the convergence of unadjusted teachers' earnings to unadjusted average earnings of college graduates in Figure 2.5 is attributable to the fact that teachers have become older and more educated relative to typical college graduates. This is summarized in Figure 2.7, which plots the ratio of what teachers would have earned had their education, experience, etc., been worth the same as college graduates, to the average earnings of college graduates. These ratios have grown substantially over the years. We conclude that relatively increasing education and experience have more than compensated for the relative declines in the returns to education and experience for teachers.

XI. THE EFFECTIVENESS OF EDUCATIONAL SPENDING

Changes in per-pupil school expenditures over the past thirty years are easy to document. Assessing the relative effectiveness of the U.S. school system is a much harder question to answer. Has greater spending per student changed school quality? What definition of school 'quality' is meaningful and empirically measurable? Economists have examined school objectives and production process (Hanushek, 1979, 1986). What these objectives are and how these have changed over time are important considerations in ascertaining efficient use of resources.

Perhaps the trend toward smaller pupil-teacher ratios in elementary and secondary schools reflects changes in school teaching objectives. Certainly it reflects increasing accommodation of handicapped and special education students in our public schools as well as more in-school class preparation time for teachers. The point is difficult to prove, but it is likely that the average class size of a typical student also has decreased over time. The nature of classroom teaching has changed: counseling, discipline, and other social issues now make higher claims on teachers' time than used to be the case. The possibilities for changing objectives to change the nature of educational output makes efficiency assessments more difficult. Much recent research has relied on standardized test scores as a measure of secondary school output in different time periods. However, not enough attention has been paid to changes in the nature of educational output, and whether average test scores reflect these changes.

The time-series patterns of standardized test scores differ by test. Average SAT scores of college-going seniors fell substantially during the 1970s, as the returns to college education fell, and rebounded slightly in the 1980s when returns increased.[4] Though this same pattern is seen in most tests, the trends vary among them. For example, average standardized reading test scores of all students displayed no significant downturn during the 1970s. Moreover, year-to-year differences in test scores often are smaller than average differences in scores between boys and girls, illustrating the difficulty of developing yardsticks to measure schools' productivity. Even if there were reliable statistics that described student competency, comparisons across time are difficult, since students in separate cohorts can differ in ability, effort, tastes, resources, subject areas of emphasis, family circumstances, and other factors that are independent of school quality.

Figure 2.6: Standardized Earnings of Teachers

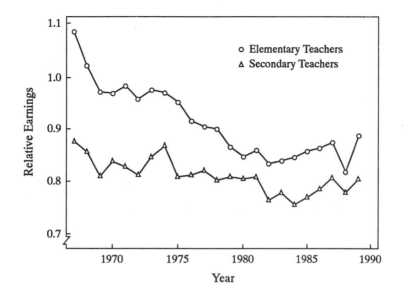

Figure 2.7: Relative Value of Teachers' Characteristics

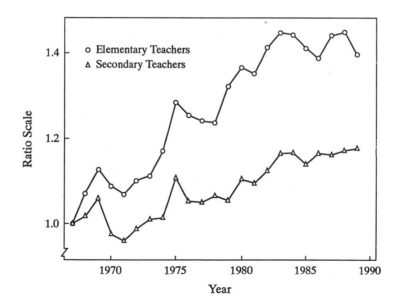

XII. DIGRESSION ON METHOD

Most of the calculations in this paper are quite straightforward and entail no sophisticated statistical techniques. However, the adjustments underlying Figures 2.5, 2.6 and 2.7 illustrate some of the methods economists employ to separate out several influences whose individual roles are likely to be concealed by the unadjusted data, thereby tempting the unwary to draw unwarranted conclusions from the raw statistics. For example, in the case we have discussed, the raw data may lead people to the unwarranted inference that the compensation of teachers has grown more generous with the passage of time. Let us see how one can investigate whether that conclusion is or is not warranted.

The adjustments presented in Figures 2.8 and 2.9 are derived from a "standardized" comparison of the average wages of teachers and average wages of college graduates. Most economic data are aggregated in some way or another. They are weighted averages of more disaggregated units. The time-series pattern of the aggregate can change for two reasons. One is that the various underlying disaggregated series used to build up the averages change. Another is that the weights change with no real change in the underlying disaggregated series. A standardized comparison basically removes the effects of changing weights on the aggregate series.

Figure 2.8: Adjusted Average Earnings of Elementary School Teachers and College Graduates

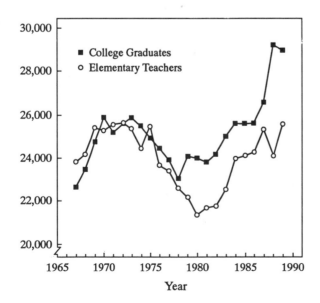

Figure 2.9: Adjusted Average Earnings of Secondary School Teachers and College Graduates

In the case in question we know that people with higher degrees and more work experience earn more than people with Bachelor's degrees and with less experience. We also know that entrants into teaching were becoming more highly educated over time, and that the average teacher became older and more experienced. Consequently the average wage of all teachers would be expected to change for these reasons, even if the wages of individual teachers with given education and experience did not change at all. Similarly for college graduates. There, the great entry of baby boom cohorts in the 1970s lowered the average experience of college educated labor and would tend to lower the average of college graduates' earning in those years, even if the earnings of individual age-experience groups had not changed at all. Basically a standardized comparison of two series adjusts for these relative weight shifts. It imposes a common set of weights on both series so that changes in weights between groups do not contaminate the comparison.

We proceeded as follows to separate the role of experience, education, etc., on teacher compensation. Regressions of the form $Y_{it} = \beta_t X_{it} + \epsilon_{it}$ were estimated separately for individual teachers and for college graduates in each year of the *Current Population Survey* from 1967-89. Here Y_{it} represents the earnings of person i in year t. X_{it} represents a vector of controls for education level (college or more), labor market experience, sex, race, city size, whether the person is a private or public sector employee, and the amount worked during the year. Experience is imputed from the person's reported age and education as experience = age - education - 6.0 and is entered as a cubic. β_t represents the vector of regression coefficients associated with these variables and ϵ_{it} is unexplained regression error, with zero expected value. Let β_{tC} denote the regression coefficient vector for college graduates in year t and let $\beta_t T$ represent the regression coefficient vector for teachers in year t. These coefficients can be interpreted as implicit prices or values of the corresponding X-variables in year t for each group.

Let Y_{tC} and Y_{tT} represent the average earnings in the samples of college graduates and teachers respectively in year t. Let X_{tC} and X_{tT} represent the average values of X for each group in year t. Figure 2.5 graphs Y_{tC} and Y_{tT}, the unadjusted mean earnings of each group. They are related to the mean X's according to the identities $Y_{tC} = \beta_{tC}X_{tC}$ and $Y_{tT} = \beta_{tT}X_{tT}$, so Y's can change because of changes in either the β's or the X's. The first standardized comparison uses a set of X's common to both series to take those changing compositional effects out of contention. Define $Y^*_{tT} = \beta_{tC}X_{tT}$ as the expected value of what teachers would have earned if their characteristics had contributed to their compensations the same amounts as those of all college graduates in each year. Compare this to $Y_{tT} = \beta_{tT}X_{tT}$, the actual average earnings of teachers. The series Y and Y* appear in Figures 2.8 and 2.9. The ratio of the two (Y_{tT}/Y^*_{tT}) is the fraction of pay that teachers give up on average each year to work as teachers rather than as general college graduates. Figure 2.6 uses the average yearly mean X's of elementary school teachers applied to college graduates β's for Y*, and the average yearly mean X's of secondary school teachers applied to β_{tC} for the Y* of secondary teachers. The X-weights vary from year to year in these figures. We have also experimented with a fixed set of X-weights, identical for all years, and with different functional forms, but the results are similar in all cases: the composition-adjusted wages of teachers declined relative to that of college graduates over the period.

Figure 2.7 shows another kind of standardized comparison. It compares Y^*_{tT} with Y_{tC} instead of with Y_{tT}. Specifically, it plots the ratios of $Y^*_{tT}/Y_{tC} = \beta_{tC}X_{tT}/\beta_{tC}X_{tC}$ for elementary and secondary teachers in each year, expressed as index numbers relative to their 1967 values. It represents the relative value of teachers' to college graduates' characteristics if both sets of characteristics had equal value in each year. In a sense it estimates what the typical teacher would have earned as a college graduate relative to the typical college graduate in each year, and shows how the X's alone affect the unadjusted means. The increasing patterns in Figure 2.7 clearly indicate that teachers were gaining relatively more experience and education compared with general college graduates over the period.

CONCLUSION

Real expenditures on secondary and elementary education more than tripled between 1960 and 1990. Rising school costs per student resulted from a decrease in the student-teacher ratio, a rise in the average age, education, and specialization level of teachers that increased their wages, and substantial growth in noninstruction labor services. A much larger share of a typical household's resources is now devoted to educating its children because per-student expenditures grew significantly more than median family income.

Despite the large rise in educational expenditures between 1967 and 1989, teachers' real wages declined relative to real wages of other college graduates, holding experience and education constant. This decline represented a relative loss of almost twenty percent (from peak to trough) for elementary teachers and less than ten percent for secondary school teachers. What impact these relative losses have had on the quality of the teaching labor force is a question that warrants further investigation. If attrition and entry rates in the teaching profession are sensitive to relative changes in the real wage, then substantial changes in the quality of the teaching force may have occurred. Some of these have been offset by increased training and experience of teachers. Also, the effects of changes in relative wages may also have varied across different subject areas, if teachers' opportunity wages varied by field. For instance, there is evidence that math and science teachers have had high attrition rates because of relatively high opportunity costs and egalitarian school pay policies (Murnane et al., 1991).

Overall, earnings of teachers have converged to the earnings of other college graduates because increases in average teacher education and experience levels have more than compensated for any loss in relative wages. Average levels of teachers' real earnings have followed the usual intertemporal pattern experienced by other college graduates, i.e. earnings declined during the 1970s and rose during the 1980s. The rebound during the last decade brought teachers' real earnings in 1989 close to its peak level some twenty years earlier.

NOTES

1. These and most other data in this paper are from various issues of the Department of Education, National Center of Education Statistics, *Digest of Education Statistics* and U.S. Department of Commerce, *Statistical Abstract of the U.S.* Estimated cost data for private schools (they account for 10 percent of aggregate enrollment) are included in the numbers reported here.

2. The data are from the Department of Education, National Center for Education Statistics, *Earned Degrees Conferred*, 1966/1967, 1979/1980.

3. A significant reason for the difference in average salary for teachers is that they work fewer hours per year than other highly educated workers. This is not an important factor for understanding the evolution of differences in earnings over time between the

two groups. The data are from the *Current Population Survey* annual March supplements over 1968-1990. Estimates are based on individuals who earned over $2000 (1990 dollars) during the year. The estimates for college graduates exclude teachers.

    4. See the two Congressional Budget Office (1986, 1987) publications for details.

REFERENCES

Anderson, M. 1992. *Imposters in the temple*. New York: Simon and Schuster.

Cohn, E. and T. Geske. 1990. *The economics of education, 3rd Ed*. Oxford: Pergamon Press.

Hanushek, E. 1979. Conceptual and empirical issues in the estimation of educational production functions. *Journal of Human Resources 14* (3): 351-388.

_____. 1986. The economics of schooling: Production and efficiency in public schools. *Journal of Economic Literature 24* (Sept.): 1141-1177.

Murnane,R., J.D. Singer, J.B. Willett, J. Kemple, and R.J. Olsen. 1991. *Who will teach?* Cambridge: Harvard University Press.

National Center for Educational Statistics, *Digest of educational statistics*, Annual, Washington, D.C.: U.S. Government Printing Office.

Parsons, D., 1974. The cost of school time, foregone earnings, and human capital formation. *Journal of Political Economy 82* (March/April): 251-266.

Peltzman, S., 1994. The political economy of the decline of American public education. *Journal of Law and Economics*: forthcoming.

Post, G. 1932. Masters' salaries and student-fees in the mediaeval universities. *Speculum* 7: 181-198.

Rashdall, H. 1895. *The universities of Europe in the middle ages*. Oxford: Oxford University Press.

Rosen, S. 1987. Some economics of teaching. *Journal of Labor Economics 5* (4,a): 561-575.

_____, 1987. Human capital. In *The new Palgrave dictionary of economics*. Eds. J. Eatwell, M. Milgate and P. Newman. London: Macmillan.

Schultz, T.W. 1960. Capital formation by education. *Journal of Political Economy 68* (December): 571-583.

Sykes, C. 1988. *Profscam: Professors and the demise of higher education*. Washington, D.C.: Regnary Gateway.

Tiebout, C. 1956. A pure theory of local expenditures. *Journal of Political Economy* (October):416-424.

U.S. Congressional Budget Office 1986. *Trends in educational achievement*. Washington, D.C:, CBO Study.

_____, 1987. *Educational achievement: Explanations and implications of recent trends*. Washington, D.C.: CBO Study.

U.S. Department of Commerce, Bureau of the Census, *Statistical abstract of the United States*, Annual, Washington, D.C.: U.S. Government Printing Office.

CHAPTER 3

MAKING U.S. SCHOOLS COMPETITIVE

Rendigs Fels

The United States offers the best higher education in the world, but there is intense dissatisfaction with our precollege system. Why? Students come to our universities from everywhere because we have the best. Why aren't our primary and secondary schools also world class?[1] What insights does economics provide for explaining the disparity between two educational systems in the same country and for devising policies to improve the quality of public schools? Economists in their studies of business and medical care stress the importance of competition. To what extent does this concept help explain the paradox? Examining the two branches of education as if they were industries comparable to other industries is enlightening.

The primary purpose of this book is to illustrate to noneconomists the research methods that economists use to study educational issues. This paper seeks to illustrate two such approaches. The body of the paper illustrates the use of economic theory for the purpose. It shows how standard economic analysis of the benefits of competition for the public interest can be extended to educational subjects. The appendix to the paper can be interpreted as a first introduction to the statistical approaches most commonly used by economists, with descriptions of the way in which those methods were used in several highly reputed investigations discussed in the text.

I. COMPETITION IN THE BUSINESS WORLD

The capitalist systems of the United States, western Europe and Japan have been hugely successful. The socialist economies of eastern Europe and the now defunct Soviet Union appear to be abject failures. Competition among producers in capitalist economies and government monopoly of production in socialist countries are by no means the only reasons, but they are   major reasons. (Bardhan and Roemer, 1992)[2]

The Lure of Profits, the Power of Bankruptcy

The lure of profits induces people to set up new businesses. Bankruptcy erases the mistakes and eliminates the obsolete. The twin processes of entry and exit, formation of new firms to exploit new opportunities and destruction of old ones that can no longer compete, serve vital functions. They stimulate existing firms to increase efficiency lest new competitors drive them into bankruptcy. They provide the means for introducing new products and eliminating production of old ones.   New firms in the early 1900s produced automobiles, driving workers out of the horse-and-buggy industry and into more useful occupations. In the awkward language of economists, organization of new firms and elimination   of unsuccessful ones facilitate the best allocation of resources: Increases in demand for old products are met by new firms as well as expansion of old ones; reductions in demand are met by bankruptcies as well as reduced output by survivors.

The contrast between the business world and public schools needs no comment.

Innovate or Perish

Monopolistic competition characterizes many American industries. Each firm has a slightly different product from its competitors. General Motors has a monopoly on Chevrolets, Ford on Fords, Chrysler on Dodges, but they all are close substitutes for each other, compete vigorously against each other, and suffer inroads from imported cars.

To survive, firms in such industries must innovate. Each seeks out its own special niche, appealing to a particular set of customers who can't be satisfied as well by any other's product. Having found a special niche, the firm must continue to innovate to hold onto it. Large firms spend immense sums on research and development. Small firms like family farms depend on research by government, universities, and other firms that produce R & D.

Again, the contrast with public schools needs no comment.

Consumer Choice

The American economy is geared to give consumers what they most want within the limits of their incomes. This is one of its great strengths. With few exceptions, consumers are the best judges of their own wants. The choices they make through their purchases force businesses to produce what the consumers want, to allocate resources in an efficient way.

Recent writings on innovations in precollege education such as those in Minnesota and East Harlem have stressed the advantages of giving parents a choice of schools. If parents can choose, the argument goes, their choices will clearly signal which schools are doing the best job, which ones the worst, and stimulate the poor schools to do better. Furthermore, parents know what kind of education best suits the differing needs of their children. As of now, only the affluent have much choice.[3] Most students have to go to the particular school determined by the school board.

Such arguments are plausible, but equal stress should be put on the supply side of competition. Consumer choice and competition among suppliers are complements. In fact, they are parts of a single process. Multiple suppliers without consumer choice is a possibility, as is choice without multiple suppliers.[4] But neither by itself is enough.[5] Competition requires both.

Consumer choice works better for some products than for others. It works well for restaurants. Diners know immediately whether they had a good meal and good service and can decide whether to go back. (True, they don't know how clean the kitchen is and must rely on the local government to protect them from unsanitary conditions.) Consumer choice works less well if consumers are poorly informed or the results of their choices will not be known for a long time or the public interest differs from consumers' private interests. All these characteristics apply to some extent to education. (Bredo, 1987; Levin, 1987.) Parents differ widely in their information about different schools; some of them know little or nothing. Parents will not know until decades later how much the education their children are getting will help them earn a living. The public has an interest in developing good citizens that is not identical with the private interest parents have in their children's welfare. The argument for parental choice of schools seems weak until we examine the alternatives. The evidence suggests that the alternatives are worse.[6]

Decision Making

Who makes what decisions -- an important problem for public schools -- varies widely in American business. In small firms like family farms, mom-and-pop grocery stores, and dental offices, the question hardly arises. The same is true of secular private schools like Groton or Exeter or Andover. Large firms like General Motors, IBM, and the big chains (A & P, Krogers, fast-food restaurants, bank holding companies, Columbia/HCA Healthcare Corporation) face the same problem as school systems: How much control should top management exercise? How much discretion should be delegated?

Answers vary widely. The chief lesson for schools from business experience is this: chains that are successful have a superior concept that can be replicated in location after location. The concept often includes hundreds if not thousands of details. The top management of a chain that has a superior concept succeeds by imposing it on all its subordinate units. But in the absence of a superior design that can be replicated again and again, especially in cases where local situations vary, lower units need authority to make their own decisions within broad guidelines.

For a long time thinking about public schools was dominated by the one-best-school concept. The current trend toward school-based decision-making reflects a failure, so far, to design a superior school that can be replicated.

Prices and Wages

The American economy relies heavily on prices to govern production. If demand for pork increases, its price goes up, inducing farmers to raise more hogs. The higher price also induces consumers to switch to beef. If the cost of producing computers goes down, prices go down also, inducing purchasers to buy more.

Wages and salaries are prices performing the same kind of function as prices of goods and services. Low incomes in agriculture throughout most of the twentieth century induced an enormous flow of population from farming to industry as rising productivity reduced the number of farmers needed to feed the population. High wages in the automobile industry attracted the workers needed during its period of great expansion. The increased demand for higher education after World War II raised the demand for professors. Salaries increased, inducing able people to go into academia. The old stereotype of the poorly-paid, absent-minded professor who could never make it in the real world became obsolete.

Competitive prices and competitive wages are vital for an efficient free-enterprise economy. Their role is muted in primary and secondary education. Public schools do not compete against each other for students on the basis of price; the price is zero. Within a school district, the schools do not compete against each other for teachers the way businesses in a city compete against each other for workers. Though school districts compete against each other for teachers, competition in the past has been limited because most teachers have had little mobility. Families that can do so take account of the quality of schools in deciding where to live. In many areas, this provides the principal competition among schools. The competition is limited because many families are not in a position to exercise this kind of option.

Economies of Scale and Scope

The most efficient size for a firm varies widely. Economies of mass production (scale) are enormous in some industries like automobiles, minuscule in others like vegetable farming. Schooling does not lend itself to mass production. The economies of scope, the advantages to producing different kinds of courses and having different grades under one roof, are limited. Some authorities think the best size for a high school is in the neighborhood of a thousand students. But limited economies of scale and scope cannot account for the limited success of American schools. American agriculture has been as much dominated by small firms as American education by small schools, yet the productivity of American agriculture has increased enormously in the last century. Its success -- in the sense of ever increasing productivity -- has come from a combination of government research, county agents who bring knowledge of the latest findings to individual farmers, and intense competition among the farmers themselves. An important difference between agriculture and schools is competition or lack of it. Although teachers colleges and universities conduct research and make it available to teachers, those who fail to adopt improved methods are not driven out of business.

A special kind of economies of scale may become significant for schools. The fast food chains -- McDonald's, Kentucky Fried Chicken, Shoney's, and many others -- consist of small units all essentially the same. Their success comes mainly from devising an attractive concept and perfecting the thousand details needed to make it profitable. Once a single unit has proved successful, it can be duplicated at thousands of other locations.[7]

Motels provide another example. In recent years chains of hospitals, e.g., Columbia/ HCAHealthcare Corporation, have proved profitable. Chris Whittle's Edison Project is an attempt to apply the chain organization to schools.

The low maximum size of schools and (to date) the absence of chains hinders the effectiveness of competition. In the business world, if Apple produces a better computer, customers buy it, and Apple expands production. In education, if all the students want to go to Superior High School, Superior High can't accommodate them. The only way out is to create new schools on the same design as Superior High. This is what East Harlem did when the success of its Central Park East (CPE) led to establishing CPE2 and CPE3 -- a kind of minichain.

Multiple Goals

A business has one goal that dominates all others, to make money. Success is measured in dollars. Schools have many goals, some measurable, some not. Standardized tests can measure students' reading skills but not their love of learning. Even if we could measure how well a school attains each of its goals, combining them into a single measure would be impossible without consensus on the relative importance of the different goals. If a school does a better job of educating blacks but does worse with whites, how should the two be weighted?

The multiplicity of goals, the impossibility of measuring some of them, and the difficulty of combining those that can be measured have two serious implications. First, the performance of a school may improve significantly without generating any clear evidence of improvement -- and vice versa: schools may get worse without any way for outside observers, or even the local board of education, to know it. Second, the best available indicator of how a school performs is the decisions of parents about which school to send their children to -- if they have the choice. If they don't have any choice, there may be no good way to evaluate schools because all other ways of evaluating them are seriously flawed.

Government Regulation

Government regulation, sometimes excessive, sometimes too little, pervades American business. The savings-and-loan fiasco is an example in which there was too little. The regulators simply did not do their job. They allowed failing banks to stay open and run up hundreds of billions of dollars in losses, to be paid for by taxpayers. Cases of alleged excessive regulation are too numerous to require recapitulation. Public policy may require a great deal of regulation, as is the case with the Food and Drug Administration, which decides whether to allow new drugs on the market. For many products, regulation is minimal, as in the case of private schools. As with public schools, government may choose to own and operate production facilities itself. Which works better, government ownership or regulation? It depends on circumstances. Since society is necessarily concerned with the content and values taught in the schools, government must either operate or regulate them.

The government particularly needs to get involved where side effects are important. Since pollution has harmful side effects, the government steps in to limit the damage. Since basic research has beneficial side effects, the government carries on a great deal of it itself and subsidizes a great deal more. Schools have large beneficial side effects. We all benefit from the education of other people's children. That is why government pays for the great bulk of education and why most of us don't mind paying our share of the taxes.

Government also gets involved in altering people's incomes. The American economic system normally operates with at least four or five percent of the labor force unemployed. Recessions from time to time raise that figure to as much as ten or eleven percent. In response, the government provides unemployment benefits. Old people used to suffer more from poverty than they do now that they get social security benefits from the government. The combination of chronic poverty of some groups and high incomes of others gives many voters the impression that the distribution of income is unfair. In response, the government operates a welfare system and collects more taxes from the rich than the poor. Requiring universal education and paying for it through taxes is another way the government alleviates the inequality of incomes.

Economic Efficiency

The private enterprise part of the American economy by and large has performed well.[8] The increase in income per person in the last hundred years has been enormous. The gains have come mainly from increased technological knowledge, increased saving and investment in capital goods, and an increasingly better educated work force. In addition, the American economic system provides strong incentives for economic efficiency, a term that includes both technical efficiency and a good allocation of resources.

An enterprise is technically efficient if it gets the most production from the resources it employs within the limits of the technological knowledge available at the time. Where competition is active, business firms that are not technically efficient tend to be driven out of business and those that are technically efficient may prosper and grow. This kind of incentive is lacking in government enterprise, leading to the widespread impression of inefficiency. Business firms that are not subject to competition have weaker incentives, but they too, like competitive firms, have the incentive of higher profits.

Economic efficiency also means producing the right outputs in the right quantities. The profit motive and the danger of bankruptcy provide strong incentives to produce what consumers most want. Examples of allocative inefficiency in the United States are by no means rare. They are apt to occur in declining industries where resources, particularly workers, are slow to move. The inefficiency is apt to be prolonged if the government props up the industry with tariffs, subsidies, or price supports. The United States produces too much sugar (it could be imported more cheaply) and too much milk.[9] Despite the exceptions, the American economy by and large does a good job of producing what consumers want, within the limits of their incomes.

Criticism of American public schools has focused mainly on their technical inefficiency -- failure to get the most out of the resources used. The argument that the United States does not devote enough resources to education is nevertheless urged repeatedly on taxpayers.

Locational Monopoly

Suppose the government decreed that grocery stores had to be at least five miles apart. In most towns, such a rule would significantly reduce competition among grocery stores. With appropriate adjustment of the number of miles, that is similar to the situation of schools. Most of them have an element of locational monopoly.[10] Even if (or where) parents were free to choose among public schools, competition would be limited except in densely populated areas like East Harlem. Since older students are more mobile than younger ones, the monopolistic element is stronger for kindergartens and elementary schools than for high schools and colleges.

While the force of competition is weaker the farther apart schools are, schools and teachers don't necessarily slack off just because they have a captive market. Schools and teachers have motives besides economic ones. They want to do a good job. That is an important source of satisfaction to them. Schools might be better if they were more competitive, but the instinct of workmanship, in Thorstein Veblen's phrase, is still at work.

Conclusion

American business has four characteristics conducive to efficiency and progress: the profit motive, competition, frequent entry of new firms and exit of old ones, and the ability to select, reward, and fire employees according to their contributions. Firms and industries vary widely in the extent to which they share these characteristics; evidently a firm or industry missing one or two of them can sometimes perform extremely well.[11] But all four characteristics help.

II. HIGHER EDUCATION

"America has the greatest university system in the world." We don't need to take the word of a distinguished foreign educator (Lord Noel Annan, former vice chancellor of the University of London) for that conclusion. The evidence for it is compelling. Students come from all over the world to study at American universities. Sixty percent of the Ph.D.s earned in the United States go to foreigners. They would not come in such numbers if we did not have the best.[12]

There is no need to exaggerate. The top hundred U.S. colleges and universities are superb by world standards, but the quality of the more than three thousand institutions of higher learning varies widely. One may shudder to think of the bottom hundred. Higher education is like medicine. At its best, medical treatment in the United States is amazing, but millions of Americans lack minimum primary care. Nevertheless, the contrast between higher education on the one hand and elementary and secondary education on the other is substantial. Explaining the disparity can throw light on educational policy.

What accounts for the great success of American universities? Why has higher education, particularly graduate training, done so much better than precollegiate public schools? There are three major reasons plus some minor ones.

Advancing Knowledge

Progress in higher education has been enormous in the last half century not because teaching is better but because the quality of the product has improved. What graduate students learned at Harvard in the 1940s would not qualify them for a faculty position at a research university today, so great has been the advance of knowledge. Because the United States has led the world in research in the last fifty years, the graduate training available here is the best in the world. The professors who teach graduate students do the research that advances knowledge.

The same is true, though to a lesser degree, of college education. Undergraduates today get a better education than their predecessors because professors have a vastly greater stock of knowledge to teach them. The advance of knowledge has improved high school and elementary education also, but to lesser degrees. Kindergarten has benefited the least. In general, the more advanced the training, the more the increased knowledge has contributed to the quality of education.

Money

Higher education in the United States is enormously expensive. Expenditures of colleges and universities -- over $12,000 per student -- are no more than half the cost. If the students were not at school, they could be working at jobs, producing goods and services, and earning income. For a number of reasons, the value of the lost output and income cannot be estimated with precision. Nevertheless, the total cost per student in higher education must be at least four times the cost of elementary and secondary schooling. The success of American colleges and universities has come in no small part from the willingness of the American people to bear the cost. In particular, the GI bill, which financed the further education of returning veterans of World War II, gave colleges and universities a big boost. The increased demand raised the salaries of professors and attracted able young faculty into academic life, increasing the quality as well as the quantity of educational output.

Competition

In the business world, successful firms expand, unsuccessful ones go bankrupt. Higher education illustrates the first effect more vividly than the second because it has been a growth industry. As demand for higher education has increased, the successful colleges and universities have expanded. Some have become gigantic. Their expansion did not have to be at the expense of weak schools. In fact, weaker schools proliferated. The cases of weak schools forced into mergers with strong ones or driven out of business altogether have been infrequent.[13] During the last half century, strong universities have been able to expand with little crowding out of others. This process helps account for the success of U.S. higher education at the top of the scale and the persistence of great variation in quality.

When we look at precollege education, we see severe restrictions on opportunities for the best schools to expand or be duplicated as well as for the worst to disappear.

Competition for students and faculty by colleges is vigorous. College students are highly mobile. Stanford and Cal Tech on the west coast compete against Yale and MIT in the east for the same high school seniors. The market is national, even international. The contrast with public schools needs no comment. Professors are also mobile. Stanford and Cal Tech compete against Yale and MIT for the best of the new Ph.D.s and raid each others' senior faculties when they can. The mobility of public school teachers and competition for the best of them is much more limited.

Competition for research professors is stiff because outsiders can tell who the good ones are. Physicists at MIT read the publications of physicists at Cal Tech, evaluate their contributions, and urge their dean to approve lucrative offers to the best.[14] This is an essential element that has made the American university system the best in the world.

In competing for faculty, universities can pay the salaries needed to attract the scholars they want. They pay physicists more than professors of fine arts, management professors more than economists, medical faculty more than anyone else. If they were restricted to paying doctors no more than fine arts professors, American medical schools would not be nearly as good as they actually are. They would lose their best people to private practice. Public schools, in contrast, cannot raise the salaries of qualified teachers of mathematics and science above teachers of history. Science and mathematics education in public schools has suffered.

The picture of vigorous competition in higher education and sluggish competition among public schools needs to be qualified. Competition for teachers in both systems is hindered because key decision makers lack good information (Hearn, 1992). The reputation of universities comes from their faculties' research, not their teaching. This is so because it is much easier for outsiders to judge the quality of the research done at a university than its teaching. Economists all over the world read the publications of economists at the University of Chicago and know that Gary Becker and his colleagues have made important contributions. Their knowledge of how well economics is taught to Chicago undergraduates is hazy. Outsiders' appraisal of research gets translated into prestige for the university. High school seniors, their parents, and others know that Princeton has more prestige than Oberlin, prestige based on research output, but their gauge of the two schools' teaching programs is derived from unreliable sources. Within a university, decisions about tenure and salaries depend much more heavily on research than on teaching because research is what makes the university's reputation and enables it to attract bright undergraduates (Hearn, 1992, 36-37). Young professors are sometimes honored for outstanding teaching in the same year they are informed their contracts are not being renewed. This curious system nevertheless works well because students learn from each other as well as from the faculty. Princeton's prestige in research attracts outstanding students, making Princeton an excellent place to learn. And employers recruit from Princeton in preference to colleges that produce less research because Princeton attracts and selects men and women of outstanding ability (Hearn, 1992, 47-48).

The difficulty of judging teaching quality is more serious for public schools than for colleges. The school boards and bureaucrats who run the schools lack reliable information about the performance of individual teachers. Principals and other teachers in the same school may know, but they don't make salary decisions. The result, abetted by unions, is a system of salaries based on experience and advanced education[15] and, in contrast to research professors, a notable absence of competition among teachers.

The three reasons just given for the success of American universities -- advancing knowledge, economic resources, and competition -- are important, but there are others. Colleges and universities make no attempt to service the bottom half of the population, the ones with the lowest intelligence, the worst preparation, the greatest disaffection for educational values. The disruptions colleges suffered in the late 1960s and the milder difficulties of recent years are nothing compared to what schools in inner cities have had to contend with. Reduction of discrimination in hiring has benefited colleges, hurt public schools. Formerly, talented women were restricted to a few "female" occupations, public school teaching among them. Now women have other opportunities. Instead of restricting their faculty mostly to white males, universities now draw on the talents of women and minorities.

Conclusion

Colleges and universities in the last half century have had great advantages that public schools have lacked. Some of the advantages (advancing knowledge, rejection of the poorly qualified, and reduced discrimination against women) are irrelevant for improving the schools. They help account for the greater success of higher education while making the lesser success of the public schools understandable and forgivable. The other two advantages (more rivalry and greater economic resources) suggest that greater spending on primary and secondary education will pay off only if it is reinforced by increased competition,

III. MEDICAL CARE

Like higher education, medical care in the United States is superb at its best. The primary reason is the same, rapidly advancing knowledge. What physicians and surgeons can do nowadays is simply amazing to anyone who remembers the medical care of the 1920s and 1930s. The care given (or not given) the thirty million Americans without insurance is another matter. Like higher education, the health care system looks less good -- and the public schools look better -- when judged by the whole range of what it does rather than by its best. It is subject to another criticism it has in common with a college education. It is enormously expensive and getting more expensive all the time.

Consumer Choice

Since choice has become one of the popular reform proposals for public schools, how well choice works in medical care is worth comment. Proposals for choice in public schools are criticized on grounds that the parents of disadvantaged students are not capable of making good choices for their children. The difficulty patients have in selecting doctors and hospitals is at least as great as the problem of selecting a school when given a choice, yet choice in medical care remains an entrenched value in the United States. For a majority of Americans, the drawbacks of a system of letting patients choose are decidedly less than having the choices made for them.

Competition

Like college education, medical care is highly competitive. Numerous physicians, practicing in small groups or individually, compete against each other for patients. Even though price competition is meager compared to department stores, groceries, and discount houses, and even though some specialties seem to get unduly high rewards compared to others, the system succeeds in rewarding the best with higher fees and/or more patients, unlike public school teachers whose salaries depend on length of service, years of education, and political lobbying.

Regulation

Government regulation of American industry is so pervasive that it is hard to say which industry is regulated most, but health care surely ranks high among those most regulated. Physicians must be licensed to practice; the federal government decides which drugs may be prescribed and which sold over the counter; doctors' fees and hospital charges are subject to pressure through

Medicare and Medicaid; erection of new hospitals is subject to government control. Evidently a system of private enterprise subject to government regulation can be made to work, a point that is relevant to proposals for reform of public schools.

Financing

Burton A. Weisbrod's (1991, 547) comparison of the financing of health care and public schools is illuminating:

> Assume that public schools had been financed differently -- in the way hospitals have been financed until recently: (1) school revenue was determined through a retrospective (cost-based) pricing system, in which (2) teachers were empowered to decide what resources should be used (a) to diagnose a particular child's educational "needs" and (b) to meet those needs, and (3) a bill for the cost of the resources used for each child was sent to the government or a private insurer and subsequently paid to the school district.

> Two questions arise: If such a system had been adopted after World War II for schools, what would have happened over the subsequent 40 years to the level of education expenditures? What would have happened to the pace of technological change in education? The lessons from health care suggest conjectures: If schooling had been "insured" on the basis of retrospective costs, expenditures would have increased far more rapidly than they did; and the pace of technological innovation in schools would have been far greater than it was.

Weisbrod's conjectures provide insights on the reasons why the medical profession has been so much more successful, so much more innovative, so much more progressive, than the public schools. Of course, the conjectures need qualification. Weisbrod was writing about health care and was using the school system to throw light on it. His purpose permitted him to neglect the ramifications of the conjectures. To his insights can be added the conjecture that medical science, capitalizing on advances in biology, chemistry, and physics, has had greater opportunities for innovation than public schools trying to capitalize on advances in psychology, sociology, computer science, and television. And Weisbrod was not making a serious policy proposal for the schools. The system of financing he sketched would have led to overspending on schools and inefficiency. But we can conclude that the way a system rewards its workers, whether laborers or professionals, can make an enormous difference.

Public Schools

The public school system in the United States lacks all four of the characteristics that spur business efficiency. Operated by government, it lacks the incentive of profit. With trivial exceptions, schools do not compete against each other for students. New schools are started and old ones closed down in response to demographic shifts, not according to how well they perform. Most debilitating of all, teachers are rewarded according to experience and education, not according to how well they do their job. There should be no surprise that the performance of an industry so organized has drawn heavy criticism and strong political pressure for reform. To an economist, it is surprising that it performs as well as it does.

Bashing the American school system has surely been overdone in recent years.[16] Nevertheless, after all qualifications have been made and the devil given everything he is entitled to, the evidence suggests that the system is inefficient. The United States has tripled its spending on schooling -- dollars per pupil after allowing for inflation -- since 1955 (see Figure 3.1).[17] What has been done with this large increase? Have taxpayers gotten their money's worth?

The money has been used to increase teachers' salaries, provide special services, and reduce class size.[18] Higher salaries relative to other workers were needed just to maintain the quality of the teaching staff.[19] Able women, formerly limited to a few "female" occupations including teaching, now have other, better opportunities. Furthermore, the working conditions in public schools have deteriorated. Teachers have to cope with increasing problems of drugs and violence, while the decline of the American family and the displacement of reading for fun by television have made teaching more difficult. Under the circumstances, we could not expect the rise in relative salaries to increase the quality of the teaching staff.

In recent decades, education of blacks has improved (Card and Krueger, 1991), and special services for the handicapped have increased. There is a presumption that money spent for these special groups is more than justified by their higher future earnings as well as by fairness.

The only real evidence that education has improved for the great majority of students in public schools (aside from the increased knowledge discussed above in connection with higher education) is the twenty percent reduction in class size (from twenty-nine in 1961 to twenty-three in 1987). But as the next section will explain, smaller classes, though better, are only a little better.

A large complex system does not change much even in two or three decades. It is hard to believe the American school system is much worse or much better than in the past. The evidence suggests that it is better.[20] Nevertheless, tripling of spending accompanied by lower test scores is disturbing. It looks as if taxpayers have spent a great deal more money without commensurate benefits.

Figure 3.1: Expenditures Per Pupil in Constant Dollars, U.S. Public Schools, 1943–44 to 1991-92

Spending has doubled since 1965, tripled since 1955, quintupled since 1945

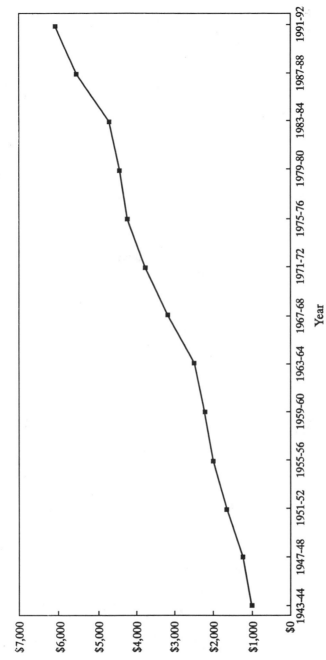

Year

Source: Digest of Education Statistics (1992, 159).

IV. PROPOSALS FOR IMPROVING PUBLIC SCHOOLS

Money

Three widely held beliefs undergird American educational policy: the schools need more money, salaries should be increased to attract better teachers, and class size needs to be reduced. That there would be benefits from spending more money to reduce class size and increase teachers' salaries is not open to doubt. (Ferguson, 1991; Finn and Achilles, 1990; Folger and Breda, 1989; Card and Krueger, 1992.) The question is whether the benefits would be worth the cost. The country has other urgent needs besides education. The federal government has a huge deficit that needs to be reduced. The infrastructure, roads and bridges in particular, urgently needs attention. State and local governments are strapped for funds. Thirty million Americans are without health insurance. Waiving for the moment the question of whether the schools are making the best use of the funds they now get, we must ask if the benefits that can be bought with more taxpayers' money are worth the cost. To rephrase the question, would another billion dollars devoted to public schools bring more benefits than a billion devoted to any of the alternatives such as tax reduction?

To reduce class size from thirty pupils to twenty would require fifty percent more teachers.[21] To attract that many teachers with qualifications equal to those already teaching would require higher salaries. More classrooms would have to be built. On the other hand, there would be some saving in administrative costs from spreading the overhead, and there would be very little increase in spending on books. The data of Folger and Breda (1989, 17) suggest that reducing class size by one-third would increase costs by one-third. In 1990-91, it would have added $73 billion to public school expenditures.

Would it be worth it? More generally, how much reduction in class size would be worth the cost? The cost of reducing average class size by a given number of students goes up the lower class size becomes. Reducing it from thirty to twenty costs about thirty-three percent more, reducing it from twenty to ten another fifty percent. There is evidence that the marginal benefits decline -- the educational gain from reducing classes from thirty to twenty is greater than from twenty to ten.[22] At some point the further gains are not worth the cost. Economically speaking, that is the optimum. Of course, we don't know where that point is. But voters may be understandably reluctant to approve increased taxes to reduce class size except in specific situations.

Teachers (eighty percent according to a Gallup poll) and parents (seventy-five percent) overwhelmingly favor small classes, but the educational value has been devilishly difficult to prove in spite of voluminous research (Hanushek, 1991). Three recent studies (Card and Krueger, 1992; Ferguson, 1991; and Folger and Breda, 1989) have finally provided convincing evidence. (See the Appendix on Research Methods for details.) Neither Card and Krueger nor Ferguson, however, dealt with the question of cost effectiveness. Folger and however, dealt with the question of cost effectiveness. Folger and Breda found that reducing class size from twenty-five to seventeen for kindergarten through grade three produced gains in reading and arithmetic that were modest. Furthermore, the gains appeared only in kindergarten and first grade. If the purpose is to improve scores on standardized tests, reducing class size is not cost effective.

That is not the end to it. In Tennessee two-thirds of the teachers said they would rather have a one-third reduction in class size than a $2,500 increase in salary. This suggests that of the thirty-three percent increase in cost, five percent could be justified as a fringe benefit for teachers that would reduce the amount of salary needed to maintain the quality of the staff. The fact that parents favor small classes also needs to be taken into consideration. In other markets economists argue that customers should be given what they want if they are willing to pay for it. In the case of public schools, the parents pay only part of the cost through their taxes. In calculating the benefits of smaller classes, we need to count something for the preferences of parents. Finally and most important, there may be -- and very likely are -- educational benefits from smaller classes that are not reflected in test scores. Still, when all the benefits of smaller classes are taken into account, the case for general reduction in class size is weak.

Stevenson and Stigler (1992) suggest a better way to use additional funds than reducing class size.[23] Their study comparing Asian and American elementary schools led them to conclude that American teachers are overworked. They are required to spend too much time in the classroom and do not have enough time to prepare lessons. Stevenson and Stigler even recommend increasing class size a little and using the saving "to expand teachers' opportunities for perfecting their teaching and for interacting with other teachers" (212). Note that they would reduce the pupil/teacher ratio without reducing class size. This implies reorganizing the way schools assign duties to teachers. Whatever the merits of the Stevenson-Stigler approach, legislators and school boards need to find better ways to use additional money as it becomes available than simply reducing the number of pupils in each classroom.

As mentioned, reducing class size means a need for higher salaries to attract more qualified teachers. There is an argument for raising salaries anyway. Stephen Jay Gould (1991, 102), has written, "If I were king, I would...double the salary of every teacher in American schools." Gould is a distinguished scientist with impressive knowledge both inside and outside his special field of evolution. He has written with sophistication about economics. No doubt he meant the sentence just quoted as a rhetorical device, not a policy proposal to be taken seriously. If he had meant it seriously, he would have thought more about it and conceded that doubling teachers' salaries would be unwise. But it represents a common point of view, and as the example of Gould illustrates, even the best share it.

The first effect of doubling teachers' salaries would be to cut down on turnover in the teaching profession.[24] Most teachers are in their present jobs because, all things considered, it is their best alternative. Double the salaries and even the few who do have better alternatives would have a powerful inducement to remain where they are. There would be even less opportunity to bring in new and better teachers. To be sure, the pool of applicants would increase. In the greater pool would be some potentially outstanding teachers. In particular, teachers with qualifications in subjects now in short supply, meaning mathematics and science, would fill existing vacancies. But over a time span of five to ten years, doubling salaries would increase the incomes of the old teachers while effecting only a little net improvement.

What would happen in a longer period, say ten or twenty or thirty years? As long as the present institutional system stays in place, the contribution to improved teaching would be limited. Excessive certification requirements now exclude many potentially good teachers, and except for an initial probationary period that weeds out utter misfits, the system has no effective way to encourage inferior teachers to change occupations and replace them with better ones.[25] A doubling of salaries would provide a tremendous opportunity to improve the quality of teaching in the long run. But until a better system of personnel management is in place, the taxpayers are justified in not wanting to pay the $79 billion a year it would take for starters.[26]

The two reasons just given show only that doubling salaries would have limited value. When it is combined with a third consideration, the enormous needs of local, state and federal governments for funds, we must conclude that Gould's proposal on balance would be detrimental to the best interests of today's school children unless it is coupled with institutional reform.

A stronger case can be made for increased spending targeted to expanding Head Start and to providing for a better transition from high school to work. Even for these purposes, skepticism is in order.

Some evidence indicates that the benefits of Head Start are temporary. But the need to help disadvantaged children early is so great that, rather than abandoning Head Start, we need to be willing to risk money to improve it.

As Marshall and Tucker (1992) argue, the United States is far behind European countries and Japan in facilitating a smooth transition from high school to the job market. Times have changed. Formerly, high school graduates and dropouts could get jobs in industry that paid well and made no great demand on academic skills. Now the job market is different. High school graduates all too often are ill-equipped to enter it.[27] Unfortunately, the United States has not yet developed a good model for remedying the problem, and school systems have shown little interest in doing so.

Competitive Policy

Chubb and Moe (1990, 219-25) sketched a proposed system for making American schools competitive. Coons and Sugarman (1992) criticized it for vagueness and drafted a more specific amendment for state constitutions. Their proposal can be criticized for the same fault they find in Chubb and Moe, since they leave many details to legislative decision within the framework of their amendment. Meanwhile, in 1992 a bill was introduced in the Tennessee legislature (Senate Bill No. 2138, House Bill No. 2662, largely the work of two businessmen, John Eason and William R. DeLoache, Jr.) that in its original version was still more specific. Though differing in details, the three proposals are similar. They are also similar to the East Harlem experience and to the system that has been in place in the Netherlands since 1917.

The Tennessee bill combined charter schools, scholarships for every student (which critics would call vouchers), parental choice, reduced certification requirements, and school autonomy, including freedom for individual schools to give teachers short-term contracts. Though the existing public schools would remain in place as long as they could meet the competition for students, the combination of features would make the system competitive. The proposal for charter schools would permit any group of citizens to found a school with minimal constraints from the government and get state or local financing.

The East Harlem experience shows what a competitive package can do when conditions are, in an ironic sense, favorable.[28] The achievement of East Harlem students at one time was just about the worst in New York City. That was a favorable circumstance for two reasons. Poor results provide a powerful incentive to change, and when you are the worst, it is comparatively easy to improve. East Harlem provided a favorable environment for competition because a large number of students were packed into a small area. With short distances to travel to different schools, locational monopoly was not a problem. The teachers were given freedom to start new schools within existing buildings with their own themes and designs. Parents could choose freely among them. Schools that did not attract enough students were shut down. Under this system, achievement scores improved dramatically. Competition worked.

A constitutional amendment adopted by the Netherlands in 1917 requires government support for all schools, public and private, religious and secular. Any group of citizens can start a new school, and parents have complete freedom of choice. The Netherlands has an entirely different attitude toward religion from the United States, which keeps state and religion separate. This feature does not seem significant for drawing lessons from the Dutch experience. Dutch children do well on achievement tests. The schools, however, are not particularly innovative. Furthermore, they appear to be economically inefficient -- too many small schools with duplication of administrative costs. The proportion of minority students in the Netherlands is much lower than in the United States. (Louis, Dodshom and

Teichler, 1990; Louis and van Velzen, 1990/91; Elmore, 1990, 308-09.) All schools follow a detailed national curriculum and pay teachers the same (Walters, 1992). The system therefore lacks a vital ingredient of competition.

While the East Harlem experience suggests that the lesson drawn from the business world is correct -- competition helps[29] -- the Netherlands experience suggests that we should not expect too much from competition alone.

Profits from Schools

Nowadays schools for grades 1-12 are almost universally nonprofit. That was not always the case. But private for-profit enterprise in schooling got wiped out partly by the great depression of the 1930s, mainly by the rise of universal free public schools. It has become almost impossible to charge enough tuition to make money by producing something that competitors are giving away. Private schools survive by maintaining their nonprofit status, enabling them to solicit gifts from alumni and subsidies from churches, options not open to organizations trying to make profits. (Cf. Brown, 1992)

Under the circumstances, Chris Whittle's Edison Project, an effort to establish a chain of private schools that would make money for its backers, would seem decidedly quixotic even if Whittle had not run into unrelated financial difficulties. At this writing the Edison Project is still alive. To predict its demise would be inappropriate. It is more appropriate to hope it succeeds. For it could succeed financially only by achieving enormous success educationally. The idea of the project is to be radically innovative in an industry not noted for radical innovation. The long odds against success illustrate vividly the contrast between schooling and business. Innovation in schooling is exceedingly difficult in part because the profit motive is not at work.

Whittle recruited a stellar group of experts to design the schools he envisioned. Benno C. Schmidt left the presidency of Yale University to head the project. Critics attacked the project because Whittle hoped to turn a profit and Schmidt left Yale for a higher salary. But the project was obviously risky even at that time. Schmidt himself optimistically put the chances of success at fifty-fifty. He had a lot to lose if it failed--his job, his reputation. He got a high salary for assuming a high risk. Early on, Whittle claimed to have commitments of close to $60 million to plan the chain of primary and secondary schools. To implement the plan he expected to need two billion dollars more. Whatever money he and his backers actually spend may all go down the drain. Only the prospect of profit would induce entrepreneurs to take such a gamble. If they did make a profit, it would be because they had made a signal contribution to American education. They would deserve it.

Most likely the experts on the Edison staff are capable of designing a better school. If not, the project will come to an abrupt end and its backers lose their millions. And this is just the point. Unlike public schools, Edison schools that fail go out of business. This is the kind of institutional arrangement America needs.[30] Unfortunately, designing a better school is not enough. The competition from free schools is a formidable obstacle.

As a practical matter, only a new organization like Edison, outside the existing institutional structure, can be expected to carry through a really radical innovation. Existing schools may adopt new methods once they have been proved in practice. But the existing education network, unlike much of private industry, is not structured to generate and put to use a steady stream of innovations, let alone a whole new system. Even private industry normally introduces radically new products through new firms (Schumpeter, 1939, 1950; Chandler, 1992). The airplane may have come out of a bicycle shop, but bicycle shops did not become airplane manufacturers. The history of industry is full of examples of established firms (like Western Union) that rejected something new (like the telephone) only to be done in by it.

More promising than the Edison Project as a way to get the profit motive, competition, and bankruptcy into the school system is the growing practice of contracting out the management of public schools to private companies. One example is Education Alternatives, Inc., a private firm that manages public schools in Baltimore and South Miami Beach and private schools in Minnesota and Arizona. As David A. Bennett (1992) points out, if Education Alternatives fails to perform well, it will lose its contracts. There are many other examples. How innovative such firms can be, given the constraints that school boards impose on them, may be doubted. But contracting management out to private firms creates the right incentives.

V. GETTING FROM HERE TO THERE

Even if we ignore the powerful political forces that defend the status quo, it would make no sense to junk the present educational system in favor of something that is theoretically ideal. The present system may not be the best in the world or the best imaginable, but it is there. It functions. There is no way the United States can educate forty-three million children without relying on the two and a half million teachers the school districts now employ. Sensible policy, even aside from politics, calls for gradual changes that may ultimately lead to major improvement.

Within the existing system, the right direction calls for more school autonomy, greater parental choice, more magnet schools,[31] charter schools, and greater recognition by superintendents and school boards that their job is to shut down inferior schools and facilitate founding of better ones. As new schools are needed to accommodate population shifts and growth, they should rely on charter schools and contracting out rather than expanding the public system. Within the public system, there seems no good way (as well as no politically possible way) to revamp the present procedures of selecting and rewarding teachers. But charter schools and public schools managed by private firms can do better provided they have autonomy and must compete for students. To sum up, we need to introduce more and more competition.

The most difficult problem is to provide equal opportunity, or at least a nearer approach to it, especially for students from poor families living in crime-ridden, drug-ridden inner cities. Experience seems to show that (1) parental choice alone may be counterproductive for this goal,[32] but (2) parental choice combined with other measures, as in East Harlem, can help quite a bit, and (3) more money is needed.

We should not expect too much. Current trends are encouraging, even exciting. But the maximum improvement we can hope for in ten years, or even twenty, is limited. To achieve what is possible requires making American schools competitive.

Appendix 3.A: Research Methods

After pointing out the difficulty of proving that lowering class size increases students' learning, the text noted three recent studies that have provided convincing evidence that it does. This appendix describes the research methods used. It illustrates how research in economics is done and why the recent findings are persuasive.

Statistical Analysis

An economist typically starts with a model. The simplest kind of model consists of an equation relating two variables such as learning (L) and class size (S) in linear form:

$$(1) \quad L = a + bS$$

where a and b are parameters that can be calculated from data for L and S. This equation, of course, is much too simple. Many other variables affect learning besides class size. They must be allowed for. Calculating b from equation (1) would probably result in a value close to zero. If not, the result would probably be produced by chance.

To take account of the other forces affecting learning, the model must be expanded to, say,

$$(2) \quad L = a + bS + cN + dP + \ldots.$$

where N is the number of days in the school year, P is the rate of pay for teachers, and the series of dots indicates other variables that the modeler will include.

The parameters (a, b, c, d, ...) can be calculated, using the method called multiple regression, provided data of good quality are available for L, S, N, P, etc. (For more on the technique of multiple regression, see, e.g., Gujarati, 1988.) Often the available data set is less than ideal, limiting the confidence we can put in the findings of any one study. Nevertheless, the method of multiple regression provides a powerful tool for extracting information from statistical data.

The work of Card and Krueger (1992) is typical of much modern research in economics. Their study explains differences in earnings of male workers in 1979 on the basis of the kind of public school education received in the 1920s, 1930s, or 1940s. The authors' selection of earnings as the measure of educational achievement is praiseworthy. Most studies use scores on standardized tests to measure how much students have learned. Such measures are woefully inadequate.

They do not tell us how productive students will be when they enter the job market or how much their education will contribute to the quality of their future life or what kind of citizens they will become. They tell something about such educational goals but not nearly enough.

Earnings data are better. Differences in earnings, as Card and Krueger have shown, measure differences in the quality of education the workers received when they were in school. They measure attainment of one of the major goals of education. Furthermore, there is a presumption that differences in earnings are correlated with differences in the attainment of the other goals. Workers who earn more probably have better lives aside from their higher incomes and probably are better citizens. While earnings data fall far short of ideal measures of what education has accomplished, they tell much more than standardized tests.

To point out one of the obvious shortcomings of earnings data, they provide information about the quality of education in the past, not the present. Card and Krueger's study reveals a great deal about education in the 1920s, the 1930s, and 1940s. It is a jump from their findings to conclusions about public education in the United States today. But what their study reveals about such variables as class size may be provisionally accepted as true generally. Or, better, it is one piece of evidence. If it can be combined with other evidence, we may reach a convincing generalization.

Many forces affected the earnings of individual workers in 1979. To disentangle the specific effects of school characteristics, Card and Krueger had to take account of the number of years of education each worker received, years of work experience, marital status, and differences in rates of pay in various localities. They proceeded in two steps. First, they estimated the rate of return to another year of education for each state of birth after allowing for other forces, using multiple regression analysis. Second, they estimated the effects of certain school characteristics on the earnings for the state in which the worker was born and presumably received his education. (The data were for men only.) They ended up with estimates of the impact, state by state, of differences in pupil/teacher ratio, the number of days in the school year, and the pay of teachers relative to other workers in the state. They found that differences in the length of the school year had no appreciable effect, but higher relative salaries for teachers and lower pupil/teacher ratios led to increased earnings of workers.

To reach these conclusions, Card and Krueger had to resort to simplifications and compromises imposed by the data available. They assumed that the workers were educated in the state in which they were born. They ignored differences in schools within the state. Although they allowed for differences in earnings opportunities within states, they differentiated only between city and country, ignoring differences among cities and differences among rural areas. They omitted women from their analysis. In view of these shortcomings, how much faith can we put in their conclusions?

Compared to other studies of this kind, Card and Krueger's deserves high marks. It uses earnings instead of test scores; its statistical technique is impeccable; the data set is large and compares favorably in quality with the data normally available. Its limitations mean that, as always in such studies, the important conclusions have not been proved beyond a reasonable doubt. On the other hand, legislators and school boards have to make decisions about class size on the basis of the best available evidence. Card and Krueger's evidence is good, but other evidence is needed.

In an important study, Ferguson (1991) used multiple regression with a large sample of students in Texas in the 1980s (more than eight hundred school districts with one hundred fifty thousand teachers and 2.4 million students). He used scores on standardized tests of reading and mathematics as the measure of student learning. Included in the explanatory variables was a measure of teacher quality, their scores on a recertification test of literacy skills. Teacher quality was the most important variable accounting for differences in mathematics as well as reading. Other important variables, in order, were the experience of the teachers, pupil/teacher ratio and master's degrees. Like Card and Krueger's, Ferguson's study deserves high marks despite its shortcomings.[33] It adds to the evidence that class size helps.

Experimental Research

Folger (1989) provides another kind of evidence. The State of Tennessee appropriated money for a longitudinal study of reducing class size by one-third in grades K-3. In a representative sample of seventy-nine schools, there were three kinds of classes: small classes with thirteen to seventeen students, regular classes with twenty-one to twenty-five without a teacher aide, and regular classes with a teacher aide. Teachers were assigned randomly; those teaching small classes were given instruction in how to take advantage of the different environment. Information was collected on other important variables, such as the amount of time spent in instruction, so that they could be controlled statistically. Pupils were given the Stanford Achievement Test and followed through the four grades and beyond. The ones in small classes performed better than those in regular classes in both reading and mathematics. The differences, however, were small, confirming the growing consensus that small classes, though better, are not cost effective. The Tennessee study reported by Folger was technically impeccable but was limited to four grades in one state in the 1980s.

The experimental approach is fundamentally different from the multiple regression analysis used by Card and Krueger, Ferguson, and dozens of other researchers. Card and Krueger used data collected for other purposes, as did Ferguson. They investigated the effects of class size (and other similar issues) by showing how differences across states appeared to be related to the subsequent earnings of the students while allowing for other major influences. In effect they held other forces constant by means of a statistical method. The experimental approach used in Tennessee compiled data especially for the purpose of learning about class size. Teachers and students were randomly assigned to the experimental or regular classes, a feature that makes the study fundamentally different from Card and Krueger's and Ferguson's.

Confidence in a result is greater if it is confirmed by different kinds of evidence. Besides the statistical method of Card and Krueger and Ferguson and the experimental approach reported by Folger, we have the evidence from polls of the opinions of teachers and parents, a large majority of whom think small classes are better. This third kind of evidence may be weak -- people's impressions are often wrong -- but it is by no means worthless. It increases confidence in the conclusion that small classes are better.

Statistical Significance

In the studies just reviewed and in much other research, the question arises whether the observed difference in learning could have been due to chance. This issue is referred to as "statistical significance", not to be confused with significance in the sense of importance. The results reported by Folger satisfy the standard criterion of statistical significance: the odds that they came about by chance are low. How important they are is another matter. The improvement in learning was small.

The usual criterion of statistical significance is odds of one in twenty, in other words, a probability no greater than five percent that the result was due to chance rather than the forces under study. This criterion has the obvious weakness that one time in twenty the conclusion will be wrong. A sterner criterion is odds of one in a hundred. There exists a body of sophisticated tests of statistical significance that determine the probability figure discussed in this paragraph. Such a probability number can be obtained quite routinely for any statistically estimated coefficient. (For further details, see, e.g., Gujarati, 1988).

If a result meets the criterion for statistical significance, we can provisionally assume, in the absence of contrary evidence, that the conclusion is correct. What if it fails the test? Then we cannot infer anything. Borland and Howsen (1993) studied the effect of competition on student achievement in Kentucky. They found that in those counties where students had the option of going to school in a different district from the one in which they lived, having two districts made no difference, but where three or more districts competed, student achievement scores were three percent higher.[34] To achieve this result, they used multiple regression, in effect holding constant other influences such as class size and teacher salaries. In their regressions, class size was not statistically significant. Should their result be considered to contradict the evidence that smaller classes are better? No. The reason for their result may have been (and almost surely was) that their sample was too small to generate a statistically significant finding.

Conflicting Studies

Borland and Howsen, Card and Krueger, and Ferguson used the same statistical technique. All of them included class size in their analyses. But the studies differed otherwise. Among the differences, Card and Krueger used earnings data, the others standardized test scores. There are dozens if not hundreds of studies of class size using the same statistical method but differing in other respects. The conclusions vary widely (Hanushek, 1991, 455). Some show that lower class size helps, others that it hurts. Most, like Borland and Howsen's, are inconclusive. How should we go about deciding what to believe?

The main principle is to select the best of the studies and ignore the rest. "Best" means a sound research design, a data set adequate in both quality and quantity, and sophisticated statistical technique. This appendix has concentrated on studies that meet these criteria.

NOTES

The author is grateful for the help of Kimberly Y. Adair, Nelson Andrews, William Baumol, Mary Pamela Beaver, William E. Becker, Melvin V. Borland, David Card, William R. DeLoache, Jr., John Eason, John Folger, Charles W. B. Fels, T. Aldrich Finegan, Malcolm Getz, Willis D. Hawley, C. Elton Hinshaw, Charles D. Robison, Clifford S. Russell, John J. Siegfried, and Jacque V. Voegeli. For permission to quote "The Health Care Quadrilemma" by Burton Weisbrod the editors of this volume wish to thank the American Economic Association.

1. The idea expressed here is only that higher education has been more successful than precollege education, a proposition that should be beyond doubt. Much of the criticism of public schools is overblown.

2. The Soviets blundered in their pricing policy. Prices promote efficiency when they reflect relative scarcities. The Soviets ignored this principle, causing great inefficiencies, among them the long lines consumers had to wait in for hours to make ordinary purchases. The Soviets also overemphasized heavy industry. The lack of competition among producers exacerbated these policy errors.

3. Families of higher socioeconomic status can and do take account of the quality of schools in choosing places of residence. (Economists call this the Tiebout effect after the author of the classic article on the subject.) In addition, well-to-do parents can send their children to private schools.

4. In a socialist economy, the government could produce everything, yet give consumers choice, adjusting output and prices in accord with consumer demand. Or a socialist economy could give consumers no choice, rationing everything, yet have autonomous producing units such as farms that compete against each other and were rewarded according to their efficiency. Neither of these hypothetical extremes would work very well.

5. The semifinal draft of this paper was completed before publication of the much-debated report of the Carnegie Foundation for the Advancement of Teaching (1992). The report alternates between skepticism about the value of choice alone ("Choice is not enough") and grudging admiration for specific instances (East Harlem, Cambridge, Montclair) where choice has been combined with other measures. Thus, it essentially supports the contention in the text above.

6. The Carnegie Foundation for the Advancement of Teaching (1992) argues that parents, when given a choice, base decisions more on convenience than quality of schools. Furthermore, parents are generally satisfied with their children's schools; few would make a change if given the option. The facts are not in dispute. They support the Foundation's contention that choice alone is not enough. But to stop analysis there is to indulge in superficiality.

It does not take a large number of parents choosing schools on the basis of quality to make a significant difference; the proportion reported by the Foundation is quite enough to have an impact. In any choice system, the school district must make an effort to provide parents with information. There is nothing wrong with choosing a school on the basis of convenience when the alternative is only a little better; convenience is one of the attractions of the much beloved neighborhood school. In any market the bulk of consumers free-ride on the choices of an informed few; we seek out friends who have made a study of the product, and we get away with the otherwise illogical practice of judging quality by price. Choice can have a bigger impact than the Carnegie Foundation infers from the data it compiled.

7. Part of the success of fast food chains (and motels) comes from an advantage not available to schools. Once you've gone to a McDonald's, you know what you will get at any other McDonald's. If you are in a strange area, you're apt to prefer not to take a chance on an unknown restaurant. A chain has a marketing advantage over independent operators. Like hospital chains, a chain of schools would not get much of
an advantage of this kind because parents and children travel more often than they move.

8. Marshall and Tucker (1992) argue persuasively that in recent years American business has not adjusted as well as business in other industrialized countries to changed conditions. American business has been slow to decentralize decision making. But it has done better in that respect than American education. Over the long haul business has done

extremely well and still is near the top.

9. To say this is not to say the government policies that perpetuate the inefficiency are wrong. Producers of sugar and milk think they are fully justified. The point is that they result in allocative inefficiency. Some of the resources used to produce sugar and milk could be used more productively in other industries.

10. The problem of locational monopoly can be reduced by housing several schools in one building, as has been done in East Harlem and elsewhere.

11. The American Telephone & Telegraph Co. is an interesting example. Before it was broken up by court order under the antitrust laws, it had a monopoly. It nevertheless performed extremely well in the sense that Americans were pleased with the service and charges. The appearance of efficiency was partly real, partly illusory. It used high charges for businesses to subsidize service for the mass of consumers. After it was broken up, charges for long distance calls fell. AT&T's performance, at least initially after the breakup, started to look lackluster because it was not used to having to compete.

12. A qualification is in order for the fellowships available in the United States that foreign students can often get.

13. Examples of schools forced into mergers or out of business include Franconia, George Peabody College for Teachers, Newark, Scarritt College, and Western College for Women.

14. Unfortunately, on account of tenure, universities can't correct all their mistakes, but the advantages of tenure in protecting academic freedom and providing faculty with security that allows them to undertake risky research projects outweigh the harm of the mistakes. Tenure in primary and secondary schools serves a somewhat different function, protecting them from the evils of political patronage. Competition could eliminate the need for tenure in precollege institutions.

15. There is, to be sure, evidence of positive correlation of education with teaching quality (Card and Krueger, 1992, 24). Basing salaries on education is not irrational. But it is not a measure of good teaching, only an inadequate proxy for it. Similarly for experience (Ferguson, 1991).

16. See Bracey (1991) for a defense of the schools. An excellent appraisal that is critical but fair is in Niskanen (1991).

17. This is the right concept for the problem discussed in the text. Education is at once a producer good, a consumer good, and a civic good. It is a producer good because it contributes to the future earnings and productivity of the students; in that respect, it is like an investment in factories and machine tools. It is a consumer good because it contributes to the quality of life of the students, aside from their earnings. And it is a civic good because it contributes to citizenship.

In consequence of these three roles, education is a normal good in the sense that as our incomes rise we spend more on it (though not necessarily a larger percentage of our incomes). Naturally when we spend more on any good or service we expect to get more -- either a greater quantity or higher quality. The question is whether, when we spend more, we get our money's worth. That is the question under discussion in the text. Spending in constant dollars per pupil is the relevant measure of how much we are spending.

Sometimes we spend more in constant dollars because the price or cost of inputs has gone up relative to other goods and services. To some extent that has happened with education (see note 18 and the text below). To the extent that it has, we can't expect better education for our money.

A different measure, viz., spending as a percentage of gross domestic product (GDP), is often cited in the literature, but it is appropriate for a different problem. The percentage of GDP devoted to education is relevant to whether we are spending the right amount on it. Even for that purpose, it does not tell much. The issue is whether spending an additional billion on education would contribute more than spending it on anything else.

18. A significant part of the increase in spending per pupil did not represent an increase in real resources devoted to education for a reason explained by Baumol (1993). Rising productivity increases wages and salaries throughout the economy over time. Salaries of teachers have to keep up with compensation of other workers or teachers will leave education.   Productivity increases more rapidly in some sectors such as manufacturing and agriculture than in others such as education. In industries with rapid productivity growth, costs per unit of output fall in spite of the increase in wages and salaries; in those with slow productivity growth, costs rise.

Crude calculations suggest that more than half of the increased spending represented an increase in real resources devoted to education. The rise in inflation-adjusted spending per pupil during 1965-91 was 116 percent. The pupil/teacher ratio was 51 percent higher at the beginning of the period than at the end. (The number of teachers rose 46 percent, while the number of pupils fell 7 percent.) There is reason to think other inputs increased more than teachers. The ratio of instructional expenses to total expenses fell from 68 percent in 1969-70 to 61 percent in 1979-80. (*Digest of Education Statistics 1992.*)

19. Teachers' salaries in constant dollars during the last two decades have risen very little, a fact that is sometimes used to argue that teachers have been treated poorly. But for the problem discussed in the text -- the salaries needed to maintain the quality of the teaching staff -- it is salaries relative to other workers' that is relevant. The ratio of instructional staff salaries to the earnings of full-time workers has risen irregularly since the early 1940s. It went from 0.85 in 1943-44 to 1.24 in 1970-71, fell to 1.11 in 1979-80, and rose to an all-time high of 1.26 in 1988-89. (*Digest of Education Statistics 1991*, 85.) In real terms, teachers have not done well in the last twenty years, but other workers have done even worse.

20. This, of course, abstracts from the more difficult environment in which the schools now operate. The personnel of a school may do just as good a job as ever, yet because drugs, crime, and pregnancies have increased, find the reputation of their school deteriorates.

21. Average class size in the United States fell from 29 in 1961 to 23 in 1987, a reduction of over 20 percent. The pupil/teacher ratio, which is not the same thing, fell from 25.6 to 17.6 in the same period, or 31 percent. (*Digest of Education Statistics 1991*.) These figures are misleading. There is great variation around the average, and there has been a substantial increase in special education with very small classes. A class size of 30 is used in the text for illustration as a ballpark figure, nothing more.

22. Ferguson (1991) found a threshold effect. In his study, there was no gain in test scores from reduction of the student/teacher ratio below 18 (equivalent to a class size in the low twenties). Without more evidence, the threshold must be regarded as a tentative hypothesis. But Ferguson's study supports the presupposition suggested by economic theory that the marginal benefits decline as class size is reduced.

23. Slavin (1990) also suggested ways to use money that would be cost effective. He pointed out that "dramatic effects can be obtained from one-to-one tutoring" (p. 7); hiring an additional teacher for each class rather than halving class size would make it possible to provide tutoring for students who need it most. He also proposed as cost effective paraprofessional tutors, peer tutoring, and cooperative learning (p. 9).

24. When Rochester raised teachers' salaries 40 percent over a three-year period, "One effect of raising teachers' salaries so much so fast was to reduce retirements to a trickle." (Marshall and Tucker, 1992, 116.) Card and Krueger (1992) in a study of school quality based on earnings data found that teachers' experience had only a negligible effect on students' future earnings (24). Ferguson (1991) on the other hand found that experience mattered.

25. Individual principals have ways to get rid of teachers they don't want, but this usually means the teachers go elsewhere in the system.

26. The estimated average salary of public school teachers in 1990-91 was $33,015, the number of teachers 2,390,771 (*Digest of Education Statistics 1991*, 71 and 81).

Stevenson and Stigler (1992, 162) point out that in Japan the ratio of teachers' salaries to per capita national income is 2.4 compared to 1.4 in the United States. Increasing the American ratio 70 percent might be an appropriate long-term goal if accompanied by personnel management reform.

27. "More than half of those people who go through elementary and secondary education...enter the workforce with virtually no vocational skills," say Marshall and Tucker, who go on, "Contrast this situation to that in most European countries, where fully 85 percent of the students who do not obtain a baccalaureate degree participate in an apprenticeship program lasting anywhere between two and four years" (1992, 153).

28. Among the numerous published accounts of the East Harlem schools, see Carnegie Foundation for the Advancement of Teaching (1992, 40-46), Fliegel (1990, 1991), and *The Economist* (1992).

29. Other evidence that competition among schools helps is reported in Borland and Howsen (1993), discussed above in Appendix 3.A.

30. Jonathan Kozol in a telecast argued that even if Edison schools survive we will never know if they are better; the issue, he charged, is not quality but salesmanship. This argument is hard to accept. It is true that judging schools is difficult; it is true that Whittle is an excellent salesman. But to succeed, good salesmen must have good products (And vice versa).

31. Blank (1990, 78) lists four characteristics of magnet schools: "(1) a special curricular theme or method of instruction; (2) a role in voluntary desegregation within a district; (3) choice of school by student and parent; and (4) access to students beyond a regular attendance zone." By 1983 there were 1,100 magnet schools in the 350 largest school districts. They have proved useful for desegregating schools and improving outcomes but do not serve the interests of at-risk students.

32. "In school districts with a substantial number of low-income, minority, and low-achieving students, public school choice programs have almost always resulted in maintaining or increasing the isolation of these students at risk in separate schools and programs. Thus, in practice, public school choice typically becomes a new form of discriminatory tracking." Moore (1990, 194-95). It is not clear what experience, other than Chicago's, Moore is referring to.

33. Among the shortcomings is the use of standardized test scores as the sole measure of what students gained; the use of averages of school districts rather than data for individual students; restriction to data for a single state that may not be typical of the country as a whole; lack of a direct measure of students' innate ability; and use of pupil/teacher ratio as a proxy for class size (by the mid-1980s, the difference between the two measures was greater than for Card and Krueger's period).

34. To be technically accurate, Borland and Howsen found "that counties that have a Herfindahl index at or above 0.50 would have student achievement scores 1.6 units [3 percent] lower than a county with a Herfindahl index below 0.50." The Herfindahl index is often used as a proxy for lack of competitiveness. The statement in the text above is a reasonably accurate simplification employed to convey the general idea to those who neither know nor care what a Herfindahl index is.

REFERENCES

Bardhan, P. and J.E. Roemer. 1992. Market socialism: A case for rejuvenation. *Journal of Economic Perspectives 6*(3): 101-16.

Baumol, W. J. 1993. *Social wants and dismal science: The curious case of the climbing costs of health and teaching.* New York: C. V. Starr Center for Applied Economics, New York University.

Becker, W. E. and D.R. Lewis., eds. 1992. *The economics of higher education.* Boston, Dordrecht, London: Kluwer Academic Publishers.

Bennett, D. A. 1992. Rescue schools, turn a profit. *The New York Times 142*(48990) June 11: A15.

Blank, R. K. 1990. Educational effects of magnet high schools. In *Clune and Witte, vol.* 2, 77-109.

Boaz, D., ed. 1991. *Liberating schools: Education in the inner city.* Washington D.C.: Cato Institute.

Borland, M. V., and R.M. Howsen. 1993. On the determination of the critical level of market concentration in education. *Economics of Education Review 12*(2): 165-169.

Boyd, W. L., and C.T. Kirchner. 1987. *The politics of excellence and choice in education: 1987 yearbook of the Politics of Education Association.* New York NY: The Falmer Press.

Bracey, G. 1991. Why can't we be like we were? *Phi Delta Kappan 73*(2): 104-17.

Bredo, E. 1987. Choice, constraint, and community. In *Boyd and Kirchner*: 67-78.

Brown, B. W. 1992. Why governments run schools. In *Levin, ed.*: 287-300.

Card, D., and A.B. Krueger. 1991. School quality and black-white relative earnings: A direct assessment. *Quarterly Journal of Economics 107*(1): 151-200.

————. 1992. Does school quality matter? Returns to education and the characteristics of public schools in the United States. *Journal of Political Economy 100*(1): 1-40.

Carnegie Foundation for the Advancement of Teaching. 1992. School choice. Princeton NJ: author.

Chandler, A. D. 1992. Organizational capabilities and the economic history of industrial enterprise. *Journal of Economic Perspectives 6*(3): 79-100.

Chubb, J. E., and T.M. Moe. 1990. *Politics, markets, and America's schools.* Washington, D.C.: The Brookings Institution.

Coons J. E., and S.D. Sugarman. 1992. *Scholarships for children.* Berkeley CA: Institute of Governmental Studies Press, University of California, Berkeley.

Clune, W. H., and J.F. Witte., eds. 1990. *Choice and control in American education. Vol. 1: The theory of choice and control in American education. Vol. 2: Thepractice of choice, decentralization and school restructuring.* Philadelphia PA: The Falmer Press.

Economist. 1992. *The rage in Harlem. June 13, 323*(7763): 26-27.

Elmore, R. 1987. Choice in public education. In *Boyd and Kerchner*: 79-98.

————. 1990. Choice as an instrument of public policy: Evidence from education and health care. In *Clune and Witte, vol.1*: 285-317.

Ferguson, R. F. 1991. Paying for public education: New evidence on how and why money matters. *Harvard Journal on Legislation 28*(2): 465-98.

Finn, J. D., and C.M. Achilles. 1990. Answers and questions about class size: A statewide experiment. *American Educational Research Journal 27*(3): 557-77.

Fliegel, S. 1990. Creative non-compliance. In *Clune and Witte, vol. 2*: 199-216.

————. 1991. The East Harlem story. In *Boaz*: 157-71.

Folger, J., ed. 1989 (published in 1992). Project STAR and class size policy. *Peabody Journal of Education 67*(1).

————and C. Breda. 1989 (published in 1992). Evidence from STAR about class size and student achievement. In *Folger*: 17-33.

Gould, S. J. 1991. *Bully for brontosaurus: Reflections in natural history.* New York: Norton.

Gujarati, D. N. 1988. *Basic econometrics. 2nd ed.* New York: McGraw-Hill Publishing Company.

Hanushek, E. A. 1991. When school finance "reform" may not be good policy. *Harvard Journal on Legislation 28*(2): 423-56.

Hearn, J. C. 1992. The teaching role in American higher education: Popular imagery and organizational reality. In *Becker and Lewis*: 17-68.

Levin, H. M. 1987. Education as a public and private good. *Journal of Policy Analysis and Management 6* (Summer): 628-41.

————, ed. 1992. Market approaches to education: Vouchers and school choice. *Economics of Education Review 11*(4): 279-451.

Louis, K. S., L. Bodstrom, and U. Teichler. 1990. *Review of educational policies: The Netherlands.* Paris: Organization for Economic Cooperation and Development.

————and B.A.M. van Velzen. 1990/91. *A Look at Choice in the Netherlands.* Educational Leadership (December/January): 66-72.

Marshall, R., and M. Tucker. 1992. *Thinking for a living: Work, skills, and the future of the American economy.* New York: Basic Books.

Moore, D. R. 1990. Voice and choice in Chicago. In *Clune and Witte, vol. 2*: 153-98.

Niskanen, W. A. 1991. The performance of America's primary and secondary schools. In *Boaz, ed.*: 51-64.

Schumpeter, J. A. 1939. *Business cycles: A theoretical, historical, and statistical analysis of the capitalist process. 2 vols.* New York and London: McGraw-Hill.

————. 1950. *Capitalism, socialism and democracy. 3d ed.* New York: Harper.

Slavin, R. 1990. Class size and student achievement: Is smaller better? *Contemporary Education* 62(3): 6-12.

Stevenson, H. W., and J. W. Stigler. 1992. *The learning gap*. New York: Summit Books.

U.S. National Center for Education Statistics, Office of Educational Research and Improvement. 1992. *Digest of education statistics, 1992*. U.S. Department of Education.

Walters, L. S. 1992. Dutch mix education and religion. *Christian Science Monitor (December 21)*:12.

Weisbrod, B. A. 1991. The health care quadrilemma: An essay on technological change, insurance, quality of care, and cost containment. *Journal of Economic Literature* 29(2): 523-52.

CHAPTER 4

THE ECONOMICS OF MARKET CHOICE AND AT-RISK STUDENTS

Masato Aoki

Susan F. Feiner

Using the market mechanism to direct K-12 education will, according to advocates, improve the quality of education for all students, and students at risk of educational failure will be especially well served by this type of institutional change. This chapter is offered as a general guide to the economics of the market choice approach. We focus on the proposal's economic content to help those not trained in economic analysis or fluent in economic grammar evaluate the market choice plan, which rests upon a particular understanding of the structure, behavior, and outcomes of competitive market dynamics as they apply to education.

Although economists build various types of models, these models share a logical structure in which markets play a central role. Through their market interactions with sellers, buyers transmit information about their tastes and preferences to sellers. Based upon observed consumption patterns and trends, sellers make decisions about what goods to produce, what quantity of each good to produce, and what price to charge. When markets send accurate information about consumer desires to producers, and when producers correctly interpret this information, markets can be shown to solve important problems of resource allocation. That is, under certain conditions markets will push producers to make available the goods and services most highly sought by consumers and at the lowest possible prices. What emerges is an effective mechanism driving the economy to serve consumer interests.

Economists generally agree that the results that actually emerge from the operation of a market in practice depend critically upon the mode of operation of the market in question, which in turn depends upon the structural characteristics of that market. There are well known sets of market attributes that a market must possess if the interactions between utility-seeking consumers and profit-seeking firms are to culminate in the production and sale of goods with the quality, quantity, and price characteristics that maximize combined consumers' and producers' benefits. Moreover, over time, as consumer preferences change and as the technology and resource availability facing firms develop, markets may, under certain conditions, adapt production and distribution in a manner that preserves their ability to maximize the combined benefits to consumers and producers. Therefore, in the economic analysis of a particular market, investigators are generally concerned over the nature of the circumstances that do in fact prevail.

This analytical approach can be applied to the research of economists on educational reform in general and the education of at-risk students in particular. If one views education as a commodity like any other, and because educational resources (like other resources) are scarce, it is possible to argue that recourse to market forces in determining the price and quantity of educational services will produce a mix of educational services that most accurately reflects what the consumers of education want.

In this chapter we examine, with the help of previous research, the extent to which the market structures in education assumed explicitly or implicitly by the discussants approximate the conditions likely to emerge in reality. For this purpose we first summarize the argument for market choice in education, stressing those aspects of the argument that rely most heavily on economic logic. We then assess the major elements of the overall argument to determine the extent to which the use of particular models is consistent with standard economic analysis.

We conclude with a discussion of the larger context within which the proposals for educational reform are debated. Here we find an interesting opportunity to use an innovative method of economic analysis. Recent developments in the methods and philosophy of economics suggest that attention to the rhetorical strategy adopted in the debate over market choice in education can be used fruitfully to supplement more traditional forms of analysis.[1] The research method of this approach rejects the view that discourse or rhetoric is a verbal veil that conceals an objective reality without altering it. On the contrary, rhetoric is regarded as a constitutive element of "reality," one that shapes our very concepts of what reality "is" by providing the language, syntax, logical connections, and metaphors for our thought processes. When applied to the task of understanding the role of economic methods in the debate over privatization, decentralization, and the education of at-risk students, the view that rhetoric is not reality-neutral forces us to consider how the structure of the economic arguments deployed in this debate molds our very conception of the problem.

Since economic models are, unavoidably, abstractions from the real world, they necessarily entail assumptions about details that are important, and therefore to be included explicitly in the model, as against those details that are deemed unimportant, and therefore can safely be left out. But are these "unimportant details" (in linguistics these are called "default assumptions") really left out, or do readers (often subconsciously) "fill in" the details according to the conventions, norms, and accepted standards of their community? In *Savage Inequalities,* Kozol (1991) exposes the poverty of the default assumption of student homogeneity by illustrating the incommensurability of the schooling experiences of poor (minority) and affluent (white) students. It is no surprise to find that schools in poor neighborhoods are not pleasant havens of learning and growth. To what extent does the rhetoric of the choice debate highlight or obscure the stark contrasts that Kozol draws? We hope that the remainder of this chapter will help the reader answer this and related questions.

I. THE ECONOMICS OF THE MARKET CHOICE ARGUMENT

Summary of the Market Choice Position

The highly influential Brookings Institution publication *Politics, Markets, and America's Schools* (Chubb and Moe, 1990) is the most recent reincarnation of the market choice position. Here we summarize the logic of the argument for institutionalization of market choice in education.

According to Chubb and Moe, "academic success is a product of effective school organization." In particular, effective organization of schools is taken to require "substantial school autonomy from direct external control."

> (I)t appears that school organization and performance are indeed related...High and low performance schools appear to be distinguished more by their leadership, professionalism, and teamwork, for example, than by their graduation requirements, or homework and writing assignments...If school success really depends on the development of a professional, teamlike organization, improvement will be harder to...achieve through the bureaucratized systems of democratic control that have governed public education for such a long time (1990, 99).

The public schools' lack of autonomy results from their very location within the public sector: the "problem of poor (school) performance is just as much a normal, enduring part of the political landscape as school boards and superintendents are. It is one of the prices Americans pay for choosing to exercise direct democratic control over their schools" (1990, 2). Direct democratic control reduces the autonomy of school principals and others in deciding curricular content, pedagogical techniques, and other matters that contribute to educational quality; and it causes public school ineffectiveness, because it gives power to special interest groups—teachers' unions, principals, school boards, superintendents, schools of education, book publishers, and testing services—all of whom have undue weight in the bureaucratic machinery of schools.

> Direct democratic control does impose a distinctive structure [that] tends to promote organizational characteristics that are ill-suited to the effective performance of America's public schools. This social outcome is the product of countless individual decisions, but it is not an outcome that any of the major players would want or intend if acting alone. It is truly a product of the system as a whole, an unintended consequence of the way the system works (1990, 21).

For Chubb and Moe, the underlying political problem can be solved by replacing the political processes governing school operations (i.e., direct democratic control) with the economic processes (i.e., indirect market control) of consumer choice and competition. The basic economic argument underlying the market choice approach is that the institutional organization of public sector schooling breeds inefficiency because the individual consumers of education—parents and students—are unable to impress their tastes and preferences upon schools. Politically directed public schools cannot produce the educational results that ensure customer satisfaction because

> the existing institutions of democratic control are simply inconsistent with the autonomous operation and effective organization of schools...In the private sector, where schools are controlled by markets—indirectly and from the bottom up—autonomy is generally high. In the public sector, where schools are controlled by politics—directly and from the top down—autonomy is generally low (1990, 183).

In other words, schools would be more effective if parents and students were allowed to interact in and with the education system as though they were shoppers in a mall; if parents and students could express their wants and if schools were allowed to respond to these wants, schools would become more effective precisely because of the power of consumers in the market place.

In this argument the logic of the market is immanent: if retailers stock the wrong sorts of wares they are driven out of business as consumers seek retailers selling the wares they want. For vendors selling the "wrong" stuff, sales fall. Two responses by the vendors are possible: suppliers can reduce the price of the goods they sell, or they can change the merchandise they offer for sale. Those vendors who fail to make the appropriate adjustment will in time disappear from the marketplace and be replaced by more responsive suppliers. According to the plan of Chubb and Moe, the various suppliers of education would compete for customers not through price changes but through the differentiated offerings of the competing schools.

In short, the market choice position views the public interest expressed by existing educational hierarchies as necessarily inferior to the self-interested and market-driven decisions of private suppliers.

> The interest group system is biased in favor of some interests over others (the organized over the unorganized especially). Politicians and administrators sometimes pursue their own interests at the expense of citizens' interests (1990, 31).

In this view, the public supply of educational services necessarily weakens the position of parents and students as consumers. In contrast, as Chubb and Moe argue, "markets work to ensure that parents and students play a much more central and influential role in private sector education" (1990, 32).

The Chubb and Moe argument stands on three legs, each intended to show how market signals will permit a better "match between what parents and students want and the kind of education their schools provide" (1990, 32). First, a market system will encourage schools to cater to consumer demand: "those who own and run the schools have a strong incentive to please a clientele of parents and students through the decisions they make" (1990, 32). Second, in a market system "people have the freedom to switch from one alternative to another when they think it will be beneficial to do so. If parents and students do not like the services they are being provided at any given school, they can exit and find another school whose offerings better meet their needs" (1990, 32). The argument's third leg invokes the Darwinian metaphor of natural selection:

> Schools that fail to satisfy a sufficiently large clientele will go out of business (or, if subsidized become an increasing burden on their patron organization, generating pressures which work in the same direction). Of the schools that survive, those that do a better job of satisfying customers will be more likely to prosper and proliferate (1990, 33).

To summarize, the basic argument of the market choice position is that public education, controlled as it is by democratic processes, cannot produce the desired convergence of parents' preferences and public school offerings: "institutions of democratic control work systematically and powerfully to discourage school autonomy and, in turn, school effectiveness" (1990, 183). What is needed, therefore, is a restructuring of the education delivery system to replace direct democratic control with market processes to liberate consumer choice and school (firm) competition. We turn now to a summary of the criticisms of the Chubb and Moe plan.

An Educator's Guide to the Economics of the Market Choice Position

It must be recognized in evaluating the work of those who advocate the market approach to education that there is a vast literature on the imperfections and failures of the market mechanism in certain circumstances. This mainstream economic analysis can help us in the analysis of the educational issue. In the Chubb and Moe argument we saw that *consumer choice* played a crucial role in generating the improvements in educational outcomes that are the stated aim of the market reform scheme.[2] To understand this connection it is necessary to understand what economists mean by consumer choice and, in turn, what market conditions are needed to ensure the desired outcomes of choice.

> During the past 30 years, the basic intellectual argument for systemic choice has not notably advanced beyond the classical economic ideas sketched by Friedman (1955, 1962). If anything, recent writing advocating choice views the matter more simplistically than did Friedman. Its seems enough today to declare that choice promotes consumer sovereignty and competition (Manski, 1992, 355).

In the classical economics way of thinking, *consumer sovereignty* is one of the fundamental attributes of competitive markets, that is, in those markets where the mechanism is effective in promoting the public welfare (see below for the criteria of competitiveness). The basic idea is that when consumers purchase particular goods from specific firms at certain prices, not only do they add to the revenue of the selling firm, they also provide market signals to the industry (i.e., the group of firms selling comparable goods) about their tastes, that is, about what the consumers desire from these commodities. Over time, firms will compete for consumers' business on the basis of either price or product quality. In effect, consumer's choices guide firms' adjustments of what price they charge (the *market price*) and what kind of product they supply. In the exercise of such leadership consumers are said to be *sovereign*. Firms' actual responsiveness or immunity to consumers' expressed preferences will depend upon the degree of competition in the industry, which in turn depends upon the industry's *market structure*. More will be said on this below.

Underlying consumer choice is each consumer's ability to choose *rationally* or according to a calculus determining which set of goods would yield the greatest enjoyment, satisfaction, or *utility* to the consumer. This calculus is based upon each consumer's unique set of *preferences*. Consumers' actual choices in markets are assumed to be rational, utility-maximizing decisions reflecting their taste-calculus or preferences.[3] In sum, preferences guide consumer demand, which in turn guides firms' supply; ultimately, it is the innate human desire to maximize consumption-derived utility that drives an industry's supply of commodities.

According to the market choice position, the absence of a *free market* in educational commodities denies consumers (and society) the principal benefits of effective expression of their preferences (through their consumption choices) to firms that openly compete for consumers' dollars. The absence of competition among the suppliers of education means that consumers can only choose from a small set of schools. Presumably this set includes only the public schools provided by the district or possibly only one public school if the district enforces a prohibition on enrollment in any but the assigned schools. In this circumstance each consumer's utility is limited by the type of education they (through their children) can consume at the available schools. Moreover, as the market choice position argues, to the extent that the dearth of options constrains the sovereignty of consumers, educational suppliers will be deprived of the market signals that they count on to adjust their product—their educational commodity—to meet consumers' utility maximizing preferences. (As with the firms' responsiveness to consumer preferences, the effects of this deprivation of market signals will depend upon the industry's market structure. See the discussion in the following section.) Therefore, parents who want schools that emphasize, for example, discipline, mathematics, or western civilization are out of luck: they must consume whatever education is produced by the locally available schools.

The advocacy of market choice in education is based upon just such an understanding of what consumers lose in the absence of a competitive schooling market. In the short term, consumers are denied maximum benefits. In the long term, the consumers' benefit continues to be curtailed by the inability of the market (i.e., the education suppliers) to respond to the expressed and changing preferences of the consumers. The market choice position interprets what's wrong with educational provision in terms of the market's responsiveness to consumer preferences, the satisfaction of which would ensure high quality education for all consumers, including at-risk students.

Given this view, the logical solution is to reform the education system to bring it to the closest possible approximation of a free market system. In such a system, schools in great demand will prosper, and in turn this prosperity will encourage similarly designed schools to enter the market. Moreover, in order to enhance their competitiveness, less popular schools will vary their product according to consumer tastes. The market will thus force schools to respond in ways that will improve the quality of the educational products available.

Voucher plans emerge from just such a vision of consumer sovereignty.

A market system relies upon permitting the establishment of schools that meet criteria set out by the state, where such entities can compete for students. The best-known version of such an approach is that proposed by Milton Friedman (1955, 1962) in the form of educational vouchers. Under a voucher approach, families would be provided with educational certificates by the state for all eligible students that could be used to pay tuition at any school that met the minimal requirements for participation in the voucher system (Levin, 1991, 141).

Although the Chubb and Moe plan differs from Friedman's in certain ways,[4] they share basic characteristics (as do the plans of the Center for the Study of Public Policy [1970] and Coons and Sugarman [1978]): all of these voucher plans seek to change the rules and range of school choice as a way of promoting the long-run, demand-led responsiveness that the market choice advocates believe is required to bring about educational improvement. In short, the logic of the argument starts with vouchers and ends with educational improvement: vouchers will allow parents as educational consumers to express their preferences; enhanced choice will stimulate competition; the competitive drive will force schools (i.e., firms) to respond to the preferences embodied in consumer demand; and, in the long run, parents (and students) will enjoy the availability of better schools from among which to choose. Consumer sovereignty will guide the market to the best of all possible outcomes, all consumers will have maximized their utility, and, when consumer demand changes, so, too, will the education supplied.

II. CRITIQUE OF THE CHUBB AND MOE ARGUMENT

Will Parents Choose the Best Schools?

In the argument for market choice, maximizing student achievement is both the asserted objective of educational policy and the assumed priority of parents. A taxpayer-funded voucher system is supposed to yield the desired result by creating a market environment that will force schools to compete for students and their vouchers. In other words, the impartial, apolitical market is supposed to push schools to become more efficient as they attempt to win "customers." In this context efficiency is taken to mean providing educational services yielding the highest achievement levels.

Recent empirical studies have challenged a particularly important assumption made by the market choice advocates: namely, given a choice, parents would place highest priority on academic quality. Frey (1992) observes that most private schools are religious schools and argues that this fact profoundly colors the argument for market choice. He asks: Is it reasonable to believe that private education, which is currently dominated by religious schools, actually delivers higher academic achievement? A survey of private school teachers provides discouraging evidence.

> In 1985-86, more teachers in non-Catholic religious schools rated the teaching of religious/moral values their highest priority than rated academics to have highest priority. In Catholic schools teaching religious/moral values was the priority of the second-largest group (NCES, 1991, 93) (Frey, 1992, 430).

So does research on parents of private school students.

> Private school parents in British Columbia cited "academic quality/emphasis" as the first reason for preferring private school in only 20.5% of the responses;

religion was cited as the top reason 22% of the time and discipline almost 17% of the time...[And] survey evidence from Minnesota [shows] that private school parents cite quality of school/education as the reason for school choice only 37.8% of the time (Frey, 1992, 431).

Willms and Echols (1992) provide additional evidence contradicting the view that expanding families' educational options leads to higher achievement levels. In the United Kingdom educational legislation has granted all parents the right to choose a school for their children; absent an explicit choice, students are assigned to "designated schools."

> Parents who exercised choice were more highly educated and had more prestigious occupations than those who sent their child to the designated school...Choosers tended to select schools with higher mean socioeconomic status and higher mean levels of attainment. However, the chosen schools did not differ substantially from designated schools in their attainment (Willms and Echols, 1992, 339).

These empirical studies raise serious questions about the criteria used by families to choose schools. Socioeconomic status and/or religious values appear to be at least as important as other attributes of the education offered by a specific school. The available evidence gathered from real world experience casts a shadow on Chubb and Moe's belief that the academic achievement of private schools as a group should be emulated by public schools.

> Chubb and Moe have interpreted available achievement data as showing that private schools, especially Catholic ones, do a better job of educating their students than do public schools. The validity of this interpretation has certainly not been accepted universally (see for example, Cain and Goldberger, 1983 and Witte, 1990). Nevertheless, choice proponents have accepted it as fact and have concluded from it that a voucher system would improve educational outcomes by inducing more students to enroll in private schools (Manski, 1992, 354).

The available evidence supports the following view.

> Private schools may be under the pressure of competition to please parents but academic achievement is not the highest priority of many parents. Enough survey evidence exists to conclude that academic achievement is far from the highest parental value (Frey, 1992, 431)

The market choice position makes two important rhetorical leaps that, when challenged, raise a host of questions. The first is exposed by the empirical evidence just reviewed, which raises doubts about a link between increased choice and improved academic achievement. To believe that market choice will improve education one must assume that there is a fundamental alignment within consumers' choice structures (preferences) between utility-maximizing education and high quality education. If and only if consumers of education have high quality education as their first priority will their utility be maximized by high quality education.

This observation may lead educators to wonder what level of educational excellence and what curricular emphases we should expect if educational consumers were indeed able to exert their sovereignty and thus "get what they want." For example, on the basis of Frey's research (1992), we may speculate that schools can be driven to emphasize religious teachings more than academic excellence. These are not mutually exclusive, of course, but they also do not imply each other. In evaluating the market choice position, it is important to realize that the educational forms consumers would rationally and freely choose may or may not correspond to what professional educators or society at large would define as educational excellence.[5] There is a question that remains: Who should be entrusted with the important task of determining what constitutes educational excellence? Implicitly, the promarket advocates would prefer parents to anyone else.

The asserted connection between competition and school autonomy rests on another unwarranted assumption. Chubb and Moe argue that market competition would augment the autonomy of schools and hence increase their ability to adjust the product to consumer preferences. Moreover, they argue that a *sine qua non* of greater school autonomy is fundamental transformation of the nation's educational system to a market-driven one, a restructuring that goes beyond decentralization.

Educators may well have reason to fear that exposing educational provision to market forces may reduce, rather than increase, school autonomy. For example, Rapple (1992) examined a 35-year English experiment (from 1862 to 1897) with a payment-by-results system, in which schools were paid "grants" according to the students' test results. He found that various aspects of English and Welsh primary schooling were profoundly corrupted by the market incentive: the curricular content was simplified and "idealized the average," the teachers were transformed from educational professionals to entrepreneurs, the teachers' pedagogy was reduced to pedantic "teaching to tests," the schools either excluded the "at-risk" students of the era or kept them at lower grades so they would not keep down the schools' test results and hence cut grant revenue. Researching the records of school "inspectors," Rapple found that "very weak students were often ignored, especially in the period immediately leading up to the examination, teachers being unwilling to waste time on those who had little chance of gaining a grant. Sometimes schools refused to accept dull children at all" (1992, 311). This research demonstrates that market incentives will impose their own, distinctive constraints on schools' and teachers' autonomy.

How Competitive Will the Envisioned Education Market Be?

Choice advocates can argue that a voucher system is inherently superior, on economic grounds, to public school finance only if they presume that education approximately fits the assumptions of classical (textbook) economics. Once this assumption is questioned, possible advantages for public school finance emerge and we are in the messy real world of trade-offs (Manski, 1992, 357).

In their advocacy of a market approach to education, Chubb and Moe predict that a high degree of competition will prevail in the education industry. However, an examination of the actual market conditions that may prevail in education is warranted, for these conditions will fundamentally determine the competitiveness of the education "industry," the degree of firms' responsiveness to consumer preferences, and the overall educational benefits of a market approach.

Economists typically use a set of four criteria in the evaluation of the market conditions that shape a given industry's behavior and outcomes. First, the number and size of the firms comprising the industry determine the degree of firms' market power, that is, their ability to influence the market price of the good or service they supply. Second, an industry's competitiveness is also influenced by the similarity and hence substitutability of one firm's commodities relative to its competitors. A third market condition, factor mobility, is the ability of firms to shift their operations from the production of one commodity to another without significant cost. Such mobility may be hindered by various barriers (e.g., patent restrictions, inaccessibility to key resources, prohibitively large scale of production, etc.) to producing a profitable good or ceasing production of an unprofitable one. Finally, competitiveness is influenced by market participants' access to relevant information. For example, consumers need information regarding the range of available goods and the prices charged by competing firms, while firms are concerned with technological advances and the availability and price of inputs.[6]

There are various reasons to doubt that the envisioned education industry will indeed be sufficiently competitive to push it to respond to consumer demand in ways that would improve educational quality. If Christopher Whittle's Edison Project provides any indication, the education market may end up being dominated by a few, powerful corporations that would be relatively impervious to market forces, including consumer demand. In addition, substitutability among schools is a function, in part, of their homogeneity. However, the explicit point of market choice and especially of promoting product rather than price competition (see above) is to encourage the proliferation of many different types of educational experiences from which parents, armed with vouchers, can choose. Moreover, the information requirement for effective consumers' sovereignty especially worries some researchers. Levin (1991) finds that the cost of collecting and disseminating the relevant information to the consuming public may add a prohibitively expensive transaction cost to the market choice plan.[7]

The conventional criteria used in the evaluation of an industry's competitiveness mainly concern the suppliers. It should be noted that when Chubb and Moe speak of the freedom to enter and exit, they usually are referring not to the suppliers but the consumers, the parents and students. Specifically, they refer to parents' ability to have their children exit one school and enter another. Indeed, consumers' ability to express their preferences in this way is important to the market signalling process discussed earlier. However, consumer mobility (what Chubb and Moe speak of) and *factor* mobility (a classical market condition) refer to different market agents and processes. A high degree of consumer mobility does not imply a high degree of factor mobility: consumers' ability to switch suppliers does not ensure that suppliers will respond to consumer preferences. The actual degree of factor mobility that we can expect of the envisioned education industry remains an open question—it is not guaranteed by promises of greater consumer mobility or choice.

Are Private Schools Better than Public Schools?

> The state will have the responsibility for setting criteria that define what constitutes a "public school" under the new system. These criteria should be quite minimal roughly corresponding to the criteria many states now employ in accrediting private schools—graduation requirements, health and safety requirements, and teacher certification requirements. *Any group or organization that applies to the state and meets these minimal criteria must then be chartered as a public school and granted the right to accept students and receive public money* (Chubb and Moe, 1990, 219; emphasis added).

Chubb and Moe's plan would thus transform the usual distinction between public and private schools. All the schools in their proposed system—even the formerly private schools—would be "public" by virtue of their eligibility for publicly funded tuition vouchers. But these nominally public schools would, like private firms, have to compete for customers. In the Chubb and Moe plan, both existing public and private schools alike would be integrated into the new "public school" market.

In making their case for market choice, proponents have held up existing private schools as evidence that schools exposed to competitive pressures provide superior education. This belief serves as a basis for the claim that private schools are *categorically* better than their public counterparts, and for the policy recommendation that public schools be made to compete and thus emulate the behavior and performance of schools in the private sector. Like the logical linkages we examined above—involving utility maximization, consumer sovereignty, and market responsiveness—the presumption of private school superiority is also questionable.

Current realities in the private school sector do not support idealized images of private schools.[8] A particularly important fact is that this sector is dominated by religious schools.

(R)eligious schools claimed the lion's share (80-90 percent) of private enrollment in the early 1980s...Roman Catholic schools, which once dominated private enrollment (see Erickson, 1986), declined dramatically in both absolute and relative terms between 1965 and 1983 to only somewhat more than half of private enrollment. The slack was taken up by the very rapid growth of evangelical Protestant (primarily fundamentalist) schools; by the mid-1980s non-Catholic religious schools (mostly Protestant evangelical) accounted for about 25 percent of total private enrollment. In the near future, religiously conservative Protestant schools might well dominate private schooling, with Roman Catholic schools in a strong second place (Frey, 1992, 428).

When private schools (excluding the Protestant evangelical schools) are compared to public schools, there is no clear difference in academic achievement.

Even restricting attention to senior-high students, private schools do not outperform public schools in all available evidence. From 1981 to 1985 public school students scored as high as or higher than private school students on the mathematics portion of the Scholastic Aptitude Test (NCES, 1991, p. 105; NCES, 1989, p. 29). This is a result unadjusted for student backgrounds, but such adjustment should tend to expand the public school advantage in mathematics...In addition, if one compares eighth and twelfth grade proficiency scores for 1990, the cross-sectional *gain* for public students exceeds that of private students in all mathematics areas (Frey, 1992, 436).

Encouragement of public schools to reproduce the performance of private schools receives little support from a growing body of evidence, which is instructive on the issue of cost effectiveness as well as student achievement.

(1) there is no systematic evidence of differences in costs for similar students and services and a given level of educational outcome; and (2) there is some systematic—though contested—evidence that private schools produce superior results in student achievement for otherwise similar students. However, the differences in results are very small on the average with little practical significance, and almost half of private school students have achievement scores below the average for public schools. Thus the overall conclusion is that private schools have a very slight advantage over public schools in terms of efficiency at the school level. Whether this very nominal difference would be exacerbated with greater competition in a market choice system is a matter of speculation (Levin, 1991, 153).

Note that Levin's research considers the comparative costs of "similar students and services." This is an important element of research design in such comparative analyses. Assertions simply presuming private school superiority have become commonplace during the past decade. Indeed, one need search no further than *A Nation at Risk*. We believe, however, that those who subscribe to this vision discount the remarkable increase in demographic diversity with which schools have had to contend over the last half-century, while ignoring the tremendous social, economic, and educational changes associated with racial desegregation, changing career expectations of female students, and recent waves of immigration.[9]

> Current enrollments in public schools reflect the fact that one in four students lives in a family whose income is below the poverty line. Another 15 percent of public school students have English as a second language, and one in three public school students are non-white (Grant, 1988, 16).

Critics of public education may be comparing apples and oranges: modern public schools are vastly more diverse and heterogeneous than either public schools of an earlier age or private schools generally.

Four categories of achievement generally accepted as criteria for assessing school success show that the system of public education has done an admirable job of bringing an increasingly diverse student population into the educational mainstream.

> 1. *High school graduation rates.* From 1970 to 1990, the percentage of all Americans aged 25 to 29 holding the high school diploma rose from 75 percent to 86 percent. For African Americans in this age cohort, the increase during this period was from 58 percent to 83 percent. Only 12 percent of this cohort held the high school diploma in 1940.
>
> 2. *Scholastic Aptitude Test.* The percentage of all American 17 year-olds taking the SAT increased from 19 percent in 1976 to 25 percent in 1992. The percentage of SAT-takers belonging to ethnic or racial minorities increased from 13 percent in 1972 to 29 percent in 1992. Not only has the pool of test-takers diversified, but the scores of minority test-takers have increased. The average score (combined) for African Americans increased from 686 in 1976 to 737 in 1992 (1976 was the year test score data disaggregated by race first became available). For Mexican Americans the average score increased from 781 in 1976 to 797 in 1992.
>
> 3. *College matriculation.* In 1970, 27 percent of European American youth in the college age cohort were enrolled in college; in 1991, 34 percent. The gains for African Americans are even more impressive: from 16 percent in 1970 to 24 percent in 1991.
>
> 4. *International comparisons.* U.S. public education also fares well when compared to other nations' outcomes in science, math, and engineering. In the United States 7.4 people in 10,000 hold a college degree (B.A. or B.S.) in a physical science, mathematics, or engineering. In Japan the comparable number is 7.3 while in the former West Germany 6.4 (Rothstein, 1993, 26-27).

Similarly impressive patterns along the lines of ethnicity, class, and gender can be discerned for a variety of other measures of educational attainment as well (Rothstein, 1993).[10]

At the least, this evidence requires any realistic evaluation of the downward trend in SAT scores to take account of the fact that the high scores of the past were a reflection of the very limited racial and ethnic composition of the college-bound population. Generally, the evidence hardly confirms the image of public education offered by its opponents. Especially when disaggregated by race, the data indicate that our institutions of public education have done far better than is widely believed in bringing various marginalized groups toward the mainstream while improving their educational attainment. More students and a more diverse group of students are awarded high school diplomas, take the SAT, earn higher SAT scores, and enroll in institutions of post-secondary education.[11] There seems to be no basis for comparable claims for private education.

As Kozol (1991) makes clear, U.S. public schools do need improvement. The available evidence, however, does not support adoption of the market choice approach on the ground that private schools are categorically better than public schools.

III. THE HISTORY AND RHETORIC OF THE MARKET CHOICE POSITION

The recent resuscitation of arguments for a voucher-based approach occurred in economic and historical circumstances that led the national debate to subordinate concern over educational quality and human betterment to the narrower goal of enhanced economic competitiveness. This change in priority has tended to subsume the at-risk student problem and concerns for education qua education to U.S. economic problems. In our view, the national discourse on the public education crisis has exerted a profound influence upon the tone, scope, and thematic content of the debates over market choice and other reform approaches. To understand the analytic content and consequences of the market choice position the nature of the discourse will be examined. We will see how the historical antecedents and analytical structure of this discussion mold our conception of educational failure, particularly as it affects at-risk students.[12]

Generally, participants in the national discourse, including market choice advocates, accept several simplistic premises. First, they tend to equate economic competitiveness and productive efficiency. That is, the complex determinants of the competitiveness of a given firm, industry, regional economy, or the national economy are reduced to the efficiency with which firms transform inputs into outputs. Second, productivity is taken to be influenced heavily by the skill level of production workers.[13] Third, workers' skill level is assumed to be affected substantially by their (formal) education. Working backwards, these premises imply that education determines workers' skill level, which in turn determines productivity, which ultimately determines U.S. economic competitiveness. This overarching view reduces a series of complex relationships into a simple cause-effect sequence, and its preoccupation with the economy can be discerned in various influential documents, including the U.S. Department of Education's *A Nation at Risk*, the Hudson Institute's *Workforce 2000,* President Bush's "America 2000" plan (the goals of which President Clinton has largely adopted), and Labor Secretary Robert Reich's policy emphasis on training.

A second key preconception implicit in this point of view is that whatever form (or reform) of education promotes economic development will concomitantly promote human development. This assumption of congruence subtly shapes the research on education reform, including research on higher-skill functions,[14] higher order thinking,[15] curriculum development,[16] and "revisioning" or rethinking of vocational education.[17] For example, it is assumed that any educational reform that promises to improve higher order thinking will necessarily benefit both the individual student as a human being and the economy.

> Changes in the economy give direction for what students need to learn, who needs to learn it, when they need to learn it, and how they need to learn it...Work increasingly requires employees both in higher and lower skill jobs to deal with uncertainty, the unfamiliar, and discontinuity; to understand the firm's marketing environment; to understand the organizational context in which the job is embedded in order to anticipate; to understand their technologies well enough to generate initial hypotheses about the source of breakdown for maintenance technicians. We see a stunning parallel between these changes in the nature and structure of work and the defining characteristics of higher order thinking (Berryman, 1989).

This statement by the director of the Institute on Education and the Economy illustrates a common position within the national discourse.

• The position under discussion grew out of recent educational and economic history in the United States. The mainstream debate emerged during the 1980s when some influential persons began to claim that there was a serious mismatch between the evolving labor force needs of U.S. industry and the labor force produced by the education system. It was implied that this was a change from the arrangement that had prevailed for 50 to 60 years.

In this view, private citizens and firms had earlier enjoyed a system of public education that contributed critically to U.S. industry and helped make this country the world's most powerful economic force. Stated briefly, the assimilation of immigrants, the political goals of expanding democracy, and the economic aims of corporate America coincided to produce a system of mass education that supplied labor for a regime of mass production, in which the competitive fulcrum was the cost-efficiency of large-scale production. Some critical histories of education have argued that the educational system that developed alongside the mass production system produced three important ingredients of profitability: first, industrial discipline, which was crucial to the widespread use of scientific management and the authoritarian, hierarchically ordered political relations characteristic of mass production; second, basic skills and trainability in basic skills, which permitted extensive on-the-job training; third, the sorting of students according to their demonstrated academic achievement. [18]

While workers bearing the stamp of such education facilitated U.S. economic growth during most of this century, these characteristics fell increasingly out of step with the labor force needs of industry. In one view, this mismatch was a by-product of the uneven and fitful supersession of mass production by an emerging regime of flexible production (Piore and Sabel, 1984). The new flexible production system is believed to impose distinct labor force requirements: workers who can be effectively deployed in a variety of ways within the production process and who are interchangeable among both the various tasks that are currently necessary and those that would become necessary as products and production processes change over time. [19]

The rejuvenation of the market choice position paralleled the emergence of this view. As official publications such as A Nation at Risk focussed attention on the needs of the economy, the stage was set for efforts to reform public education by "breaking the mold." Market choice advocates judged that U.S. industry had been damaged by educational failure (that was widely alleged to have handicapped its competitiveness), but that the market held the key to repairing the education system: if educational production and distribution could be made to work like competitive markets, education would be improved, and U.S. firms would gain a ready supply of appropriately skilled workers. Thereby, market choice would allow education to help the economy escape from a path of continued stagnation.

Educators have recently demonstrated the limitations of evidence of public education's demise. Some of the key points in the public educators' self-defense have already been summarized here. [20] The case for the educators appears even stronger when we consider the contradictory position of public education in relation to the educational needs of U.S. industry. On one hand, public education's sorting function requires increased inclusion of students who have been historically kept outside of the educational mainstream—African Americans, Hispanic Americans, and, of particular importance, students whose educational progress was stunted by inadequate health and social support services. Before such students could be sorted, they had to be brought into the arena of public education. However, effective inclusion requires the provision of a host of extra-curricular support services. During the last 25 years, the public school system has been a prime means for delivery of such support services, and this role has been expanded to include services related to teenage pregnancy, drug and alcohol abuse, violence, and AIDS. In other words, the public schools were asked both to bring traditionally excluded students into the mainstream and to become the providers of an ever-expanding set of extra-curricular services. Of course, both objectives—inclusion and support service provision—are worthy goals, but the combination of the two in the absence of increased resources for instruction per se has made the teachers' principal responsibility of pedagogy much more difficult. As a result, public education was torn between two objectives:

production of the kind of labor force increasingly called for by the changing economy and alleviation of the at-risk student problem. In effect, public education was supposed to enhance the labor force and, at the same time, provide the means for at-risk students to climb out of poverty.

Generally, the national discourse has failed to recognize that the category "at risk" extends far beyond education: to be at risk also entails cultural, medical, political, and economic attributes. Considered from just the economic perspective, by the time they enter school, most at-risk students are already losers in the economic competition. Some researchers have long suspected that the best predictor of student performance is the level of parental education and income (Bowles and Gintis, 1976), while more recent findings confirm that "educational results have been found to be especially weak among the increasing numbers of students from poor, minority, immigrant and single parent families" (Levin, 1992, 279). The person at risk of school failure often also is engaged in a struggle with a variety of social and medical conditions that are closely associated with poverty: homelessness, abuse by parents or caretakers, and various, fragmented family-school-community relations, HIV, cancer, low birthweight, and various other causes of a "medically fragile" state, and exposure (either direct or via parents) to alcohol, cocaine, lead, and other toxic substances.[21] Moreover, these social and medical conditions are linked to various attributes of the "cognitive and social performance of students": noncompliance ("aggressiveness, failure to comply with teacher directives, or loss of control"); self-regulation difficulties ("ability to attend to, take in, use information; to organize a calm, regulated state; and to adapt to the needs of a situation"); language and communication difficulties; difficulties with social relationships; and difficulties in judgment and decision making (Stevens and Price, 1992).

These traits are precisely those that mark the students who are least desirable to employers.[22] If there is any truth to the notion that public schools perform labor market triage for U.S. industry—that is, separating the trainable and potentially productive from the others who populate the at-risk category—and if a prime objective of education reform is to improve worker skills, productivity, and ultimately economic competitiveness, then we should not expect such education reform to provide much relief for at-risk students. The issue of how to help at-risk students is no less complicated than the issue of how to reduce poverty.[23]

The title *A Nation at Risk* signifies that at-risk students will be forced to compete with the national economy as the objective of the education reform. As long as economic improvement is at the center of the national discourse's sights, then reform schemes such as market choice and vouchers, at best, advocate a faith in the reform's potential benefits for at-risk students *as secondary effects* of the principal objective of improving economic competitiveness; at worst, they relegate the concern for at-risk students to the status of an afterthought or a marketing ploy to sell a reform proposal.[24]

IV. CONCLUSION

Those concerned about both education and at-risk students may wish to challenge the subordination of education to economic imperatives. If education reform is simply manpower policy, then we should investigate where at-risk students will fit within the changing occupational structure. We may find that our economy, left to its own devices, will not provide any more or any better occupational roles for those traditionally at risk; that the labor-supply needs of U.S. industry will be satisfied in ways that fail significantly to integrate poor, socially fragmented, and/or medically fragile students; and that, therefore, labor market triage, which is a by-product of public education's sorting function, will continue to leave the most needy students in economic and social isolation.

Those who, like Kozol (1991), understand the at-risk student problem as inseparable from educational and economic inequality should be concerned by recent empirical studies that suggest that market choice and vouchers may have the unintended effect of exacerbating current inequalities. Evidence suggests that "parents seem to be motivated to increase the economic segregation of the educational environment beyond that already existing as a result of residential location" (Lankford and Wyckoff, 1992); the strength of parents' desire for quality schooling is linked positively to their own educational attainment and occupational status (Willms and Echols, 1992); choice systems may not have the claimed equalizing effects on educational opportunity (Manski, 1992); school segregation may not be decreased by choice plans (Chriss, Nash, and Stern, 1992); and parents' active participation in the search for information and the ability to use it in educational choices are related to their educational attainment, occupational status, and race (Levin, 1991). These empirical results cast additional doubts on the benefits promised by market choice for at-risk students. Analysis of the economic assumptions underlying the market choice position fuels skepticism about the panacea choice is supposed to provide. Educators concerned about the conditions and prospects of at-risk students have much to ponder and study before supporting the market choice position.

NOTES

1. For a description of rhetorical analysis, see Solow, Klamer, and McCloskey (1988); and McCloskey (1985, 1990, and 1994).

2. We will italicize technical terms of economists when they are first used. The purpose is to help noneconomists identify specialized terms, a proper understanding of which is necessary for a critical evaluation of the market choice plan.

3. These choices can be traced backward to individual tastes and preferences, which are the origin of the familiar demand curves of elementary economics.

4. There is an important distinction between the Chubb and Moe plan and the approach Friedman supported decades earlier. While the Friedman system would allow parents to supplement established vouchers levels with private funds, the Chubb and Moe

plan would prohibit any such supplementation. This progressive element of the Chubb and Moe plan runs counter to the libertarian spirit of Friedman's approach, which exalts the individual freedom to choose. Prohibiting voucher supplements is intended to discourage schools (firms) from competing on the basis of price by forcing them to compete on the basis of product quality. The rationale is that allowing price competition may exacerbate the educational inequality that the market choice plan aims at ameliorating. As Frey (1992) clearly demonstrates, however, such *de jure* prohibitions will not effectively prevent price competition, especially as long as parents can make private donations to schools, or school districts can set tuition levels above voucher allowances, or districts can rebate portions of vouchers in excess of tuition. Such mechanisms will serve to subvert the Chubb and Moe plan and violate its progressive spirit. "Inequality of education expenditure would unambiguously rise under the subverted Chubb and Moe plan. Current high-spending districts would become high-voucher districts, and vice versa. Grafted on top of unequal vouchers, which would presumably perpetuate present inequalities, would be the additional inequality chosen by families and implemented through supplemental 'donations.' That families might choose to receive rebates in order to spend less than the voucher would also increase inequality if parents with low income or low preferences for education tended to live in low-voucher districts—a highly likely prospect" (Frey, 1992, 433).

5. Levin (1991) couches this consideration in terms of the conflicts between the private benefits accruing to individual consumers and the various social benefits of schooling.

6. See the following standard texts: Baumol and Blinder (1994), Case and Fair (1994), and Samuelson and Nordhaus (1994).

7. Levin sees an irony here: market choice aims at eliminating bureaucrats and special interest groups from the center of decision-making and replacing them with thousands of consuming families, but this decentralization would necessitate a highly centralized information distribution system.

8. For many Americans, the term private school is likely to conjure images of elite boarding schools like those attended by Holden Caulfield, dramatized in movies such as "School Ties," or depicted in novels such as *A Separate Peace*. Most students in the private sector attend schools very different from those.

9. See Hodgkinson (1985).

10. See also Jaeger (1992).

11. Moreover, the sanguine implications of the SAT data are enhanced by the recent acknowledgment that SAT scoring procedures have tended increasingly to understate student achievement and that, therefore, the scale will have to be "recentered." The acknowledged reason for the adjustment—increases in the size and diversity of the SAT-taking population—is evidence of public education's partial success in bringing marginalized students into the educational mainstream.

12. This discourse is manifested in many writings beside Brookings Institute publications. Those active in the dialogue are both economists and noneconomists. These participants include federal agencies (e.g., U.S. Departments of Education and of Commerce), government-funded research agencies (e.g., the National Center on Education and the Economy and the National Center for Research in Vocational Education), private research centers (e.g., the Hudson Institute), business groups (e.g., the Conference Board

and various national and regional business "roundtables"), and the business and popular presses (e.g., *Fortune* and *The Wall Street Journal*).

13.   The most sophisticated expressions of this reduction recognize that productivity is conditioned by various factors other than workers' skill levels, including inventory control techniques, the extent of worker participation and teamwork, and the quality of the materials and equipment used. But even these relatively elaborate analyses theorize how these other factors contribute to productivity as dependent upon workers' skill level.

14.   See Bailey (1990).

15.   See Resnick (1987).

16.   See Berryman (1989).

17.   See Cantor (1989).

18.   See Bowles and Gintis (1976) and Spring (1976, 1989).

19.   See the rapidly expanding literature on the labor force requirements of flexible production, including Bailey (1990), Carnevale (1991), and Osterman (1988, 1990).

20.   See also Jaeger (1992), Bracey (1992), and Rotberg (1990), who critically analyze the statistical bases underlying the mainstream discourse's attack on U.S. public education.

21.   The September 1992 issue of *Phi Delta Kappan* includes a series of articles describing these various dimensions of being at risk.

22.   Compare this list, for example, to the "Five Competencies" and "Three-Part Foundation" as listed in the U.S. Department of Labor's 1991 SCANS report, *What Work Requires of School*.

23.   This complexity is recently being raised more often and more forcefully by the education community. For example, Bracey (1992) challenges the direction of causality in the view that the claimed (though unsubstantiated) decline in school quality contributed materially to social and economic decline in the 1980s. Hamby (1989) argues that schools alone do not cause students to drop out, and, therefore, schools alone cannot prevent students from dropping out. Jaeger (1992) argues that education's performance must be assessed within the broad social context of modern life in the United States, which is constituted by multiple crises. Tye (1992) warns against basing a decentralization movement upon oversimplified and oversimplifying assumptions about education in America.

24. Manski (1992) and Jaeger (1992) argue that choice and privatization schemes would benefit a subset of educational consumers and not education as a whole. Manski writes about "systemic choice," "The intention clearly is to subsidize enrollment at secular private schools and, courts permitting, at religiously affiliated schools as well" (352). Moreover, when the calculus of value-added and cost-per-pupil are placed center-stage, those already at risk are put at further risk of being rejected and barred from private schools, which will continue to be allowed to admit selectively. For evidence of this Jaeger points to the experiment in Milwaukee, where nearly one-quarter of the 317 participants in a voucher/choice system were returned to the public schools because the private schools "found them too difficult to handle or incompatible with the schools' goals" (126).

REFERENCES

Bailey, T. 1990. Jobs of the future and the skills they will require. *American Educator* 14 (1): 10-15, 40-44.

Baumol, W. 1982. *Contestable markets and the theory of industry structure.* New York: Harcourt Brace Jovanovich.

Baumol, W. and Blinder, A. 1994. *Economics: Principles and policy.* Fort Worth: Dryden Press.

Berryman, S. 1989. Economic change: The implications for student learning. *NASSP Bulletin* February: 59-70.

Bowles, S. and Gintis, H. 1976. *Schooling in capitalist America: Educational reform and the contradictions of economic life.* New York: Basic Books.

Bracey, G. 1992. The condition of public education. *Phi Delta Kappan* 74 (October): 104-27.

Cain, G. and Goldberger, A. 1983. Public and private schools revisited. *Sociology of Education*: 208-18.

Cantor, L. 1989. The 're-visioning' of vocational education in the American high school. *Comparative Education* 25 (2): 125-32.

Carnevale, A. 1991. *America and the new economy.* San Francisco: Jossey-Bass.

Case, K. and Fair, R. 1994. *Principles of economics.* Englewood Cliffs: Prentice Hall.

Catterall, J. 1992. Theory and practice of family choice in education: Taking stock—review essay. *Economics of Education Review.* 407-416.

Center for the Study of Public Policy. 1970. *Education vouchers: A report on financing elementary education by grants to parents.* Cambridge, MA.

Chriss, B.; Nash, G.; and Stern, D. 1992. The rise and fall of choice in Richmond, California. *Economics of Education Review.* 11 (4): 395-406.

Chubb, J. and Moe, T. 1990. *Politics, markets, and America's schools.* Washington, D.C.: The Brookings Institution.

Coons, J. and Sugarman, S. 1978. *Education by choice.* Berkeley: U. of California Press.

Erickson, D.A. 1986. Disturbing evidence about the 'one best system.' In *The public school monopoly,* ed. R.B. Everhart. San Francisco: Pacific Institute for Public Policy Research.

Frey, D. 1992. Can privatizing education really improve achievement? An essay review. *Economics of Education Review.* 11 (4): 427-38.

Friedman, M. 1955. The role of government in education. In *Economics and the public interest,* ed. Solo, R. New Brunswick: Rutgers U. Press.

_____. 1962. *Capitalism and freedom.* Chicago: U. of Chicago Press.

Garner, W.T. and Hannaway, J. 1982. Private schools: The client connection. In *Family choice in schooling,* ed. Manley-Casmir, M. Lexington, MA: D.C. Heath.

Grant, C. 1988. Race, class, gender, and schooling. *Education Digest.* 54 (December): 15-18.

Hamby, J. 1989. How to get an "A" on your dropout prevention report card. *Educational Leadership.* 46 (February): 21-28.

Hodgkinson, H. 1985. *All one system: Demographics of education—kindergarten through graduate school.* Washington, D.C.: Institute for Educational Leadership.

_____. 1989. *The same client: The demographics of education and service delivery systems.* Washington, D.C.: Institute for Educational Leadership, Center for Demographic Policy.

Hudson Institute. 1987. *Workforce 2000.* Washington, D.C.: U.S. Government Printing Office.

Jaeger, R. 1992. Weak measurement serving presumptive policy. *Phi Delta Kappan* 74 (October): 118-28.

Kozol, J. 1991. *Savage inequalities: Children in America's schools.* New York. Harper Collins.

Lankford, H. and Wyckoff, J. 1992. Primary and secondary school choice among public and religious alternatives. *Economics of Education Review.* 11 (4): 317-37.

Levin, H. 1991. The economics of educational choice. *Economics of Education Review.* 10 (2): 137-58.

_____. 1992. Market approaches to education: Vouchers and school choice. *Economics of Education Review.* 11 (4): 279-85.

Manski, C. 1992. Educational choice (vouchers) and social mobility. *Economics of Education Review* 11 (4): 351-69.

McCloskey, D. 1985. *The rhetoric of economics.* Madison, Wis.: University of Wisconsin Press.

_____. 1990. *If you're so smart: The narrative of economic expertise.* Chicago: University of Chicago Press.

_____. 1994. *Knowledge and persuasion in economics.* Cambridge: Cambridge University Press.

Miller, L.S. 1986. The school-reform debate. *Journal of Economic Education* 17 (Summer): 204-209.

National Center for Education Statistics. 1989. *1989 education indicators.* Washington, D.C.: U.S. Government Printing Office.

_____. 1991. *Private schools in the United States: A statistical profile, with comparisons to public schools.* Washington, D.C.: U.S. Government Printing Office.

Osterman, P. 1988. *Employment futures: Reorganization, dislocation, and public policy.* New York: Oxford University Press.

_____. 1990. Elements of a national training policy. In *New developments in worker training: A legacy for the 1990s,* eds. L. A. Fermin, M. Hoyman, J. Cutcher-Gershenfeld, and E. J. Savoie, 257-82. Madison: Industrial Relations Research Association.

Pickering, J. and Bowers, J. 1990. Assessing value-added outcomes assessment. *Measurement and Evaluation in Counseling and Development* 22 (January): 215-21.

Piore, M. and Sabel, C. 1984. *The second industrial divide: Possibilities for prosperity.* New York: Basic Books.

Rapple, B. 1992. A Victorian experiment in economic efficiency in education. *Economics of Education Review* 11 (4): 301-16.

Resnick, L. 1987. *Education and learning to think.* Washington, D.C.: National Academy Press.

Rotberg, I. 1990. I never promised you first place. *Phi Delta Kappan* 72 (December): 296-303.

Rothstein, R. 1993. The myth of public school failure. *The American Prospect*. (Spring): 20-34.

Samuelson, P. and Nordhaus, W. 1994. *Economics*. New York: McGraw-Hill.

Scherer, F. 1980. *Industrial market structure and economic performance*. Boston: Houghton Mifflin.

Shepherd, W. 1979. *The economics of industrial organization*. Englewood Cliffs, NJ: Prentice-Hall.

Solow, R., and Klamer, A., and McCloskey, D. 1988. *The consequences of economic rhetoric*. Cambridge: Cambridge University Press.

Spring, J. 1976. *The sorting machine: National education policy since 1945*. New York: McKay.

_____. 1989. *The sorting machine revisited: National education policy since 1945*. New York: Longman.

Stevens, L. and Price, M. 1992. Meeting the challenge of educating children at risk. *Phi Delta Kappan*. 74 (September): 18-23.

Tye, K. 1992. Restructuring our schools: Beyond the rhetoric. *Phi Delta Kappan* 74 (September): 8-14.

U.S. Department of Education, National Commission on Excellence in Education. 1983. *A nation at risk: The imperative for educational reform*. Washington, D.C.: U.S. Government Printing Office.

U.S. Department of Labor, The Secretary's Commission on Achieving Necessary Skills. 1991. *What work requires of schools: A SCANS report for America 2000*. Washington, D.C.: U.S. Government Printing Office.

West, E. 1982. The prospects for education vouchers: An economic analysis. In *The public school monopoly*, ed. R. Everhart. San Francisco: Pacific Institute for Public Policy Research.

_____. 1992. Autonomy in school provision: Meanings and implications—review essay. *Economics of Education Review*. 11 (4): 417-25.

Willms, J. and Echols, F. 1992. Alert and inert clients: The Scottish experience of parental choice of schools. *Economics of Education Review*. 11 (4): 339-50.

Witte, J. 1990. *Understanding high school achievement: After a decade of research, do we have any confident policy recommendations?* Dept. of Political Science, U. of Wisconsin-Madison.

CHAPTER 5

INCENTIVES TO STUDY
AND THE ORGANIZATION
OF SECONDARY INSTRUCTION

John H. Bishop

The scientific and mathematical competence of American high school students is generally recognized to be low. The National Assessment of Educational Progress (NAEP) reports that 92 percent of high school seniors cannot "integrate specialized scientific information" and do not have "the capacity to apply mathematical operations in a variety of problem settings." (NAEP, 1988a, 51; 1988b, 42)

At the end of high school there is a large gap between the science and math competence of American students and their counterparts overseas.[1] The Americans who participated in the Second International Math Study were high school seniors in college preparatory math courses. This group, which represented only 13 percent of American 17 year olds, was roughly comparable to the 15 percent of youth in Finland and the 50 percent of Hungarians who were taking college preparatory mathematics. In Algebra, the score of 40 percent correct for this very select group of American students was about equal to the score of the much larger group of Hungarians and substantially below the Finnish score of 79 percent correct (McKnight, et al., 1987).

The findings of the Second International Science Study are similar. Take Finland, for example. The 41 percent of the Finnish students who were taking some biology in their senior year of secondary school got 50 percent correct. The 12 percent of Americans taking a second biology course in senior year got 38 percent correct. The 16 percent of Finns taking chemistry knew almost as much as the 2 percent of American high school seniors who were taking their second year of chemistry (many of whom were in "Advanced Placement") (Postlethwaite and Wiley, 1992). Only in reading are American students in the middle rather than the bottom of the international league tables (Elley, 1992, 108-9).

The poor performance of American high school students in mathematics and science is sometimes blamed on the nation's "diversity". However, the U.S. is not the only country challenged by ethnic diversity. The share of the students who are taught in a language different from their own mother tongue is 6 percent in both France and the United States, 5 percent in Scotland, 12 percent in Canada, 15 percent in Northern Italy and 20 percent in Switzerland (IAEP, 1991a). It is true that secondary schools do a particularly poor job educating African-Americans, Hispanics and children from low income backgrounds. But the affluent nonminority parents who believe that their children are doing acceptably by international standards are misinformed. In Stevenson, Lee and Stigler's (1986) study of fifth grade math achievement, the best of the 20 classrooms sampled in Minneapolis was outstripped by every single classroom studied in Sendai, Japan and by 19 of the 20 classrooms studied in Taipei, Taiwan. The nation's top high school students rank far behind much less elite samples of students in other countries. Substantially larger shares of 17-18 year old Belgians, Finns, Hungarians, Scots, Swedes and Canadians are studying advanced algebra, pre-calculus and calculus and their achievement levels are significantly higher than American high school seniors in such classes. In math and science, the gap between American high school seniors from middle class suburbs and their counterparts in many northern European nations and Japan sometimes exceeds the two to three grade level equivalent gap between whites and blacks in the U.S. (NAEP, 1988b; McKnight, et al., 1987).

It is sometimes said that low achievement is the price one must pay for greater access. The U.S. does have larger stocks of secondary school graduates than other nations, but on a flow basis, the American advantage has vanished. Table 5.1 presents data on the ratio of secondary school diplomas awarded to population for a variety of industrialized countries. The ratio is over 100 percent in Denmark, Finland and Germany, 90 percent in Japan, 82 percent in the Netherlands, 76 percent in France and 65 percent in England. Despite the minimal standards for getting a diploma in the United States, the ratio of secondary school diplomas awarded to population eighteen years of age was only 73.7 percent in 1988, slightly below its level in 1968.[2] Standards were lowered in the 1970s, but access did not improve.

Participation in postsecondary education is higher in the United States (see Table 5.1), but most college freshmen are studying material that European university students studied in secondary school. Many Europeans doubt that BAs from second rank American universities are equivalent to the French *Licence* or the Dutch *Doctoraal examen*. In the economically critical fields of science, mathematics, computer science and engineering, the degree production relative

Table 5.1:   1991 Graduation Rates for Secondary and University Education

	Sec. Dipl/ Pop18	Bachelors/ Pop22	Sci, Eng, Math Deg/ LF2534
Australia	---	24.4	8.2
Canada	73	33.3	6.2
Denmark	100	16.5	6.7
Finland	125	17.2	7.0
France	76	16.3	7.2
Germany	117	13.3	6.8
Ireland	51	16.0	8.8
Italy	76	9.2	2.6
Japan	91	23.7	9.7
Netherlands	82	8.3	2.5
Norway	89	30.8	7.9
Sweden	80	12.0	4.0
United Kingdom	74	18.4	7.7
United States	74	29.6	6.5

Source: OECD, *Education at a Glance* (1993; pp. 176, 179 & 185). Column 1 is the ratio of secondary school diplomas and credentials awarded in 1991 to population eighteen years of age. It exceeds 100 percent in Denmark, Finland and Germany because older individuals from larger birth cohorts are completing their secondary schooling and because some individuals obtain two secondary level credentials (eg. In Germany some recipients of the Abitur pursue three year apprenticeships that yield vocational qualifications). The third column is 10 multiplied by the ratio of science, mathematics, computer science and engineering degrees awarded in 1991 at all levels (BS, MS and PhD) to the labor force twenty-five to thirty-four year-olds.

to population exceeds U.S. levels in Japan, Norway, France and Ireland. Finland, Canada, Denmark and Germany produce proportionately just about as many people trained in these fields as the United States. Only Italy, the Netherlands and Sweden are distinctly below the U.S. Many observers believe that the abundance and quality of scientists and engineers has historically been an important source of competitive advantage for American companies. This advantage is diminishing.

The poor quality of American secondary schools has economic consequences. The high school graduates of 1980 knew about 1.25 grade level equivalents less mathematics, science and English than the graduates of 1967. This decline in the academic achievement is estimated to have lowered the nation's output by $86 billion in 1987 and will lower it by more than $200 billion annually in the year 2010 (Bishop, 1989).

A high school diploma no longer signifies functional literacy. Most schools do not help their graduates obtain employment and many do not even send transcripts to employers when their graduates sign the necessary waivers while applying for a job. This is probably one of the reasons why, for the last six years, an average of 28 percent of noncollege-bound white high school graduates and 55 percent of the black graduates had no job four months after graduating from high school (Bureau of Labor Statistics, 1989; 1991). It also probably contributed to the 14 percent decline in real wages of recent high school graduates since 1971 (Katz and Murphy, 1990).

The deteriorating achievement levels of those completing high school in the late 1970s did not cause college entrance rates to decline, but it was accompanied by a decrease in college completion rates. The share of high school graduates 25 to 29 years old who complete four years of college, which rose dramatically in the 1950s and 1960s, peaked at 28 percent in 1976/7 and then fell to 25 percent in 1981/2. It has since crept back to 27.2 percent in 1991/92 (NCES, 1992a, Table 22.3).

Demand for highly educated workers has grown rapidly during the last forty years and wage premiums for college graduates are now at post war highs. The very high payoff to completing a college degree has stimulated a modest increase in rates of college completion by recent high school graduates but completion rates are still low. By February 1986, for example, only 18.8 percent of 1980 high school graduates had obtained a bachelors degree. Even for students with A averages in high school, the BA completion rate was just 49 percent. For C students, 2.5 percent had completed college (National Center for Education Statistics, 1992b, Table 299). If the academic preparation of those completing high school does not improve, college drop out rates will probably remain high and, as a result, the supply of college educated workers will fall short of the forecasted demand and wage gaps between educational haves and educational have nots will remain very high (Bishop and Carter, 1991).

Why does the mathematics and science achievement of American high school students compare so unfavorably to achievement levels in other advanced countries? The first three sections of the paper offer a diagnosis. Section I examines the proximate causes of low achievement levels: the low priority that students, parents and the public place on learning. Section II demonstrates that the rewards for learning are particularly weak in American secondary schools and suggests that this is the primary reason why students, parents and the public commit so few resources to teaching and learning mathematics and science. Section III examines how school organization and external assessment influence student learning. Section IV and V offer practical policy recommendations for strengthening student incentives to learn and parental incentives to demand higher quality instruction.

I. LOW EFFORT: PROXIMATE CAUSE OF THE LEARNING DEFICIT

There is evidence indicating that this poor record of achievement is caused by the limited amount of time, money and psychic energy devoted to academic learning in American high schools. Students, parents and the public are all responsible.

Student Effort

Time on Task: Learning is not a passive act; it requires the time and active involvement of the learner. In a classroom with one teacher and 20 students, there are 20 learning hours spent for every hour of teaching time. Student time is, therefore, the critical resource, and how intensely it is used affects learning significantly. Numerous studies have found learning to be strongly related to time on task (Wiley, 1986).

Studies employing a time diary method have found that American middle school students spend 28.7 hrs/wk in school and senior high students spend 26.2 hrs/wk in school. European students spend a similar amount of time in school. The Japanese, however, spend 46.6 hrs/wk for junior high school and 41.5 hours for senior high school (Juster and Stafford, 1990).

Classroom observation studies reveal that U.S. students are engaged in a learning activity for only about half the time they are scheduled to be in school. A study of schools in Chicago found that schools with high-achieving students averaged about 75 percent of class time for actual instruction; for schools with low achieving students, the average was 51 percent of class time (Frederick, 1977). Overall, Frederick, Walberg and Rasher (1979) estimated 46.5 percent of the potential learning time is lost through absence, lateness, and inattention.

Homework: Harris Cooper's (1989) meta-analysis of randomized experimental studies found that students assigned homework scored about one-half a standard deviation higher on post tests than students not receiving homework assignments.

The impact of homework on the rate at which middle school students learn was also significant, though somewhat smaller. There was no evidence of diminishing returns as the amount of homework increased. Nonexperimental studies indicate that the relationship between homework and learning is linear.

In the High School and Beyond Survey, students reported spending an average of only 3.5 hours per week on homework (National Opinion Research Corporation, 1982). Time diaries yield similar estimates for the early 1980s: 3.2 hours for junior high school and 3.8 hours for senior high school. Time diaries for Japanese students reveal that they spend 16.2 hours per week studying in junior high school and nineteen hours a week studying in senior high school.

In the early 1980s, many American high school classes gave no homework assignments. Arthur Powell described one school he visited:

> Students were given class time to read *The Scarlet Letter, The Red Badge of Courage, Huckleberry Finn,* and *The Great Gatsby* because many would not read the books if they were assigned as homework. Parents had complained that such homework was excessive. Pressure from them might even bring the teaching of the books to a halt....[As one teacher put it] "If you can't get them to read at home, you do the next best thing. It has to be done....I'm trying to be optimistic and say we're building up their expectations in school." (Powell, Farrar and Cohen, 1985, 81)

It's not just reading that teachers feel they cannot require. A high school history teacher who had previewed PBS's 11 hour series on the Civil War and who had participated in developing teaching materials associated with the series was asked by a reporter whether he was assigning it to his class. The teacher replied that unfortunately he could not because 11 hours was way beyond what most high school students were willing to commit to an assignment.

The educational excellence movement appears to have resulted in an increase in homework assignments during the 1980s. In 1982 27 percent of 13 year olds and 30 percent of 17 years olds reported not being assigned any homework. Another 11.5 (6.0) percent of 17 (13) year olds reported not doing it. By 1990 only 5-6 percent of 13 and 17 year olds reported getting no homework and only 4 to 8 percent reported not doing what was assigned (National Center for Education Statistics, 1993, 351-2). In the 1991 IAEP survey, 29 percent of American 13 year olds said they were doing two or more hours of homework daily. The proportion doing more than two hours of homework was equally low in Canada and Portugal and even lower in Scotland and Switzerland. In most countries, however, the proportion was higher: 79 percent in Italy, 63-64 percent in Ireland and Spain, 50-58 percent in Israel, Hungary, France, Jordan and the former Soviet Union, and 41-44 percent in Brazil, Korea, Taiwan and China (NCES, 1992b, Table 387).

Other Uses of Time: When homework is added to engaged time at school, the time devoted to study, instruction, and practice in the U.S. totals only 18-20 hrs/wk -- between 15 and 20 percent of the student's waking hours during the school year. By way of comparison, typical seniors spend nearly 10 hours per week in part-time jobs (NORC, 1982) and 19.6 hours per week watching television. Thus, TV occupies as much time as learning. Numerous studies conducted in a variety of countries have found that time spent watching TV is negatively correlated with student achievement in mathematics, reading and science (IAEP, 1992, Elley, 1992).[3]

In Table 5.2 we can see that secondary school students in other industrialized nations use their time very differently. Reading takes up six hours per week of a Finnish student's nonschool time, 4.8 hrs/wk of Swiss and Austrian student's time but only 1.4 hrs/wk of an American student's time. They watch much less television: 55 percent less in Finland, 70 percent less in Norway and 44 percent less in Canada. In other countries high school students watch less TV than adults; in the United States they watch more.

Trends do not appear very favorable. The share of American 17 year olds who report they watch more than three hours of TV a day rose from 31 percent in 1978 to 55 percent in 1986, then fell slightly to 49 percent in 1990. In 1990 16 percent of 13 year olds said they were watching six or more hours of TV a day (NCES, 1993, 354-55).

Table 5.2: Time Use by Students (hours per week)

	T.V.		Reading Time
	Students	Adults	Students
U.S.	19.6	15.9	1.4
Austria	6.3	10.6	4.9
Canada	10.9	13.3	1.5
Finland	9.0	9.0	6.0
Netherlands	10.6	13.4	4.3
Norway	5.9	7.2	4.3
Switzerland	7.7	9.0	4.8

Source: Hours derived from time diary studies. Organization of Economic Cooperation and Development, *Living Conditions in OECD Countries* (1986; Tables 18.1 & 18.3).

Avoidance of Demanding Courses: Science and mathematics deficits are particularly severe because most students do not take rigorous college preparatory courses in these subjects. Of those graduating from high school in 1990, only 50 percent had taken chemistry, only 21.5 percent had taken physics, only 13.5 percent had taken pre-calculus and only 6.6 percent had taken calculus (National Center for Education Statistics, 1991, 54). Advanced Placement courses in Biology, Chemistry and Physics are each taken by only about 1 percent of high school graduates.

States have attempted to deal with this problem by increasing the number of mathematics and science courses required for graduation. What impact does the number of courses taken in a subject have on learning? To answer this question, an analysis was conducted of longitudinal data on the sophomore cohort of *High School and Beyond*. The dependent variables were the change between sophomore and senior years in overall grade point average and test scores in four subjects: English, mathematics, science and social studies. The specific model estimated was:

$$Y_{it} - Y_{it-1} = \beta X_{it-1} + \phi C + \theta Y_{j=i,t-1} \qquad i = 1....5$$

where

Y_{it}	=	the i th outcome variable measured at the end of senior year. (e.g. math test score)
Y_{it-1}	=	the sophomore year measure of the i th outcome variable
$Y_{j=i,t-1}$	=	a vector of sophomore year measures of outcome variables other than the i th
X_{it-1}	=	a vector of variables characterizing background and curriculum course-work variables measured in the sophomore year
C	=	a vector of variables describing the courses taken in junior and senior year
ϕ	=	a vector of coefficients measuring effects of course work on learning and career aspirations

The control variables included an array of socioeconomic background variables, sophomore year GPA, sophomore year test scores, sophomore year attitudinal variables, sophomore year educational and occupational expectations, and the parents' career expectations for their child. Numerous measures of curriculum were used to assess curriculum effects, including sophomore year self-reported curriculum track (vocational and academic), self-reported number of courses taken between the sophomore and senior year in a variety of subjects, and self-reported data on whether the respondent had taken a number of specific courses. Chemistry, physics, algebra II, trigonometry and calculus were selected from a more complete list of courses to represent rigorous math and science course work generally taken during or after the sophomore year in high school (Bishop, 1985).

Results are presented in Table 5.3. Holding background characteristics and the rigor of the math and science courses constant, an additional three courses in math and science during high school increased the gain in math competency between 10th and 12th grade by only .19 of a grade level equivalent and *reduced* science gains by .09 of a grade level equivalent and *reduced* English and social studies gains by .17-.18 of a grade level equivalent. Holding background characteristics and the total number of courses taken in specific fields constant, taking five college preparatory math and science courses--chemistry, physics, algebra II, trigonometry and calculus--increased the gain during the two year period on math and science tests by .74-.76 of a grade level equivalent and increased the gain in English and social studies by .34-.44 of a grade level equivalent. The crucial difference is apparently that these college preparatory classes are more demanding than other classes. This is clearly the case in our data, for the students who took all five of the more difficult college preparatory classes suffered a significant decline in GPA between sophomore and senior year.

Table 5.3: **Change in Academic Achievement Resulting from Modifying Curriculum** (in percent of a grade level equivalent)

Achievement on	Taking Rigorous College Prep Courses	Taking 3 Additional Courses in Math and Science	Taking 3 Additional Courses in Business and Office	Taking 3 Additional Courses in Technical
Verbal Test	34***	17***	20***	4
Math Test	76***	19***	-9	15**
Science Test	74***	-9***	-6	-1
Civics Test	44*	-18***	15**	1
Grade Point Average	-.12**	0.0	.06**	.05*

*Statistically significant at the 95 percent level. **Statistically significant at the 99 percent level. ***Statistically significant at the 99.9 percent level.

Source: Entries are averages of coefficients from separate regressions for males and females. For the four test scores, entries are coefficients scaled as a percent of a grade level equivalent under the conservative assumption that the test's standard deviation is equal to three grade level equivalents. The results for GPA are in percents of one point on a four point GPA scale. The dependent variable was the change between the end of sophomore and senior years. The models used to derive these estimates contained a total of 75 control variables. Included among the control variables were the sophomore values on the 10 other outcome measures, a great variety of specific courses, years of courses in specific subjects taken during freshmen and sophomore year and during junior and senior year, family background, self-assessed ability to succeed in college, and parental pressure to attend college.

These results clearly imply that learning rates are determined more by the *rigor* than the number of courses taken in a subject. Consequently, state requirements that students take more math and science courses to graduate will have little effect on learning if students meet the requirement by taking undemanding courses. Too many students avoid the more rigorous science and math courses because such courses increase their workload and lower their grade point average.

Psychic Energy: Even more important than the time devoted to learning is the intensity of the student's involvement in the process. At the completion of his study of American high schools, Theodore Sizer (1984) characterized students as, *"All too often docile, compliant, and without initiative.* (p. 54)" John Goodlad (1983) described: *"a general picture of considerable passivity among students...(p. 113)"*. The high school teachers surveyed by Goodlad ranked "lack of student interest" as the most important problem in education.

Implicit Contracts between Teachers and Students: The student's lack of interest makes it difficult for teachers to be demanding. Sizer's description of Ms. Shiffe's biology class, illustrates what sometimes happens:

> She wanted the students to know these names. They did not want to know them and were not going to learn them. Apparently no outside threat--flunking, for example--affected the students. Shiffe did her thing, the students chattered on, even in the presence of a visitor....Their common front of uninterest probably made examinations moot. Shiffe could not flunk them all, and, if their performance was uniformly shoddy, she would have to pass them all. Her desperation was as obvious as the students cruelty toward her. (1984, 157-158)

How do teachers avoid this treatment? Sizer's description of Mr. Brody's class provides an example.

> He signaled to the students what the minima, the few questions for a test, were; all tenth and eleventh-graders could master these with absurdly little difficulty. The youngsters picked up the signal and kept their part of the bargain by being friendly and orderly. They did not push Brody, and he did not push them....Brody's room was quiet, and his students liked him. No wonder he had the esteem of the principal who valued orderliness and good rapport between students and staff. Brody and his class had agreement, all right, agreement that reduced the efforts of both students and teacher to an irreducible and pathetic minimum.(p. 156)

Some teachers are able to overcome the obstacles and induce their students to undertake tough learning tasks. But for most, the student's lassitude is demoralizing. Teachers are assigned responsibility for setting high standards but they are not given any tools that might be effective for inducing student observance of the academic goals of the classroom. They must rely on the force of their own personalities. All too often teachers compromise academic demands because the bulk of the class sees no need to accept them as reasonable and legitimate.

Nevertheless, American students do not appear to realize how poor their performance is. **Even though American 13 year olds were one-fourth as likely as Korean students to "understand measurement and geometry concepts and [to be able to] solve more complex problems," Americans were three times more likely to agree with the statement, "I am good at mathematics"** (Lapointe, Mead and Phillips, 1989).

Past efforts to improve secondary education have focused on stricter graduation requirements, more rigorous courses, greater emphasis on the basics (English, math, science, social science, computer science), and improvements in the quality of teaching through higher salaries, career ladders, and competency tests for teachers. Upgrading the content and quality of school offerings is a necessary but not a sufficient condition for improved achievement. New York State, for example, tried to increase the rigor of high school curricula by upgrading the requirements for the Regents diploma, but the result has been a drop in the number of students getting the Regents diploma and an increase in the number of students receiving local diplomas. **Motivating** students to take rigorous courses and to study harder needs to receive much more attention from reformers.

Parental Effort

There is evidence that a second major reason for the low levels of achievement by American students is parental apathy. High school teachers rank "lack of parental interest" as the second most important problem in education (Goodlad, 1983). An NSF funded survey of 2222 parents of 10th graders found that 25 percent thought their child should take only one or two science classes in high school (Longitudinal Survey of American Youth-LSAY, Q. BH165). When 2829 high school sophomores were asked whether "My parents...think that math (science) is a very important subject," 40 percent said no with respect to mathematics and 57 percent said no with respect to science (LSAY, Q. AA19Q-AA19R). Only 30 percent of 10th graders reported their parents "want me to learn about computers" (LSAY, Q AA19D).

Despite the poor performance of Minneapolis 5th graders in mathematics, their mothers were much more pleased with the performance of their local schools than the Taiwanese and Japanese mothers. When asked "How good a job would you say ___'s school is doing this year educating___", 91 percent of American mothers responded "excellent" or "good" while only 42 percent of Taiwanese and 39 percent of Japanese parents were this positive (Stevenson, Lee and Stigler, 1986). Table 5.4 presents data from this study.

Despite the small size of Japanese and Taiwanese homes, 95-98 percent of the fifth graders in these two countries had a desk of their own specifically for studying, while only 63 percent of the Minneapolis children had a desk. Mathematics workbooks had been purchased for their children by 56-58 percent of Taiwanese and Japanese parents but by only 28 percent of American parents. Science workbooks had been purchased by 51 percent of Taiwanese parents, 29 percent of Japanese parents, and by only 1 percent of American parents. This is not because they love their children any less. American parents have different priorities such as teaching responsibility and work habits by requiring that they do chores around the house. Taiwanese parents place such a high priority on school performance that their children are expected to devote themselves to studying and are, therefore, relieved of household duties. Clearly, American parents hold their children and their schools to lower academic standards than Japanese and Taiwanese parents.

If American parents were truly dissatisfied with the academic standards of their local public schools, tutoring after school would be common (as in France and Japan) and enrollment in private schools offering an enriched and rigorous curriculum would be higher (as in Australia). It is the better discipline, religious education and absence of disruptive students that appears to attract students to most private day schools, not more rigorous academics and better qualified teachers. Private school students do not learn at an appreciably faster rate than public school students (Cain and Goldberger, 1983).

Table 5.4: Learning is a Low Priority of Parents (in percents)

	Minneapolis U.S.A.	Sendai Japan	Taipeh Taiwan
Mother attended college	58	22	13
Fifth grader has study desk	63	98	95
Parents purchased workbook for additional homework in: mathematics	21	58	56
science	1	29	51
Fifth grader has assigned chores	95	76	28
Parents believe their school is doing an "Excellent or Good Job"	91	39	42

Source: Stevenson, Lee & Stigler "Mathematics Achievement of Chinese, Japanese and American Children", *Science* (February, 1986; pp. 693-699).

Public Effort: Educational Expenditure--A Deceptive Indicator

Graduation Requirements: Graduation requirements have been raised but they are still not very high. While most states require four years of English, no states require four years of mathematics and only eight require three years of mathematics. In most states the mathematics requirement can be fulfilled without learning any geometry or algebra. For science the norm is a two year requirement. Only three states require three years of science and three require only one year (NCES, 1992, Table 145). In some states the science requirement can be met by taking horticulture courses.

Pressure on Teachers to Pass Students: Many teachers feel they are being pressured to give students passing grades. When asked "Is there pressure on your teachers to pass students who don't earn a passing grade?", 58 percent of local teacher union leaders in New York State responded YES. The primary source of this pressure was school administrators.

> Some school districts have a policy that each teacher's student grades are printed out and distributed among the faculty. Those teachers with the lowest student averages are singled out for "discussions" about why their students are lower. (New York State United Teachers, March 3, 1994, 2).

Teachers who set expectations too high get in trouble. For example, Adele Jones, an Algebra II teacher in Georgetown Delaware, was fired because she failed too many of her students (42 percent one year and 27 percent the next). The principal justified his decision with the following:

> "I have made it very clear that one of my goals is to decrease the failure rate, to make sure the kids feel good about learning, stay in class, stay in school and do well.... Math is just a big body of knowledge; what is Algebra II across the nation anyway?" he asks. When he taught band, he adds, he certainly didn't expect kids to finish the year as musicians-- but he did want them to know more about music than they did before....All the talk about preparing students for college struck him as "ludicrous." Instead the goal should be to keep students studying math (Bradley, Sept 19, 1993, 19, 20).

Jodie Edwards, a student who passed Algebra II felt:

> All the principal talks about is making us feel good,...but I feel better when I know I actually did it than when I'm just given an A....I've been in classes where I just sit there and pass with no problem. But [Ms Jones is] the best math teacher I ever had. I actually learned something in her class, and I can remember it (Bradley, 20).

Walter Hall Jr., a student who had flunked the course, testified:

> "I guess some of it could be attributed to a lack of study, because I
> wasn't really like into the books hour after hour, But in the rest of my
> classes, I was doing fairly well, and it was only testing that gave me a
> problem." (Bradley, 20).

Spending per Pupil: When comparisons of schooling costs are made by
deflating school expenditure by a cost of living index, the U.S. comes in third
behind only Sweden and Switzerland (OECD, 1993, 92). Such comparisons are
not very informative, however, because the cost of providing instruction of given
quality is only weakly correlated with a cost of living index. The cost of
recruiting quality teachers is higher in the U.S. because college graduates (the
pool of workers from which teachers must be drawn) are better paid than in
Europe and East Asia. Since labor compensation accounts for the bulk of
education costs, the proper deflator for schooling expenditure is not a general cost
of living index, but a wage index that reflects the cost of recruiting competent
teachers. In the absence of such an index, deflation by GDP per worker is the
next best thing. OECD's estimates of the ratio of public and private expenditure
on secondary education per student to GDP per capita and GDP per worker are
given in Table 5.5. This way of comparing expenditure per student places the

Table 5.5: Public and Private Expenditure per Secondary School Student Relative to GDP per Worker and GDP per Capita

| | Relative to GDP per | |
	Worker	Capita
Australia	10.6%	20.5% (voc ed excl)
Belgium	12.0%	28.7%
Denmark	17.0%	30.7%
Finland	15.0%	30.2%
France	12.2%	28.1% (apprenticeship exp. excl.
Germany	15.1%	34.1% (apprenticeship incl.)
Italy	9.3%	22.2%
Japan	10.2%	19.5%
Netherlands	10.9%	24.7%
Norway	16.0%	32.0%
Sweden	21.1%	40.7%
Switzerland	15.8%	30.2%
United Kingdom	9.8%	20.0%
United States	14.0%	28.5%

Source: Data on the ratio of expenditure per secondary student to GDP per capita is from OECD, *Education
at a Glance* (1992, 63; 1993, 95). Column 1 deflates expenditure per student by GDP per worker. Data
on the ratio of workers to population is from Nelson and O'Brien (1993, 90-91).

U.S. roughly in the middle of the table, below Germany, Switzerland and the Scandinavian countries but above Japan, France, the United Kingdom, Australia, Netherlands and Italy.

Because vocational education is more expensive than traditional academic courses, providing vocational education through schools as is done in Sweden, Holland, France and the United States raises the costs that must be born by taxpayers. Dual systems of education like the German, Austrian and Swiss systems arrange for employers to provide most of the vocational instruction and thus place lower demands on the taxpayer. In 1980, German employers invested an average of $6000 per year in the training of each apprentice they took on as part of the dual system of vocational training (Noll, et al., 1984). The German government estimates that private expenditure on education of youth (almost all of which is employer spending on apprenticeship training of secondary school students) is equal to **1.5 percent of GDP** (OECD, 1993, 65-66). This implies that German employers account for 38 percent of the nation's spending on elementary and secondary education. Employer spending on apprenticeship training is part of the spending estimates for Germany in Table 5.5. Other countries, however, have not included employer investments in apprenticeship training in the spending estimates reported to the OECD.

A Broader Mission: Even with the correct deflator and apprenticeship spending included, expenditure per pupil remains a deceptive indicator of a nation's investment in education. Countries budget school costs differently and assign public schools different functions some of which have little to do with academic instruction. American schools often perform functions such as after school sports, bus transportation, psychological counseling, medical check ups, after school day care, hot meals, and driver education that many other countries assign to other institutions. Costs of transportation are generally not included in school budgets in Japan and Europe where students use the public transportation system to go to school. In many European countries after-school sports are sponsored and organized by local government, not the school. This removes the capital costs of extensive school-based sports facilities and the salaries of coaches and maintenance personnel from the school budget. The additional functions performed by American schools are one of the reasons why nonteaching staff account for a much larger share of employment in U.S. public education than in most other countries (see column 5 of Table 5.6; OECD, 1992, Table P9.e). If adjustments were made for service mix, and a cost of education index reflecting compensation levels in alternative college level occupations was used to deflate expenditure, the ranking of the U.S. in Table 5.5 would probably drop somewhat.

American education budgets are spent differently than European and Japanese education budgets. Computers are more plentiful and physical facilities are generally better. Libraries are larger and textbooks more colorful and up to date. In part, this reflects the fact that books, computers and buildings are cheaper (relative to teachers of constant quality) in the United States. Pupil-teacher ratios in U.S. secondary schools are close to the OECD average. They are below those in Japan but above those in Belgium, Denmark, Italy, Norway and Sweden (see column 4 of Table 5.6).

What is unique about the way Americans organize and budget their schools is the heavy investment in nonteaching staff and the relatively low levels of teacher compensation. Nonteachers account for one half of the employees in public elementary and secondary education in the U.S. Nonteachers account for less than a quarter of employees in Belgium, Germany, Japan and Netherlands and only 36 percent of secondary school employees in France (see column 5 of Table 5.6). Howard Nelson's (1990) examination of this issue concluded that teacher compensation was between 45.5 and 53.5 percent of current expenditures in the U.S.[4] These ratios are higher in most other OECD countries. The mean for OECD countries reporting this statistic was 68 percent (OECD, 1993, 88).

Teacher Compensation: Relative to the norms that prevail in Europe and Asia, secondary school teaching in the United States is a poorly-paid low-prestige occupation. Data on the relative wage of experienced lower and upper secondary teachers is presented in the first two columns of Table 5.6. Most countries pay their experienced upper secondary teachers between 60 and 70 percent more than the average worker. Denmark pays them 83 percent more, Germany pays them 98 percent more and the Netherlands pays them 132 percent more. The United States pays its secondary teachers only 33 percent more than the average worker. The lower pay in the United States is not compensation for more attractive conditions of work (see column 3 of Table 5.6). American upper secondary teachers spend a good deal more time providing instruction to students than teachers in Europe and Japan. Annual figures are 825 hours in the U.S., 696 hours in Canada and Japan, 556 hours in Finland and 536 hours in France (Nelson and O'Brien, 1992).

The key salary comparison, however, is not with the wage of the average worker, but with the salaries of other occupations requiring similar amounts of education. When college graduate salaries are compared, education majors in the U.S. come out at the very bottom. Data from the 1984, 1987 and 1990 Surveys of Income and Program Participation (SIPP) (see column 1 of Table 5.7) indicate that for 18 to 64 year olds, the wage premium over education majors was 78 percent for physical science and mathematics majors and 106 percent for economics majors. Social science majors earned 32 percent more and humanities majors earned 9 percent more than education majors. Relative to individuals with graduate degrees in education, those with MBAs earned 65 percent more, those with law degrees earned 104 percent more, and those with advanced degrees in physical science earned 75 percent more (Kominski, 1987, 1990; Kominski and Sutterlin, 1992).[5]

Not all nations pay their teachers so poorly. Australian university graduates with education degrees start at the same salary as graduates in economics/business, 8 percent ahead of those who majored in humanities and only 2 percent behind those who majored in physical science (Guthrie, 1990). In Canada starting salaries of education graduates are 11 percent higher than the salaries of humanities graduates, 7 percent higher than economics and business graduates. Five years after graduation, education graduates in Canada were still 13 percent better paid than humanities graduates, 3 percent better paid than economics graduates and only 13 percent less well paid than business graduates. In the United States in 1981 starting salaries of education graduates were 14 percent higher than humanities graduates, 10-11 percent higher than business

Table 5.6: Teacher Compensation and Student-Teacher Ratios

	Teacher Salary (15 yr Exp)/ Earnings of All Workers[1]		Yrly Hrs of Instruction[2]	Ratio Sec. Pupils to Teachers[3]	Share of Non Teachers[4]
	Lower S.S.	Upper S.S.	Upper S.S.		
Australia	1.60	1.60	---	18.6	29%
Belgium	1.25	1.61	637	7.7	19%
Canada	1.68	1.68	696	15.3	---
Denmark	1.16	1.83	615	10.7	43%
Finland	1.61	1.67	556	----	46%
France	1.44	1.66	532	14.0	36%
Germany	1.82	1.98	810	16.5	18%
Italy	1.31	1.35	745	9.2	- - -
Japan	1.71	1.73	696	17.3	23%
Netherlands	1.58	2.32	943	15.9	20%
Norway	1.33	1.65	586	8.9	---
Spain	1.40	1.72	536	16.9	---
Sweden	1.14	1.32	593	10.7	---
United Kingdom	1.63	1.63	776	14.7	---
United States	**1.33**	**1.33**	**825**	**15.5**	**47%**

[1] Compensation of secondary teachers was calculated by multiplying their salary by the ratio of compensation to wages for manufacturing workers. This estimate of teacher compensation was then divided by average compensation of all workers. The figure for French upper secondary teachers is a weighted average of salaries for Agrege (20%) and others (80%). (Nelson and O'Brien, 1993; pp. 73, 74, 90 & 91).

[2] Mean number hours teaching a class per day times the mean number of workdays for teachers. (Nelson and O'Brien, 1993, Table II.3. & II.4.)

[3] The ratio of the number of full-time-equivalent pupils enrolled in public and private secondary schools to the number of full-time-equivalent secondary school teachers (OECD, 1993; 104).

[4] Share of all staff employed in publicly funded elementary and secondary schools and ministries of education that are not classroom teachers. The nonteaching staff includes administrators at all levels, teachers aides, guidance counselors, librarians, nurses, custodial staff, food service workers, bus drivers, and clerical workers. Figures for most nations are for all three levels of schooling (OECD, 1993; 100). The French figure is for secondary education only (Ministere de l'Education Nationale et de la Culture, 1992; 184). If the staff of primary schools had been part of the calculation, the estimate would have been lower. The U.S. figure is for public elementary and secondary schools and does not include people working for State Departments of Education (NCES, 1992; 88). In the U.S. teachers aides account for 8.8 percent of school staff.

Table 5.7: Relative Salaries by Field of Study in University

	United States		Australia		Canada		United Kingdom	
Date of Earning..	1984,87	1991	1979	1989	1988	1987	1981	1985
Field of Study	BA/BS 18+ Adults	1990 Grad Female	Prev. Yr. Grads	Yr. Grad	1986 Grad	1982 Grad	1980 Grad	1980 Grad
Bachelors' Degree								
Education	100	100	100	100	100	100	100	100
Humanities	108	99	86	92	89	87	86	118
Phys Sci &Math	177	137	97	102	107	113	101	146
Biological Sci	146	110	----	----	85	90	91	121
Health	117	167	----	----	115	113	86	128
Engineering	226	163	102	110	111	116	104	141
Soc Sci not Econ	139	108	---	---	93	110	87	119
Economics	229		91	100	93	97	90	156
Business (BA)	206	126	----	----	93	113	89	145
Advanced Degree								
Humanities	85	----	----	----	64	67	----	----
Phy. Science	175	----	----	----	80	82	----	----
Engineering	171	----	----	----	84	103	----	----
Soc Sci not Econ	112	----	----	----	77	80	----	----
Business (MBA)	164	----	----	----	95	115	----	----
Law	204	----	----	----	114	128	----	----

The index numbers hold the level of the degree constant and compare the salary of degree recipients in specified major to the salary of those who majored in education. For advanced degrees the United States data were for all advanced degrees (incl. PhDs), while the Canadian data were for Masters and First Professional Degrees (not PhDs).

Source: Column 1 is based on averages of real monthly earnings data for 1984, 1987 and 1990 (Kominski, 1987; 1990; Kominski and Sutterlin, 1992). Column 2 is derived from NCES (1993b). Column 3 and 4 are derived from Guthrie (1990). Column 5 is calculated from Clark, *The Class of 1986,* (1992; Table C-4 & C-5). Column 6 is from Clark, *The Class of 1982 Revisited,* (1991; Table E-3 & E-4). Column 7 and 8 are derived from Dalton and Makepeace (1990; Table 1 & 2).

graduates and only 1 percent below math and physical science graduates. By comparison, starting salaries of U.S. mathematics and physical science majors who entered teaching were 42 percent below the salaries of those who obtained computer programming and system analyst jobs and 35 percent below the starting salaries of those obtaining jobs in mathematics or physical science (NCES, 1993b, 26).

This suggests one reason why it is so difficult in the United States to attract the best and brightest into teaching, and why it is particularly difficult to recruit competent science and mathematics teachers. SAT test scores are lower for education majors than for any other major. The gap is particularly large in mathematics. In 1990-91 the Math SAT of intended education majors was thirty-three points below the overall average, 107 points below engineering majors and 131 points below majors in the physical sciences. The Verbal SAT of intended education majors was sixteen points below the overall average, thirty-four points below arts and humanities majors and thirty-one points below social science majors (NCES, 1992, Table 124).

In Europe and Japan, by contrast, there is often fierce competition to enter university programs specializing in the preparation of secondary school teachers. In France, for example, secondary school teachers must pass rigorous subject matter examination. In 1991 only 31.3 percent of those who took the written exam for the *Certificat d'Aptitude au Professorat de l'Enseignement du Secondaire* (the most common of these examinations) passed it. The best teaching jobs go to those who pass an even more rigorous examination, the *Agregation Externe,* which had a pass rate of 17.7 percent in 1991 (Ministere de l'Education Nationale et de la Culture, 1992, 205-206).

The quality of the people recruited into teaching is very important. The teacher characteristic that most consistently predicts student learning are tests assessing the teacher's general academic ability and subject knowledge (Hanushek, 1971; Strauss and Sawyer, 1986; Ferguson, 1990; Ehrenberg and Brewer, 1993; Monk, 1992). Ferguson, for example, found that holding community characteristics, class size, teacher experience and the proportion of the teaching staff with masters degrees constant, that a one standard deviation increase in the TECAT test scores of a school districts teachers increased the reading exam scores of students in third and higher grades by about .20 to .25 of a standard deviation (about one grade level equivalent for senior high students). Since teacher test scores had no relationship with student test sores in first grade, there is a strong presumption that teachers with higher test scores improve the reading ability of their pupils in the early grades and that these gains are maintained through high school (Ferguson, 1990, Table A).

Because Americans with university training in mathematics and science can earn much more in jobs outside the education sector, those with talent in these areas are difficult to recruit into high school teaching. This results in most teachers being poorly prepared in science and mathematics. This, in turn, helps explain why American students lag behind European and Japanese students in mathematics and science but not in reading.

The question that tends to be raised by statistics such as these is **"Why do American voters choose to pay teachers so little?"** Why do voters not demand higher standards of academic achievement at local high schools? Why do school boards allocate scarce education dollars to interscholastic athletics and the band rather than better mathematics teachers and science laboratories? It is to questions such as these that we now turn.

Voter Apathy Regarding Academic Achievement

One of the unique characteristics of the American education system is that all the really important decisions--budget allocations, hiring selections, salary levels, teaching strategies, grading standards, course offerings, pupil assignments to courses and programs, disciplinary policies, etc.--are made by classroom teachers and school administrators who are responding to local political pressures. Federal and state officials are far removed from the classroom, and the instruments available to them for inducing improvements in quality and standards are limited. They do not have effective control of the standards and expectations that prevail in the classroom. They do not control the allocation of school funds between academics and athletics.

State aid can be increased; but econometric studies suggest that increases in state aid reduce local property tax collections by a significant amount (Carroll, 1982; Ehrenberg and Chaykowski, 1988). For every extra dollar of noncategorical state aid to local school districts only about 50 cents is spent on education by the locality: the rest either lowers tax rates or enables the community to spend more on other public functions. For categorical programs like Title I, the increase in local education spending is larger, but some leakage appears to be inevitable (Tsang and Levin, 1983; Monk, 1990).

School boards are the primary mechanism by which the voters exercise authority over local schools. In most parts of the country only bond issues need go to the voters for approval. The board determines the budget and sets the property tax rates necessary to fund that budget. Parents are typically a minority of voting age adults in the community, but only about 10 percent of the nonparents in a community typically vote in school board elections. Parents are more likely to vote in school board elections, so they have effective control of the school board in many communities. In other communities they could easily gain control if they turned up at the polls and voted in concert. Parents pay less than a third of school taxes in most communities, so voting for school board members who promise to support increased educational spending and higher standards is, for them, a low cost way of improving the school attended by their child. Why hasn't this power been exercised to raise academic standards and teacher salaries? Why do less than a third of parents vote in most school board elections? Why do so many parents vote against increases in school taxes? When additional money is available, why is so much of it spent on upgrading the sports program and the band, not on hiring a physics teacher?

If, as indicated above, the parents of a community are satisfied with academic outcomes that leave their children years behind students of other nations in mathematics and science, federal and state efforts to raise standards will have no lasting effect.

II. THE ABSENCE OF REWARDS FOR EXCELLENCE: A ROOT CAUSE OF THE LEARNING DEFICIT

The evidence supports the conclusion that a fundamental cause of the low effort level of American students, parents, and voters in school elections is the absence of good signals of effort and learning in high school and a consequent lack of rewards for effort and learning. In the United States the only signals of learning that generate substantial rewards are diplomas and years of schooling. In most other advanced countries mastery of the curriculum taught in high school is assessed by essay examinations that are set and graded at the national or regional level. Grades on these exams signal the student's achievement to universities, colleges and employers and influence the jobs that graduates get and the universities and programs to which they are admitted. How well the graduating seniors do on these exams influences the reputation of the school and in some countries the number of students applying for admission to the school. In the United States, by contrast, students take aptitude tests that are not intended to assess the learning that has occurred in most of the classes taken in high school. The primary signals of academic achievement are grades and rank in class--criteria which assess achievement relative to other students in the school or classroom, not relative to an external standard.

Consequently, *the students who do not aspire to attend highly selective colleges benefit very little from working hard while in high school, and parents have little incentive to vote the tax increases necessary to upgrade the academic quality of local schools.* This is a consequence of eight phenomena.

Gresham's Law of Course Selection

Easy and entertaining courses drive out rigorous courses. Because their student bodies are so diverse, American high schools offer a variety of courses at vastly different levels of rigor. The rigor of the courses taken is not well signaled to employers and most colleges, so taking rigorous courses is seldom rewarded. Most parents are uninformed about course options and their consequences and fail to influence the choices made. In Ithaca, New York, for example, less than one-fifth of parents attend the meeting in 8th grade at which the student and guidance counselor plan the student's ninth through 12th grade course sequence. Most students choose courses that have the reputation of being fun and not requiring much work to get a good grade. As one student put it:

> My counselor wanted me to take Regents history and I did for a while.
> But it was pretty hard and the teacher moved fast. I switched to the
> other history and I'm getting better grades. So my average will be better
> for college. Unless you are going to a college in the state, it doesn't
> really matter whether you get a Regent's diploma. (Ward, 1994)

Another student who had avoided the harder courses even though she was sure she could do the work explained her decision with, *"Why should I do it,* [the extra work], *if I don't have to?"* (Ward, 1994) Teachers know this and adjust their style of teaching and their homework assignments with an eye to maintaining enrollment levels. Attempts to induce students to take tough courses seldom succeed:

> An angry math teacher [who remembering] the elimination of a carefully
> planned program in technical mathematics for vocational students simply
> because not enough signed up for it,...[said] 'Its easy to see who really
> makes decisions about what schools teach: the kids do.' (Powell, Farrar
> and Cohen, 1985, 9)

Making graduation contingent on passing a minimum competency exam does not solve the problem because the minimum is set low and most students pass it early in their high school career.

Achievement in High School is not Necessary for College Admission

Most American colleges and universities do not set rigorous standards for admission. While college attendance is correlated with high school achievement, not even functional literacy is required for admission to most community colleges and a number of four year colleges. High school students know that taking undemanding high school courses and goofing off in these courses will not prevent them from being admitted to a college.

In the United States access to higher education is rationed primarily by student aptitude and parental willingness to pay. Most financial aid to undergraduates is awarded solely on the basis of need, not the student's past academic achievements. The most selective universities and colleges are also the most expensive. Doing well in high school typically results in parents paying more for the college education of their child, not less. In Japan, the most prestigious universities are also the cheapest, so doing well in high school lowers the amount of money parents have to pay for college.

In Europe, universities are free and most governments provide college students with a stipend to cover living costs. Places in higher education are rationed not by price or aptitude, but by achievement in the core subjects studied in secondary school.

Admission to Selective Colleges is Based on Aptitude and Class Rank Not Achievement

Where admission to college does depend on high school performance, it is not based on an absolute or external standard of achievement in high school subjects. Rather, it is based, in part, on aptitude tests that do not assess the high school curriculum, as well as on measures of student performance such as class rank and grade point averages, which are defined relative to classmates' performances. Selective colleges do look at the rigor of the high school program a student has pursued in high school and evaluate grades in that light. Many students are unaware of this practice and choose courses that they know they will have no difficulty in getting an A. Selective colleges give preference to students who take Advanced Placement courses. Seniors applying to selective colleges are aware of this and often sign up for AP classes. The AP exams come after colleges announce their admission decisions, however, so many students do not put the required energy into the course and decline to take the AP exam when the time comes.

Difficulties in Signaling Upgraded Standards to Colleges and Employers

Setting higher academic standards or hiring better teachers does not on average improve the signals of academic performance--rank in class, GPA and SAT scores--that selective colleges use for making admission decisions and a few employers use to make hiring decisions. Higher standards for graduating are not likely to be supported by the parents of children not planning to go to college, because they would put at risk what is most important, the diploma. Higher standards do not benefit students as a group, so parents as a group have little incentive to lobby strongly for higher teacher salaries, higher standards and higher school taxes.

Local Monopolies in the Provision of Secondary Schooling

In most American communities, students and parents cannot choose which public high school to attend. In Europe and Japan, by contrast, the family can often select which secondary school a student attends. Barriers to attending a school other than the closest one are lower in these countries because schools are smaller and more numerous, public transportation is available, opportunities to participate in sports and music are often organized by the community not the school, and centralized funding of schools means that spending per pupil varies little and money follows the student even when a school in a nearby community is selected. The centralization of funding and the free choice of schools results in stronger competitive pressure on schools to excel and smaller quality differentials between schools of the same type than in the U.S. This is one of the reasons why, despite the comprehensive character of American schools, variations in achievement among individuals and schools are larger in the U.S. than in most other advanced countries. In science at 14-15 years of age, the U.S. ranks 2nd among 15 advanced countries in the inequality of student achievement and 5th in the inequality of school mean achievement levels (IAEEA, 1988, Table 5 and 7).

If American parents and students were allowed to choose their high school, however, the Gresham's law of course selection might become a Gresham's law of school selection. If college admissions decisions continued to be based on grades and rank in class, it might be preferable to be a big fish in a low standards pond than an average fish in a high standards pond. Even though American high schools differ greatly in standards and quality, employers do not appear to be using high school reputation as a signal when making hiring selections (Hollenbeck and Smith, 1984). Some colleges take high school quality into account when evaluating a student's GPA, but most colleges do not. In such an environment it is not clear what will impel parents to send their children to a school that promises a rigorous academic program involving a great deal of homework rather than to a school with a reputation for excellence in hockey.

School choice will induce schools to upgrade the rigor and quality of their program only if substantial rewards--better jobs and admission to selective college programs--go to those who graduate from schools with higher standards, better teachers and longer homework assignments. Including high school "reputation" in the factors considered when making hiring and college admission decisions is not a satisfactory solution, however, because the reputations of U.S. high schools are based more on the socioeconomic background of the students, where they go to college and (for private schools) the percentage of applicants rejected than on the actual academic achievement of the students (about which little is known). Schools would respond by hiring PR firms to produce flashy videos about the school and by becoming more selective in admissions.

In order for school choice to generate an environment that induces schools to focus on upgrading instruction and improving learning, (1) the skills and competencies of individual graduates must be assessed relative to an external standard that is comparable among schools and (2) individual rewards--e.g., access to preferred university programs and better jobs--must be attached to these results. Only then are students and parents encouraged to select schools on the basis of their expected value added, rather than on the basis of reputations that school staff are unable to change by doing a better job teaching. Most advanced nations have such an assessment system. The United States does not. Without such assessments, school choice might well cause academic expectations and standards to decline.

Difficulties in Assessing Teacher Performance

There is no effective way of holding most high school and middle school teachers individually accountable for the learning of their students. Unionization is not the critical barrier, for unionized European and Japanese secondary school teachers and most American primary school teachers feel accountable for the learning of their students. The lack of accountability in American secondary schools stems from: (1) the rarity of high or medium stakes examinations assessing student achievement in particular subjects relative to an external standard, and (2) the fact that most secondary school students receive instruction in English, mathematics, history, and science from many different teachers. The exceptions to this norm are the coaches of the athletic teams, the band conductor, teachers of advanced placement classes, and vocational teachers (who are often evaluated for their success in placing students in good jobs). In Europe, students who are preparing to take the exit exam in a particular subject typically remain together in one class and are taught by just one or two teachers during the upper secondary years. In most Japanese junior high schools, a team of teachers, each responsible for a different subject, teach all the 7th graders one year, the 8th graders the next year, and the ninth graders the third year. Examinations taken during ninth grade determine admission to competitive high schools so teachers feel responsible for how well their students do on these examinations.

Peer Group Norms

In the United States, the peer group actively discourages academic effort. No adolescent wants to be considered a "nerd, brain geek, grade grubber or brown noser" or to be "acting white," yet that is what happens to students who study hard and are seen to study hard. Because the school's signals of achievement assess performance relative to fellow students through grades and class rank, not relative to an external standard, peers have a personal stake in persuading each other not to study.

The primary reason for peer pressure against studying is that pursuing academic success forces students into a zero-sum competition with their classmates. Their achievement is not being measured against an absolute, external standard. In contrast to scout merit badges, for example, where recognition is given for achieving a fixed standard of competence, the school's measures of achievement assess performance relative to fellow students through grades and class rank. Students who study hard for exams make it more difficult for close friends (other members of the class) to get an A or be ranked at the top of the graduating class. Since devoting time to studying for an exam is costly, the welfare of the entire class is maximized if no one studies for exams that are graded on a strict curve. The cooperative solution is "no one studies more than the minimum." Participants are generally able to tell who has broken the "minimize studying" code and reward those who conform and punish those who do not. Side payments and punishments are made in a currency of friendship, respect and ridicule that is not limited in supply. For most students the benefits that might result from studying for the exam are less important than the very certain costs of being considered a "brain geek", "grade grubber," or "acting white," so most students abide by the "minimize studying" "don't raise your hand too much" norm.

The peer norms that result are: *It is OK to be smart. You cannot help that. But, it is definitely not OK to spend alot of time studying. Instead, use your free time to socialize, participate in athletics or earn money.* This is illustrated by the following story related by one of my students:

> Erroneously I was lumped into the brains genus by others at [high] school just because of the classes I was in. This really irked me; not only was I not an athlete but I was also thought of as one of those "brain geeks". Being a brain really did have a stigma attached to it. Sometimes during a free period I would sit and listen to all the brains talk about how much they hated school work and how they never studied and I had to bite my lip to keep from laughing out loud. I knew they were lying, and they knew they were lying too. I think that a lot of brains hung around together only because their fear of social isolation was greater than their petty rivalries. I think that my two friends who were brains liked me because I was almost on their level but I was not competitive (Tim, 1986).

Note how those who broke the 'minimize studying' norm tried to hide the fact from classmates. They did not espouse an alternative "learning is fun and important" norm.

The costs and benefits of studying vary among students because interest in the subject varies, ability varies and parental pressure and rewards vary. This heterogeneity means that some students choose to break the "minimize studying" norm. When they are a small minority, they cannot avoid feeling denigrated by classmates. In the top track and at schools where many students aspire to attend competitive colleges, numbers will be sufficient to create a subculture with its own norms denigrating those who disrupt classroom instruction or have difficulties in the course. This is the structural basis of the "brains" and "preppie" cliques found in many high schools. Most high school students, however, are in cliques that denigrate studying.

Peer pressure not to study does not derive from a general desire to take it easy. In jobs after school and at football practice, young people work very hard. In these environments they are part of a team where individual efforts are visible and appreciated by teammates. Competition and rivalry are not absent, but they are offset by shared goals, shared successes and external measures of achievement (i.e., satisfied customers or winning the game). On the sports field, there is no greater sin than giving up, even when the score is hopelessly one sided. On the job, tasks not done by one worker will generally have to be completed by another. For too many students in too many high schools, when it comes to academics, there is no greater sin than trying hard.

A second reason for peer norms against studying is that most students perceive the chance of receiving recognition for an academic achievement to be so slim they have given up trying. At most high school awards ceremonies the recognition and awards go to only a few--those at the very top of the class. By ninth grade most students are already so far behind the leaders, that they know they have no realistic chance of being perceived as academically successful. Their reaction is often to denigrate the students who take learning seriously and to honor other forms of achievement--athletics, dating, holding your liquor and being "cool"--which offer them better chances of success.

The Labor Market Does Not Reward Achievement in High School

The labor market fails to reward effort and achievement in high school. Analysis of the Youth Cohort of the National Longitudinal Survey indicates that *during the first eight years after leaving high school, greater competence in science, language arts and mathematical reasoning lowers wages and increases the unemployment of young men.* Table 5.8 presents estimates of the percentage increase in wage rates that results from a one population standard deviation (or five grade level equivalent) improvement on tests assessing competence in mathematical reasoning, English, science, technology and computational speed (Bishop, 1989, 1992). *For young women, verbal and scientific competencies have no effect on wage rates and a one grade level increase in mathematical reasoning competence raises wage rates by only one-half of 1 percent.* As a result, students who plan to look for a job immediately after high school see very little connection between how much English, mathematics and science they learn and their future success in the labor market. Less than a quarter of 10th graders believe that geometry, trigonometry, biology, chemistry, and physics are needed to qualify for their first choice occupation (LSAY, 1988, BA24B-BA25D).

Although the economic benefits of higher achievement to the employee are quite modest and do not appear until long after graduation, the benefits to the employer (and, therefore, to national production) are immediately realized in higher productivity. Over the last 80 years, industrial psychologists have conducted hundreds of studies, involving hundreds of thousands of workers, on the relationship between productivity in particular jobs and various predictors of that productivity. They have found that competence in reading, mathematics, science and problem solving are strongly related to productivity in almost all of the civilian and military jobs studied (Ghiselli, 1973; Hunter, Crossen and Friedman, 1985). Table 5.9 presents the results of one study predicting a hands-

Table 5.8: Effect of Competencies on Log Wage Rates and Earnings

	Technical	Clerical Speed	Computation Speed	Math Reasoning	Verbal	Science	R^2	Number of obs.	F Test on Academic Coef.
Males									
Wages-1986	0.80*** (6.10)	.005 (051)	.064*** (5.75)	-.007 (.51)	-.021 (1.49)	-.008 (.60)	.264	4272	4.35** neg
Earnings-1985	.133*** (6.26)	.004 (.21)	.119*** (6.55)	-.037* (1.78)	.014 (.61)	-.021 (.93)	.358	4564	2.4
Females									
Wages-1986	.006 (.31)	.028*** (2.60)	.024** (2.04)	.027* (1.94)	.027* (1.75)	.012 (.81)	.275	4080	12.6*** pos
Earnings-1985	-.020 (.64)	.022 (1.14)	.053*** (2.60)	.065*** (2.66)	.039 (1.40)	.009 (.34)	.328	3888	11.8*** pos

* $p < .05$ on a one tail test ** $p < .025$ on a one tail test *** $p < .005$ on a one tail test

Coefficients estimate the effect of a five grade level equivalent or one population standard deviation change in the test composite. T Statistics are in parenthesis under the coefficient.

Source: Analysis of the 1986 National Longitudinal Survey of Youth. Sample excluded individuals who were in the military in 1979 but included students both full and part time if they had a job in 1985 or 1986. School attendance was controlled by four separate variables: a dummy for respondent is in school at the time of the interview; a dummy for respondent has been in school since the last interview; a dummy for part time attendance and the share of the calendar year that they youth reported attending school derived from the NLS's monthly time log. Years of schooling was controlled by four variables: years of schooling, a dummy for high school graduation, years of college education completed, and years of schooling completed since the ASVAB tests were taken. Reports of weeks spent in civilian employment were available all the way back through 1975. For each individual, these weeks worked reports were aggregated across time and an estimate of cumulated civilian work experience was derived for January 1 of each year in the longitudinal file. This variable and its square was included in every model as was age, age squared and current and past military experience. The individual's family situation was controlled by dummy variables for being married and for having at least one child. Minority status was controlled by a dummy variable for Hispanic and two dummy variables for race. Characteristics of the local labor market were held constant by entering the following variables: dummy variables for the four Census regions, a dummy variable for rural residence and for residence outside an SMSA and measures of the unemployment rate in the local labor market during that year.

on measure of job performance in the military. Technical competence had no effect on job performance in clerical jobs but very substantial effects on performance in skilled technical, general maintenance and skilled electronics jobs. A five grade level equivalent improvement in mathematical reasoning ability raised performance by .447 standard deviations (SD) in clerical jobs, .34 SD in general maintenance jobs (eg. truck driving and construction), and .18-.24 SD in skilled technical and skilled electronics jobs. The proportionate change in productivity that results is somewhere between 25 and 40 percent of these numbers.[6] Science and word knowledge also have substantial effects on job performance in skilled technical, general maintenance and clerical jobs (Bishop, 1989, 1992).

Despite their significantly higher productivity, *young workers who have achieved in high school have not been receiving appreciably higher wage rates after high school.* Apparently, when a non-college-bound student works hard in school and improves his or her competence in language arts, science and mathematical reasoning, the youth's employer reaps much of the benefit.

Employers appear to believe that school performance is a good predictor of job performance. Studies of how employers rate job applicant resumes that contain information on grades in high school have found that employers give substantially higher ratings to job applicants with high grade point averages (Hollenbeck and Smith, 1984). However, they have great difficulty getting information on school performance. If a student or graduate has given written permission for a transcript to be sent to an employer, the Federal Education Rights and Privacy Act obligates the school to respond. Many high schools are not, however, responding to such requests. In Columbus Ohio, for example, Nationwide Insurance sent over 1,200 requests for transcripts signed by job applicants to high schools in 1982 and received only 93 responses.

An additional barrier to the use of high school transcripts in selecting new employees is that when high schools do respond, it takes a great deal of time. In most high schools, the system for responding to transcript requests has been designed to meet the needs of college-bound students rather than the students who seek jobs immediately after graduating. The result is that a 1987 survey of a stratified random sample of small-and medium-sized employers who were members of the National Federation of Independent Business (NFIB) found that transcripts had been obtained before the selection decision for only 14.2 percent of the high school graduates hired.[7] Only 15 percent of the employers had asked high school graduates to report their grade point average. The absence of questions about grades on most job application forms reflects the low reliability of self-reported data, the difficulties of verifying them, and the fear of EEO challenges to such questions.

Table 5.9: Effect of Competencies on Job Performance (SQT)

	Mechanical Comprehension	Auto. Info.	Shop Info.	Electr. Info.	Attention to Detail	Comp. Speed	Word Knowl.	Arith Reasoning	Math Knowl.	Science	R^2
Skilled Technical (1324)	0.092*** (3.07)	0.017 (0.58)	0.132*** (4.28)	0.174*** (5.09)	0.024 (1.12)	0.031 (1.17)	0.215*** (6.77)	0.062** (1.96)	0.121*** (3.76)	0.057* (1.83)	0.54
Skilled Electronic (349)	0.086 (1.30)	0.098 (1.49)	0.246*** (3.64)	0.045 (0.60)	0.084 (1.81)	-0.013 (0.22)	-0.004 (0.06)	-0.021 (0.30)	0.261*** (3.67)	0.072 (1.05)	0.42
General (const.) maintenance (879)	-0.004 (0.11)	0.082** (2.34)	0.117*** (3.25)	0.121*** (3.05)	0.043* (1.76)	0.068*** (2.19)	0.066* (1.80)	-0.101*** (2.73)	0.441*** (11.70)	0.134*** (3.67)	0.59
Mechanical Maintenance (131)	0.042 (0.38)	0.314*** (2.88)	0.206* (1.84)	-0.089 (0.71)	0.055 (0.72)	0.325** (2.43)	-0.004 (0.03)	-0.068 (0.59)	0.031 (0.52)	0.096 (0.85)	0.41
Clerical (830)	-0.068 (-1.59)	0.087*** (2.05)	-0.030 (-0.69)	0.065 (1.33)	0.015 (0.50)	0.085** (2.24)	0.118*** (2.61)	0.241*** (5.33)	0.206*** (4.46)	0.064 (1.44)	0.42
Operators and Food (814)	0.109* (2.50)	0.179*** (4.11)	0.062 (1.39)	0.100** (2.02)	0.050 (1.62)	-0.037 (0.96)	0.061 (1.33)	0.114* (2.47)	0.106** (2.25)	0.076* (1.66)	0.41
Unskilled electronic (2545)	0.004 (0.14)	0.027 (0.87)	0.062* (1.93)	0.077** (2.15)	0.036 (1.65)	0.053* (1.92)	-0.010 (0.31)	0.058* (1.75)	0.018 (0.55)	-0.025 (0.76)	0.05
Combat (5403)	0.147*** (8.28)	0.060*** (3.38)	0.080*** (4.42)	0.058*** (2.86)	0.048*** (3.82)	0.035** (2.23)	0.069*** (3.71)	0.070*** (3.74)	0.139*** (7.29)	0.070*** (3.82)	0.35
Field Artillery (534)	0.059 (1.10)	0.047 (0.89)	0.030 (0.56)	0.134** (2.21)	0.088** (2.33)	-0.009 (0.19)	0.000 (0.01)	0.186*** (3.28)	0.230*** (3.99)	0.061 (1.10)	0.42

Source: Reanalysis of Maier and Grafton's (1981) data on the ability of ASVAB 6/7 to predict Skill Qualification Test (SQT) scores. The correlation matrix was corrected restriction of range by Maier and Grafton.

After a worker has been at a firm a while, the employer presumably learns more about the individual's capabilities and is able to observe performance on the job. Workers assigned to the same job often produce very different levels of output (Hunter, Schmidt and Judiesch, 1988). Why, one might ask, are the most productive workers (those with just the right mix of specific competencies) not given large wage increases reflecting their higher productivity? The reason appears to be that workers and employers prefer employment contracts that offer only modest adjustments of relative wages in response to perceived differences in relative productivity. There are a number of good reasons for this preference: the unreliability of the feasible measures of individual productivity (Hashimoto and Yu, 1980), risk aversion on the part of workers (Stiglitz, 1974), productivity differentials that are specific to the firm (Bishop, 1987a), the desire to encourage cooperation among coworkers (Lazear, 1986) and union preferences for pay structures that limit the power of supervisors. In addition, compensation for differences in job performance may be nonpecuniary -- praise from one's supervisor, more relaxed supervision, or a high rank in the firm's social hierarchy (Frank, 1984). A study of how individual wage rates varied with initial job performance found that when people hired for the same or very similar jobs are compared, someone who is 20 percent more productive than average is typically paid only 1.6 percent more. After a year at a firm, better producers received only a 4 percent higher wage at nonunion firms with about twenty employees, and they had no wage advantage at unionized establishments with more than 100 employees or at nonunion establishments with more than 400 employees (Bishop, 1987a).

If relative wage rates only partially compensate the most capable workers in a job for their greater productivity, why don't they obtain promotions or switch to better paying firms? To some degree they do, particularly in managerial and professional occupations. This explains why workers who score high on tests and/or get good grades are less likely to be unemployed and more likely to be promoted, and why, many years after graduation, they eventually obtain higher wage rates (Wise, 1975; Bishop, 1990). Because worker productivity cannot be measured accurately and cannot be signaled reliably to other employers, this sorting process is slow and only partially effective (Bishop, 1987b).

Incentives To Learn In Other Nations

The tendency not to reward effort and learning in high school appears to be a peculiarly American phenomenon. Marks in school are a major determinant of who gets the most preferred apprenticeships in Germany. Japanese and European educational systems administer achievement exams that are closely tied to the curriculum. While the Japanese use a multiple choice exam, all other nations use examinations in which students write essays and show their work for mathematics problems. Generally, regional or national boards set the exams and oversee the blind grading of the exams by committees of teachers. These are not minimum competency exams. In many subjects the student may choose to take the exams at two different levels of difficulty. Excellence is recognized as well as competence (Noah and Eckstein, 1988).

Performance on these exams is a major (sometimes the sole) determinant of admission to a university and to oversubscribed fields of study such as medicine and law.   In many countries, good grades on the toughest exams-- physics, chemistry, advanced mathematics--carry particularly heavy weight. Exam grades are included in resumes and are asked for on job applications.

In Japan, clerical, service, and blue collar jobs at the best firms are available only to those who are recommended by their high school. The most prestigious firms have long term arrangements with particular high schools to which they delegate the responsibility of selecting new hires for the firm. The criteria by which the high school is to make its selection are, by mutual agreement, grades and exam results. In addition, most employers administer their own battery of selection tests prior to hiring. The number of graduates that a high school is able to place in this way depends on its reputation and the company's past experience with graduates from the school. Schools know that they must be forthright in their recommendations because if they fail just once to make an honest recommendation, the relationship will be lost and their students will no longer be able to get jobs at that firm (Rosenbaum and Kariya, 1989).

This system has the consequences one might expect. Rosenbaum's (1990) study of the high school to work transition in Japan finds that good grades, no discipline problems, and participation in extracurricular activities all have significant positive effects on obtaining jobs at large firms and entering a white collar (rather than a blue collar) occupation. In the U.S., by contrast, the job outcomes of males are not improved by good grades, fewer absences from school, a lack of discipline problems or participation in extracurricular activities. For female high school graduates, obtaining a white collar job is associated with high grades, but it is also positively associated with being a discipline problem in school.

Parents in Japan, Australia, and Europe know that a child's future depends critically on how much is learned in secondary school. In many countries the options for upper secondary schooling depend primarily on the child's performance in lower secondary school, not on where the parents can afford to live, as in the US. Since the quality and reputation of the high school is so important, the competitive pressure often reaches down into lower secondary school. National exams are the yardstick, so achievement tends to be measured relative to everyone else's in the nation and not just relative to the child's classmates. As a result, parents in most other industrialized nations demand more and get more from their local schools than we do and, nevertheless, they are more dissatisfied with their schools than American parents.

Japanese teenagers work extremely hard in high school, but once they enter college, many stop working. For students in nontechnical fields a country club atmosphere prevails. The reason for the change in behavior is that when employers hire graduates with nontechnical majors, they base their selections on the reputation of the university and a long series of interviews and not on teacher recommendations or other measures of academic achievement at the university. Students in engineering and other technical programs work much harder than their liberal arts counterparts largely because job opportunities depend largely on the recommendation of their major professor. **Studying hard is not a national character trait; it is a response to the way Japanese society rewards academic achievement.**

American students, in contrast, work much harder in college than in high school. This change results, in part, from the fact that academic achievement in college has important effects on access to high paid occupations such as medicine and law and on the quality of the job obtained at graduation. When higher level jobs requiring a bachelors or associates degree are being filled, employers pay more attention to grades and teacher recommendations than when they hire high school graduates. The NFIB survey found that when college graduates were hired, 26 percent of the employers had reviewed the college transcript before the selection, 7.8 percent had obtained a recommendation from a major professor and 6.3 percent had obtained a recommendation from a professor outside of the graduate's major or from the college's placement office.

III. THE LACK OF CONTINUITY IN RELATIONSHIPS

Schools must be challenging places, but they must be supportive places as well. School is a stressful experience and students need emotional support from fellow students and from teachers. Most European countries appear to believe that the way to create a supportive environment is to form students into classes that remain together for most of the school day and from one year to the next. In Scandinavia and Germany, for example, elementary school classes typically remain intact and have the same teacher for three years. In Denmark pupils can have the same teacher for up to nine years. Lower and upper secondary schools are typically smaller than in the U.S. At the beginning of lower secondary school, a class is formed that stays together for most of the day and remains intact (except for normal turnover) from one year to the next. Secondary teachers of French, chemistry or history would typically teach a particular class three years in a row. It is reasonable to hypothesize that the continuity of teacher and peer relationships and the fact that assessment is primarily relative to an external standard not relative to others in the class might affect student perceptions of how friendly the school's atmosphere is. Thus, the anomie and competitiveness (student against student) of American secondary schools might be the real reason why, despite minimal graduation standards, American dropout rates are so high.

This hypothesis is supported by an experiment conducted in a high school attended by disadvantaged minority students. Sixty-five of the entering ninth graders were randomly assigned to a unit that took homeroom and most core classes together in classrooms that were located in close physical proximity to one another. The homeroom teacher (who also taught one of the core subjects) was assigned the guidance and counseling duties normally handled by guidance counselors and other specialized school staff. The experiment focused on ninth graders because student vulnerability to developing academic and emotional difficulties appears to be greatest during transitions from one school to another. The organization of 10th through 12th grade was not changed. This very modest step towards a European style student assignment system had remarkably large effects on absenteeism, grades and retention. Nineteen percent of the controls dropped out in ninth or 10th grade, but only 4 percent of the experimental group. During the ninth and 10th grades, the experimental group was absent significantly less and got significantly higher grades. By the end of high school 43 percent of controls had dropped out; only 21 percent of experimentals (Felner, Ginter and Primavera, 1982; Felner and Adan, 1991). The research is being replicated in other schools. The experimental evaluation of New York City's Career Magnet schools tends to support Felner's findings: the magnets that most completely isolated themselves from the rest of the high school in which they were located had more positive effects (Crain, Heebner and Si, 1992). These results suggest that inexpensive restructuring of how entering students are assigned to classes (to reduce the anomie that students experience in our large secondary schools) can produce salutary effects. The results also call into question the nation's heavy investment in specialized school staff.

Teachers as Coaches Rather Than Judges

Most students do not develop strong personal ties with any teacher and those relationships that develop typically expire at the end of the academic year. When a mentoring relationship develops it is usually with a coach, a band conductor, a dramatics teacher, debate team sponsor, yearbook advisor, vocational teacher or an advanced placement teacher. There are reasons why these important but infrequent relationships usually develop with these types of staff. The intensive multi-year interaction with a small stable group of students helps to create a supportive atmosphere. More important still is the effects of a coaching relationship in which the teacher is helping the student prepare for a "performance" (a play, concert or AP exam) or a competition with students from another school (basketball game, debate or VICA contest). These teachers are not the high stakes judges of the student's performance and achievement. They give guidance and feedback while the student prepares for the game or exhibition, but summative evaluations are made by others. As a result, the mentor/coach is able to set high performance standards without losing the crucial role of advocate, confident and friend.

External assessment of accomplishment is thus crucial to the development of mentoring relationships between teachers and students. Without it, the effort to become friends with one's students and their parents tends to deteriorate into extravagant praise for mediocre accomplishment. In courts of law, judges must disqualify themselves when a friend comes before the bar. Yet, American teachers are placed in this double bind every day. Often the role conflict is resolved by lowering expectations or hiding failure with charitable phrases such as "does good work when he chooses to participate." Other times the choice of high standards means that close supportive relationships are sacrificed.

It is these considerations that account for the support that most European secondary school teachers give to externally graded exams and external reviews of a student's completed projects. When changes in this system were proposed in Ireland, the Association of Secondary Teachers of Ireland wrote:

Major strengths of the Irish educational system have been:

(i) The pastoral contribution of teachers in relation to their pupils

(ii) the perception of the teacher by the pupil as an advocate in terms of nationally certified examinations rather than as a judge.

The introduction of school-based assessment by the pupil's own teacher for certification purposes would undermine those two roles, to the detriment of all concerned....

The role of the teacher as judge rather than advocate may lead to legal accountability in terms of marks awarded for certification purposes. This would automatically result in a distancing between the teacher, the pupil and the parent. It also opens the door to possible distortion of the results in response to either parental pressure or to pressure emanating from competition among local schools for pupils (ASTI, 1990, 1).

IV. A STRATEGY FOR TRANSFORMING SECONDARY EDUCATION

It is easy to list changes that can increase educational achievement: greater attention in class, more reading, less TV, more homework, more challenging courses, better teaching, more competent teachers and longer school years (see Appendix 5.A). There are, however, no magic bullets and no clear recipes for introduction of some of these changes. Young people in other nations learn more than ours because they work harder at it. What is difficult is identifying practical ways of inducing 47,000,000 students to study harder and 80,000,000 parents to demand higher quality and higher standards in the education of their children.

There are 22,731 public secondary schools in the United Sates that are run by 15,358 largely autonomous local education agencies. Mandates from above have been tried and have failed. This section of the paper outlines a strategy of change built around increased rewards at both the individual and community levels for improvements in academic achievement.

The key to motivating students to learn and parents to demand a quality education is recognizing and rewarding learning effort and achievement. Some students are attracted to serious study of a subject by intrinsic fascination with the subject. They must, however, pay a heavy price in the scorn of their peers and lost free time. Society offers them little reward for their effort. Most students are not motivated to study by love of the subject. The sentiment expressed by one student, *"You're going to work your whole life,...[High school should be a place to] enjoy life and have fun"* (Powell, et al., 1985, 43) is quite common. Sixty-two percent of 10th graders agree with the statement, "I don't like to do any more school work than I have to" (Longitudinal Survey of American Youth or LSAY, Q. AA37N). As a result, far too few high school students put serious time and energy into learning.

If this is to change, a strategy for reducing peer pressure against studying needs to be devised and rewards for learning need to be increased. The full diversity of types and levels of accomplishment need to be signaled so that everyone--no matter how advanced or far behind--faces a reward for greater time and energy devoted to learning. Learning accomplishments need to be described on an absolute scale so that improvements in the quality and rigor of the teaching and greater effort by all students in a school makes everybody better off. Colleges need to be induced to select students on the basis of externally validated measures of achievement, not by "aptitude" test scores or rank in class.

If employers know who is well educated in these fields, they can be expected to provide the rewards needed to motivate study. Ninety-two percent of 10th graders say they "often think about what type of job I will be doing after I finish school"(LSAY, Q. AA13C). If the labor market were to begin rewarding learning in school, many high school students would respond by studying harder and local voters would be willing to pay higher taxes so as to have better local schools. The Secretary of Labor's Commission on Workforce Quality and Labor Market Efficiency advocates such a change:

> The business community should...show through their hiring and promotion decisions that academic achievements will be rewarded (1989, 9).
> High-school students who excel in science and mathematics should be rewarded with business internships or grants for further study (1989, 11).

Some might respond to this strategy for achieving excellence by stating a preference for intrinsic over extrinsic motivation of learning. This, however, is a false dichotomy. Nowhere else are masses of people expected to devote thousands of hours to a difficult task while receiving *only* intrinsic rewards.

Public recognition of achievement and the symbolic and material rewards received by achievers are important generators of intrinsic motivation. They are, in fact, one of the central ways a culture symbolically transmits and promotes its values.[8]

Recommendations for policy initiatives have been grouped into three categories:
* Better signals of learning accomplishment,
* Inducing students to pursue a more rigorous curriculum,
* Generating additional recognition and rewards for learning.

Better Signals of Learning Accomplishment

• Instituting Statewide Achievement Examinations

Of the 50 states, only New York has a system of achievement exams where students are required to write essays and solve long mathematics problems. This appears to have raised achievement levels in New York State. When the family income, parental education, race and gender of SAT test takers are controlled, New York State has the highest adjusted mean Scholastic Aptitude Test score of the sample of 38 states with an adequate numbers of test takers to be included in the study (Graham and Husted, 1993). This benefit occurs *despite* the fact that Regents exam grades account for less than half of the course grade and influence only the type of diploma received. A passing score on Regents exams is not necessary for admission to local community colleges and out-of-state colleges and employers ignore exams results when they make hiring decisions. If the rewards for doing well on Regents exams were greater, incentive effects would be even larger.

Statewide assessments of competency and knowledge that are keyed to the state's core curriculum (e.g., New York State's Regents Examinations and California's Golden State Examinations) should be made a graduation requirement. All students would be assessed in core subjects such as English, mathematics, history and science but students would also be able to select additional subjects--e.g., foreign languages, art, economics, psychology, auto repair, electronics, computer programming--for assessment. Results of these assessments would replace SAT and ACT test scores in the admission and selection process and determine the award of state merit based scholarships.[9] Students would be given a credential certifying performance on these exams and employers should be encouraged to factor examination results into their hiring decisions.

This approach to signaling academic achievement to employers is preferable to extensive use of employment testing of job applicants. By retaining control of exam content, educators and the public influence the kinds of academic achievement that are rewarded by the labor market. Societal decisions regarding the curriculum (e.g., all students should read Shakespeare's plays and understand the Constitution) tend to be reinforced by employer hiring decisions. Tests developed solely for employee selection purposes do not ask questions about Shakespeare and the Constitution.   Because it is centralized and students undertake the assessments over the course of their final years in high school the quality and comprehensiveness of the assessment can be much greater.

• **Externally Assessed Achievement Should Determine College Admissions**

Albert Shankar, President of the AFT, and Robert Samuelson, editorial writer for *Newsweek*, have argued that college admission and financial aid should go only to those who have demonstrated some minimum level of achievement on an external assessment.   Such a policy would indeed dramatically strengthen incentives to study in high school, but undoing the open admissions policies of most community colleges would generate intense opposition.   It would mean sacrificing a feature of American society--second, third and fourth chances for getting a good education regardless of whether earlier educational opportunities were squandered--that most Americans hold very dear.

There is, however, a more modest proposal that is consistent with open admissions at community colleges and voc/tech institutions, and which would have stronger and more widespread incentive effects.   **The proposal is to use externally assessed achievement as the basis for deciding who is admitted to particular colleges, to particular fields of study (e.g., an electronics technician program might admit only those with a minimum level of competence in algebra and physics) and into degree credit programs generally.**   Entering students who did not meet these requirements would be able to fulfill them at community colleges but the credits received in remedial courses would not count towards an associates or bachelors degree.

This is not really a radical proposal because most colleges already offer remedial courses that students with deficiencies in their background must take without getting degree credit.   The proposal is to increase what we expect students to have learned **before** they are admitted into bachelors or associates degree programs, and to require poorly prepared students to spend additional time getting a degree.

Colleges and universities are already stratified in their rigor and prestige. The economic rewards for graduating from the finest colleges are very substantial (Solomon, 1975; Symonette, 1981; Karabel and McClelland, 1987; Mueller, 1988; James, Alsalam, Conaty and To, 1989).   Graduates with scientific and technical training are much better remunerated than graduates with humanities and social science degrees.   This means that strong incentives to compete for admission to the best colleges and the high wage majors already exist.   The problem is not a lack of competition, but the basis of that competition--teacher assessments of achievement relative to others in your high school and aptitude tests which do not assess what has been learned in most high school courses.   If college admissions decisions were made on the basis of external assessments of achievement in the subjects studied in high school, student incentives to study in high school and parental incentives to press for higher standards would improve dramatically.

If, however, external assessments of achievement are to be used in the college admissions decision, the results of these assessments need to be available in time to affect these decisions. **This means that assessments should be graded by the end of April and announcements of admission to college delayed until late May.** Advanced Placement exams, for example, would have to be taken a month earlier than they are now and must be graded in the space of a couple of weeks.[10] Colleges would have to be forced to stop competing for students by offering early guarantees of admission. These changes would have a number of salutary effects. Ask any teacher about second semester seniors and you will hear complaints about their unwillingness to work hard. This would end. They would, in fact, become the hardest workers in the high school, thereby becoming good role models for the younger students. More significantly, the whole structure of incentives to study would be strengthened.

• Develop Better Assessment Mechanisms

If student recognition and rewards depend on the results of assessments of competency made by the education system, it is essential that all the competencies that we believe students should be developing be assessed. Since curriculum objectives differ somewhat from state to state, a variety of assessment mechanisms will be needed. Means of assessing higher order thinking skills, hands on performance and portfolios of the student work need to be developed. Written exams might include some multiple choice items but other types of questions--essays, short explanations, showing your work in multi-step math problems--should become more common.

• Certifying Competencies and Releasing Student Records

> Schools should develop easily understood transcripts which at the request of students, are readily available to employers. These transcripts should contain documentable measures of achievement in a variety of fields as well as attendance records. State governments should provide assistance to facilitate the standardization of transcripts so that they will be more easily understood. (Commission on Workforce Quality and Labor Market Efficiency, p. 12)

Schools should provide graduates with certificates or diplomas that certify the students' knowledge and competencies, rather than just their attendance. Competency should be defined by an absolute standard in the way Scout merit badges are. Different types and levels of competency need to be certified. Minimum competency tests for a high school diploma do not satisfy the need for better signals of achievement in high school. Some students arrive in high school so far behind, and the consequences of not getting a diploma are so severe, we have not been willing to set the minimum competency standard very high. Once they satisfy the minimum, many students stop putting effort into their academic courses. What is needed is a more informative credential that signals the full range of student achievements (e.g., statewide achievement exam scores, competency check lists).

One of the saddest consequences of the lack of signals of achievement in high school is that employers with good jobs offering training and job security are unwilling to take the risk of hiring a recent high school graduate. They prefer to hire workers with many years of work experience. One important reason for this policy is that the applicant's work record serves as a signal of competence and reliability that helps the employer identify who is most qualified. In the United States recent high school graduates have no such record and information on high school performance is not available, so the entire graduating class appears to employers as one undifferentiated mass of unskilled and undisciplined workers. A common employer's view of 18 year olds was expressed by a supervisor at New York Life Insurance (a company that recently moved some claims processing work to Ireland) who commented on television **"When kids come out of high school, they think the world owes them a living"** (PBS, March 27, 1989).   Surely this generalization does not apply to every graduate, but the students who are disciplined and academically well prepared currently have no way of signaling this fact to employers.

The school can help students get good jobs by adopting an equitable and efficient policy for releasing student records. School officials have the dual responsibility of protecting the student's right to privacy and helping them find good, suitable jobs. The student and his or her parents should receive copies of transcripts and other records that might be released so that they may make them available to anyone they choose. Schools can also develop a sheet explaining to parents and students their rights, as well as the pros and cons of disclosing information.

According to the Federal Education Rights and Privacy Act, all that a student/graduate must do to have school records sent to a prospective employer is sign a form specifying the purpose of disclosure, which records are to be released, and who is to receive the records. The waiver and record request forms used by employers contain this information, so when such a request is received, the school is obliged to respond. Requiring that graduates fill out a school devised form, as some high schools do, results in the employer not getting the requested transcript and the graduate not getting the job. Many high school graduates do not realize that they failed to get a job they were hoping for because their high school did not send the transcript that was requested.

• Credential Data Bank and Employee Locator Service

It may, however, be unrealistic to expect more than 20,000 high schools to develop efficient systems of maintaining student records and responding quickly to requests for transcripts. An alternative approach would be to centralize the record keeping and dissemination function in a trusted third party organization. The student would determine which competencies are to be assessed and what types of information are to be included in his/her competency portfolio. Competency assessments would be offered for a variety of scientific, mathematical and technological subjects, languages, writing, business and economics, and occupational skills. Tests with many alternate forms (or administered by computer using a large test item bank) would be used so that students could retake the test a month later if desired. Only the highest score would remain in the system. Students would be encouraged to include descriptions of their extracurricular activities, their jobs and any other accomplishments they feel are relevant, and to submit samples of their work such as a research paper, art work, or pictures of a project made in metal shop. Files could be updated after leaving high school.

Students would receive copies of their portfolio that they could carry to job interviews or mail to employers. They would also be able to call a 900 number and request their portfolio be sent to specific employers. Finally, they could put themselves in an employee locator data bank similar to the student locator services operated by the Educational Testing Service and American College Testing. A student seeking a summer or post graduation job would specify the type of work sought and dates of availability. Employers seeking workers could ask for a printout of the portfolios of all the individuals living near a particular establishment who have expressed interest in that type of job and who pass the employer's competency screens. Student locator services have been used heavily by colleges seeking to recruit minority students and an employee locator service would almost certainly be used in the same way. Pilot programs are underway in Hillsborough County, Florida, Orange County, California, Fort Worth, Texas, and New Jersey and a number of other locations. State governments should consider becoming sponsors of such systems.

• Acting as a Source of Informal Contacts

School personnel can be a reference and a source of job contacts for their students. Some students may feel that they do not have and cannot develop good employment contacts. School personnel can help out by building and maintaining trusting relationships with local employers and then helping to match employer and student needs. Students from disadvantaged backgrounds have special need for this kind of help, because their relatives and neighbors typically lack the employment contacts of middle-class families.

Whenever possible, there should be a one-on-one relationship between a specific teacher or administrator and an employer. A study by McKinney et al. (1982) found that *when schools formalize this relationship by creating a placement office, fewer vocational students found jobs.* The best example of an informal contact system is the one that exists for many vocational students. Vocational teachers often know local employers in related fields; they also know their students well enough to recommend them. This kind of informal system can be expanded to include all students not planning to attend college.

Inducing Students to Pursue a More Rigorous Curriculum

The analysis of the causes of American apathy toward teaching and learning has important implications for the curriculum. Many of the weaknesses of math and science curricula--the constant review and repetition of old material, the slow pace and minimal expectations--are adaptations to the low level of effort most students are willing to devote to these subjects. When considering proposed revisions of the curriculum, **one must remember that motivating students to take tough courses and to study hard must be a central concern.**

A second constraint that must be recognized is the great diversity of the learning goals and capabilities of high school students. On the NAEP reading and mathematics scales 15-16.5 percent of 13 year olds have better skills than the average 17 year old student, and 7-9 percent of 13 year olds score below the average nine year old (NAEP 1988b, NCES 1992a). Consequently, it is neither feasible nor desirable for all senior high school students to pursue the same curriculum. While many nations have a common curriculum with no tracking in elementary school and lower secondary schools, no country requires all senior secondary students to take the same courses. Some students will want to pursue subjects like mathematics and science in greater depth and rigor than others. Some students will want to concentrate on technology, not pure science. Some courses will be easier than others and students will inevitably be able to choose between more demanding and less demanding courses.

How then does one convince students to take tough courses and study hard? The previous analysis suggests the following: (1) develop rigorous courses that teach students concepts and material that they will use after leaving high school, (2) convince students that the material being taught is useful by presenting it as solutions to practical real world problems, (3) honor them for choosing more challenging courses, (4) define accomplishment in a way that students who work hard will perceive themselves as successful, and then (5) recognize and reward accomplishment.

Usefulness is an important criterion for selecting topics in a curriculum for three reasons. First, the social benefits of learning derive from the use of the knowledge and skills, not from the fact they are in someone's repertoire. Secondly, skills and knowledge that are not used deteriorate very rapidly. In one set of studies, students tested two years after taking a course had forgotten 1/3 of the high school chemistry, 1/2 of the college psychology and zoology, and 3/4 of the college botany that had been learned (Pressey and Robinson, 1944, 544). Skills and knowledge that are used are remembered. Consequently, if learning is to produce long term benefits, the competencies developed must continue to be used after the final exam (either in college, the labor market or somewhere else). Finally, usefulness is essential because students are not going to put energy into learning things they perceive to be useless. Furthermore, the labor market is not in the long run going to reward skills and competencies that have no use. Indeed, selecting workers on the basis of competencies that are not useful in the company's jobs is in most circumstances a violation of Title VII of the Civil Rights Act.

• Making a Differentiated Senior High Curriculum Work

By 10th grade most students have a pretty good idea of what kinds of jobs they want after finishing their education. Ninety-seven percent can select a particular occupation they expect to have at age 40 and 77 percent agree with the statement: "I am quite certain about what kinds of jobs I would enjoy doing when I am older" (LSAY, Q. AA13C & AA22A). Students who are planning careers in science and engineering need to be able to take college preparatory biology, chemistry and physics courses that prepare them for the core courses they will face in college. The students not planning on scientific careers, however, quite often fail to see how these courses will be useful to them. Less than a quarter of 10th graders believe that geometry, trigonometry, biology, chemistry, and physics are needed to qualify for their first choice occupation (LSAY, Q. BA24B-BA25D).

In senior high school an effective way to motivate students to take demanding courses and to study hard is to tailor courses to the student's career interest and ensure that prospective employers are aware that the student took challenging rigorous courses. An experimental evaluation of New York City's Career Magnet schools suggests that they have increased both reading scores and retention (Crain, Heebner and Si, 1992).

• Teaching Science and Math by Infusing it into Technology Courses

Analyses of labor market success of young men and of job performance in the military indicate that young people who expect to have jobs in which they use or maintain complicated pieces of equipment should receive a thorough technology education (Bishop, 1989b, 1992; Hunter, Crossen and Friedman, 1985). Computer classes are one example of the kinds of courses needed. High school sophomores described their computer classes as "Very Useful" for their career 53 percent of the time and as of "No Use" only 6 percent of the time (LSAY, Q. AACOMF).

The *Principles of Technology* (PT) course developed by a consortium of vocational education agencies in 47 states and Canadian provinces in association with the Agency for Instructional Technology and the Center for Occupational Research and Development is another example of a course that meets this need very well. This two-year applied physics course is both academically rigorous and practical. Each six day subunit deals with the unit's major technical principle (e.g., resistance) as it applies to one of the four energy systems--mechanical (both rotational and linear), fluid, electrical, and thermal. A subunit usually consists of two days of lectures and discussion, a math skills lab, two days of hands-on physics application labs, and a subunit review. This approach appears to be quite effective at teaching basic physics. When students enrolled in regular physics and Principles of Technology courses were tested on basic physics concepts at the beginning and end of their junior and senior year in high school, the PT students started out behind the regular physics students but obtained an average score of 81 at completion as compared to an average of 66 for those completing a physics course (Perry, 1989). Another study by John Roper (1989) obtained similar results. Comparable courses need to be developed for other fields of technology. This is an area of study that needs much more attention than it has been getting from educational reformers and curriculum developers.

• Expand Advanced Placement Courses

The Advanced Placement program is a cooperative educational endeavor that offers course descriptions, examinations, and sets of curricular materials in twenty-eight different academic subjects. Students who take these courses and pass the examinations receive college credit for high school work. Unlike the SAT, the ACT and all other standardized aptitude and achievement tests that employ the multiple-choice answer format exclusively, students are expected to write essays and to work out complicated science and mathematics problems. Hence they are similar in format and roughly comparable in difficulty to French Baccalaureates, English A Levels, and other exams taken by European secondary school students. The College Board is developing a parallel set of exams for high school level courses such as principles of technology, algebra, history, English and other subjects. This will give larger numbers of 10th and 11th graders and students not planning to attend four year colleges a chance to have their accomplishments certified.

Expanding the AP program should be a centerpiece of any effort to promote excellence in American high schools. The proportion of 11th and 12th graders taking AP exams more than doubled between 1983 and 1988 and grew a further 46 percent by 1992 . Nevertheless, only 8,022 of the 22,902 U.S. high schools participate in the Advanced Placement Program and only 52 AP exams are taken on average in each participating high school. Of the 11th and 12th graders in 1993, only 2.8 percent took an AP English exam, 2.3 percent took an AP history exam, 1.7 percent took the AP calculus exam, 1.7 percent took an AP science exam. (The College Board 1988, NCES 1993).

Federal and state governments can facilitate the growth of the AP program by underwriting the development of AP exams for new subjects, by financing summer institutes for the teachers of AP courses, by subsidizing the fees charged for taking the exam and by offering AP Excellence Awards to students who achieve passing scores on the exam. The amount of the scholarship award might depend both on the level of student's pass and the eligibility of the student for Pell grants. In 1990, 326,025 students would have been eligible for an AP excellence award, so a scholarship program awarding an average of $250. per recipient would have cost only $82 million.

Students and their parents are generally unaware that taking one or more AP course is almost a requirement for admission at many selective colleges. At Cornell's Engineering College, for example, over 90 percent of the freshman class had taken an AP calculus and/or science course(s) in high school. If a large group of colleges were to announce and publicize this policy, high schools that do not currently offer AP courses would be pressed to offer them and enrollment in the courses would increase.

• School Choice

Once external examinations of achievement at the end of high school become common place, school choice will considerably strengthen pressures for higher standards. European education systems typically allow students a good deal of latitude in selecting which school to attend. School funding is generally independent of where the student lives and follows the student to the school. Consequently, schools experiencing an increase in applications have an incentive to expand up to the capacity of their physical plant. Schools with strong reputations get more applications than they can accept and are, in effect, rewarded by being allowed to admit the "best" from their pool of applicants. School reputations are heavily influenced by the school's results on the external exams taken by students at the end of secondary education.

About a decade ago England and Scotland gave parents the right to send their children to schools outside the normal attendance area. Two years after choice became operational in Scotland, 9 percent of pupils entering secondary school (11 to 14 percent in urban areas) attended a school outside their cachement area (Adler and Raab, 1988). Scottish parents who made this choice appeared to be behaving rationally for they tended to choose schools that were more effective than the school in their own cachement area. An analysis of school choice in the Fife Education Authority found that the schools chosen by those leaving their cachement area had better examination results than would have been predicted given the pupil's primary school test scores and family background and the average SES of pupils at the school.[11]

To help parents evaluate schools, each grant maintained school in England is required to report its GCSE and A level exam results to the Department of Education and after checking the results are published and made available to the newspapers (see Exhibit 3). These school league tables apparently have big effects on school reputations. Kenilworth School, for example, was ranked number one among comprehensive schools in Warickshire in 1991 and the following year its applications and first year enrollment increased nearly 30 percent. Administrators seeking to strengthen their school's reputation are thus induced to give teaching effectiveness (as assessed by the external exam) first priority.

Generating Additional Recognition and Rewards for Learning

• Cooperative Learning

One effective way of inducing peers to value learning and support effort in school is to reward the group for the individual learning of its members. This is the approach taken in cooperative learning. Research results (Slavin 1985) suggest that the two key ingredients for successful cooperative learning are the following:

> A cooperative incentive structure--awards based on group performance-- seems to be essential for students working in groups to get really involved in tutoring and encouraging each other to study.

> A system of individual accountability in which everyone's maximum effort must be essential to the group's success and the effort and performance of each group member must be clearly visible to his or her group mates.

For example, students might be grouped into evenly matched teams of four or five members that are heterogeneous in ability. After the teacher presents new material, the team works together on work sheets to prepare each other for periodic quizzes. The team's score is an average of the scores of team members, and high team scores are recognized on a class bulletin board or through group certificates of achievement.

What seems to happen in cooperative learning is that the team develops an identity of its own, and group norms arise that are different from the norms that hold sway in the student's other classes. The group's identity arises from the extensive personal interaction among group members in the context of working toward a shared goal. Since the group is small and the interaction intense, the effort and success of each team member is known to other teammates. Such knowledge allows the group to reward each team member for his or her contribution to the team goal.

• Honoring Academic Achievement

The medals, trophies, and school letters awarded in interscholastic athletics are a powerful motivator of achievement on the playing field. Academic pursuits need a similar system of reinforcement. Awards and honors systems should be designed so that almost every student can receive at least one award or honor before graduation if he or she makes the effort.[12] The standard for making an award should be based on absolute criteria: if greater numbers achieve the standard of excellence, more awards should be given. The trophy case and bulletin board at the entrance of the school should be used to recognize academic achievements not athletic achievements.

• Award Scholarships on the Basis of Past Academic Achievement as Well as Need

In addition to need based scholarship programs, states should award scholarships on the basis of academic achievements assessed by criteria external to the school such as the Advanced Placement exams, New York State's Regents Exams and California's Golden State examinations. The purpose of scholarships is to reward effort and accomplishment not "talent" or IQ; so aptitude tests should not be used to select winners. Rank in class and GPA should also not be the basis for these awards. The size of the award would depend on financial need.

• League Competitions between Schools in the Academic Arena

Band and athletic programs receive very generous support from the community because the band and the team are viewed as representing the entire high school to neighboring communities and the rest of the state and because their accomplishments are highly visible. A similar spirit of competition between communities needs to be developed in the academic arena. States should examine the feasibility of establishing a system of highly visible competitions for each academic subject and for extracurricular activities like debate, school newspaper, and the stock market game. As many students as possible should participate. This can be accomplished by arranging separate competitions for each grade, requiring (where possible) the school to field a team that includes all students taking a particular course and having the share of the student body that is on the team be one of the criteria by which schools are judged. As in sports, fair competition can be ensured by placing small schools and schools serving disadvantaged populations in a separate league or by establishing a handicapping system.

The competitions should not be a glorified Trivial Pursuits game. While cable TV broadcasts of High School Bowl-like contests can be a component of the program, most of the points obtained by a school's team should come from assessments of the performance of the entire team on authentic tasks like writing an essay, giving a speech, determining the chemical composition of a compound, working out long mathematics problems, writing a computer program, or fixing a car. As much as possible, the tasks should be aligned with the state curriculum for that subject.

• Mastery Learning

Students who are not learning at the desired rate can be expected to commit additional time to the task before or after school, on Saturday, during the summer or by giving up free periods. Students who have not been performing at grade level in required core subjects would be scheduled in the fall to receive additional instruction in the subject(s) they are having problems with. This can be accomplished in a number of ways: coming to school early, staying after school, Saturday school or extra periods devoted to the subject substituting for study hall or an elective class. Mac Iver's (1991) analysis of NELS:88 data on 8th graders suggests that these interventions may have significant and substantively important effects on student mathematics and reading ability. The student and his parents would also be told in the fall that if performance does not improve considerably that summer school would be required as well. Progress would be assessed primarily by course grades and teacher evaluations, but there should be an external yardstick as well. The external yardstick might be a competency check list, a mastery test keyed to the textbook, or an exam specified by the state, the school or collectively by the teachers in that grade level or department.[13] Since students will want to avoid being required to spend additional time in classes after school, on Saturday or during the summer, the policy will be a powerful incentive for them to pay attention and complete homework in their regular classes.

V.   EFFECTS OF PROPOSED REFORMS ON UNDERREPRESENTED MINORITIES

The two blue ribbon commissions that recommended improvements in the signaling of academic achievement to colleges and employers included substantial representation from the minority community.[14] Nevertheless, the reader may be wondering about the likely effects of the reform proposals just described on the labor market chances of minority youth. Because minority students receive lower scores on achievement tests, it may appear at first glance that greater emphasis on academic achievement will inevitably reduce their access to good colleges and to good jobs. This is not the case, however, for four reasons.

If academic achievement becomes a more important basis for selecting students and workers, something else becomes less important. The consequences for minorities of greater emphasis on academic achievement depends on the nature of the criterion that becomes deemphasized. Substituting academic achievement tests for aptitude tests in college admissions **improves minority access** because minority-majority differentials tend to be smaller (in standard deviation units) on achievement tests (e.g. the NAEP reading and math tests) than on aptitude tests (e.g. the SAT). Greater emphasis on academic achievement **improves the access of women** to high level professional, technical, craft, and managerial jobs because it substitutes a criterion on which women do well for criteria--such as sex stereotyped beliefs about which jobs are appropriate for women--that have excluded women in the past.

For the same reason, greater emphasis on academic achievement when selecting young workers will not reduce minority access to jobs if it substitutes for other criteria that also place minority youth at a serious disadvantage. The current system in which there is almost no use of employment tests and little signaling of high school achievements to the labor market clearly has not generated jobs for minority youth. In October 1985, 1986, 1987, 1988, 1989 and 1990, an average of only 46 percent of the previous June's black high school graduates not attending college were employed (Bureau of Labor Statistics 1989). One reason why minority youth do poorly in the labor market is that most of the criteria now used to make selections--previous work experience, recommendations from previous employers, having family friends or relatives at the firm, proximity of one's residence to stores that hire youth, performance in interviews, and prejudices and stereotypes--work against them. These criteria will diminish in importance as academic achievement becomes more important. One cannot predict a priori whether the net result will help or hinder minority youth seeking employment. In some models of the labor market the relative position of minority workers improves when academic achievement is better signaled (Aigner and Cain, 1975).

The second way in which minority youth may benefit from improved signaling of school achievements is that it will give recent high school graduates, both black and white, the first real chance to compete for high-wage, high-training content jobs. At present all youth are frozen out of these jobs because primary labor market employers seldom consider job applicants who lack considerable work experience. Experience is considered essential partly because it contributes to productivity but also because it produces signals of competence and reliability that employers use to identify who is most qualified. A black personnel director interviewed for a CBS special on the educational reform proudly stated, "We don"t hire high school graduates any more, we need **skilled workers**" (CBS, September 6, 1990). State exams, competency portfolios and informative graduation credentials would change this situation and give students a way of demonstrating that the stereotype does not apply to them. Young people from minority backgrounds must overcome even more virulent stereotypes and they often lack a network of adult contacts who can provide job leads and references. By helping them overcome these barriers to employment, competency portfolios are of particular help to minority youth.

The third way in which these proposals will assist minority students is by encouraging greater numbers of firms to undertake affirmative action recruitment. The creation of a competency portfolio data bank that can be used by employers seeking qualified minority job candidates would greatly reduce the costs and increase the effectiveness of affirmative action programs. Affirmative action has significantly improved minority representation in managerial and professional occupations and contributed to a substantial increase in the payoff to schooling for blacks (Freeman, 1981). One of the reasons why it has been particularly effective in this labor market is that college reputations, transcripts and placement offices provide brokering and pre-screening services that significantly lower the costs of recruiting minority job candidates. The competency portfolio data bank would extend low cost brokering and pre-screening services to the labor market for high school graduates. The creation of such a data bank would almost certainly generate a great deal of competition for the more qualified minority youth in the portfolio bank.

The final and most important way in which these reforms will benefit minority youth is by bringing about improvements in academic achievement and productivity on the job. Student incentives to study hard, parental incentives to demand a better education, and teacher incentives to both give more and expect more from students will all be strengthened. Because of the way affirmative action is likely to interact with a competency profile data bank, the rewards for learning will become particularly strong for minority students. Learning will improve and the gap between minority and majority achievement will diminish. Society has been making considerable progress in closing achievement gaps between minority and majority students. In the early National Assessment of Educational Progress (NAEP) assessments black high school seniors born between 1952 and 1957 were 6.7 grade level equivalents behind their white counterparts in science proficiency, 4 grade level equivalents behind in mathematics, and 5.3 grade level equivalents behind in reading. The most recent National Assessment data for 1989-90 reveal that for blacks born in 1972, the gap has been cut to 5.2 grade level equivalents in science, 2.4 grade level equivalents in math, and 3.5 grade level equivalents in reading (NAEP, 1989; NCES, 1992, Table 102, 112 & 118). Koretz's (1986, Appendix E) analysis of data from state testing programs supports the NAEP findings. Hispanic students are also closing the achievement gap. These desirable trends suggest that despite their limited funding, Head Start, Title I, and other compensatory interventions have had an impact. The schools attended by most minority students are inferior to those attended by white students (Ferguson, 1990), so further reductions in the school quality differentials can be expected to produce further reductions in academic achievement differentials.

The student body of James A. Garfield High School in Los Angeles is predominantly made up of persons from disadvantaged minorities; yet in 1987 only three high schools in the nation (Alhambra High School in California and Bronx Science and Stuvesant High School in New York City) had a larger number of students taking the AP calculus exam. This high school and its two calculus teachers, Jaime Escalante and Ben Jimenez, were responsible for 17 percent of all Mexican Americans taking the AP calculus exam and 32 percent of all Mexican Americans who pass the more difficult BC form of the test (Matthews, 1988). There is no secret about how they did it; they worked extremely hard. Students signed a contract committing themselves to extra homework and extra time in school and they lived up to the commitment. What this success establishes is that minority youngsters can be persuaded to study just as hard as the academic track students in Europe and that if they do, their achievements will match those in other countries.

Appendix 5.A: The Payoff to Lengthening the School Year

Studies in which mathematics tests have been administered to students both in the spring and the fall of a calendar year find that mathematics competence declines during the summer months (Heyns, 1986, 1987). Entwisle and Alexander's (1989 Table 1) study of first and second graders in Baltimore, for example, found no gain in mathematics skills between the April test administration and the October test administration, even though that period contained two full months of classroom study of arithmetic. If children were learning during the two months of classes included in the summer gap period at anything like the rate they learn during the rest of the school year, their reading and math skills must have declined during the summer months. The learning loss is particularly large for disadvantaged students and for minority students (Heyns, 1987).

Direct evidence on this issue can be found in the evaluation of Summer Training and Employment Program. In this study the initial test was administered after the end of school in June and the end of summer administration was prior to the beginning of school in the fall. In this study the control group that received no instruction during the summer experienced very large declines in mathematics and substantial declines in reading.

In most classrooms the first few weeks are spent reviewing and practicing skills taught in previous years. Old material can probably be relearned at a more rapid rate than new material is learned, so this is likely to be a period of particularly rapid rise in test scores. Mc Knight et al., (1988) severely criticize this practice of allocating so much time to review of old topics rather than to the presentation of new material. These findings suggest that school attendance is essential if math and reading skills are to improve and that a longer school year would not only increase learning time but also reduce forgetting time. Adding a month to the school year could very well produce a more than proportionate increase in learning.

Studies of the effect of summer school confirm the educational impact of additional instruction time. The best study of this issue used a random assignment control group methodology to evaluate STEP, a program for disadvantaged youth that combines a part time summer job with about 90 hours of remedial instruction. It found that adding the instruction to the summer job raised academic achievement by .5 grade level equivalents above that of youth receiving only a part time job. (Sipe, Grossman and Milliner, 1988). The success of the STEP intervention has resulted in its replication (with federal support) in 33 different school systems.

This evidence indicates that extending the school year would not only raise educational standards generally, it would also help children from educationally and economically disadvantaged backgrounds keep up with their more advantaged peers.

Accelerating the Pace of Instruction

Increasing the time devoted to learning by one-ninth or more has major implications for the curriculum. The learning objectives specified for each year would need to be changed. In subjects which follow a sequence such as mathematics, reading, and spelling, material taught at the beginning of third grade might be moved to the end of second grade, eighth grade topics might be taught in seventh grade, etc. In mathematics, for example, coverage of probability and statistics might be greatly increased. For students headed for college, the final two years would be given over to AP courses. College freshman would arrive much better prepared than they are now. A decision would have to be made whether (a) the bachelors degree should become a three year degree, (b) the number of credits for graduation should be increased, or (c) college courses should be made more rigorous with a corresponding reduction in the number of credits that students can carry per semester.

The Costs and Benefits of Lengthening of the School Year

The most significant barrier to this reform is the cost. If teachers are to spend more time teaching, yearly salaries must be increased by a comparable percentage. Lawrence Picus (1993, 14) has estimated that a 24.4 percent increase in the time spent in school (by switching from the current 6.25 hrs*180 days/yr to a 7 hrs*200 days/yr) would cost $34.4 billion or roughly 16 percent of 213.2 billion spent for public elementary and secondary education. This is not really as big a number as one might think. For comparison, between 1986 and 1991, real spending on education by state and local governments rose by $53.4 billion and real gross domestic product was growing at an annual rate of more than $100 billion dollars per year. Since more than half of the mothers of school children work, the savings in day care costs would be substantial. If one-fifth of the 38.4 million public school children no longer required day care for 275 hours per year costing $4.00 per hour, the savings would be $8.45 billion. Since most teachers and students do not work in the summer, the increase in learning time would come primarily out of leisure not work time. GDP would immediately increase because the rise in teacher pay and labor released by the reduced demand for child care would be larger than the induced decline in summer job earnings of teachers and students. When GDP rises, taxes rise as well, so the change would be partially self-financing.

The long term benefits would be very large. Because a longer school year reduces summer forgetting as well as increasing learning time, it is quite possible that a more than proportionate learning response (on a grade level equivalent scale) would result. Let us, however, make the conservative assumption that the 24.4 percent increase in learning time increases 12th grade achievement scaled in grade level equivalents by 20 percent or 2.6 U.S. grade level equivalents. Student cohorts experiencing the longer school year for 13 years would have their compensation increased by about 10.4 percent or $2184 a year.[15] The productivity effects of test score increases are 50 percent larger than wage rate effects (Bishop, 1987a, 1987b). Consequently, increasing time in school by 275 hours per year is estimated to eventually raise the productivity of adults by $3276 per year (15.6 percent of mean compensation). Because a one year age cohort contains 3.5 million people, the benefit is about $ 11.5 billion dollars per year. The real rate of return on the taxpayer contribution to the additional learning investment is 33 percent per year.[16] Only investments in R&D have real social rates of return this high. If the real rate of social discount is 6 percent and the growth of labor productivity is projected at 2 percent per year, the ratio of present discounted benefits to costs is 5.3 to 1.[17] Even if the increased time in school produces only a third of my assumed learning gains, the investment has a higher payoff than most other uses of tax dollars.

NOTES

For permission to quote *Horace's Compromise* (Copyright (c) 1984 by Theodore R. Sizer) and *The Shopping Mall High School* (Copyright (c) 1985 by Arthur G. Powell, Eleanor Farrar and David K. Cohen) the editors of this volume wish to thank Houghton Mifflin Co.

1. In science the gaps between American students and European students appear to develop during middle school and high school, not elementary school. In the IEA study of science achievement in 1983-84, American 10 year olds did about as well as students

in Australia, Italy and Norway and at least 4 percentage points better than students in England, Hong Kong, Israel, Poland, and Singapore. The U.S. was significantly behind the following countries: Canada (percent correct 3.5 points higher), Hungary (a gap of 5.4 points), Sweden (a gap of 6.3 points), and Finland, Japan and Korea (a gap of roughly 9 points) (Postlethwaite and Wiley, 1992, Table 3.1). Since the standard deviation of test scores is 19.0, the deficit with respect to Finland, Japan and Korea at this age is slightly less than one-half a US standard deviation. In the 1991 IAEP study of 9 year olds, the 64.7 percent correct for U.S. students was exceeded only by the students of Northern Italy, Korea and Taiwan (66.7-67.9 percent correct). Percent corrects for Canada, England, Hungary Israel, Scotland, the former Soviet Union, and Spain ranged between 61.5 and 62.9. Slovenia, Ireland and Portugal scored between 54.8 and 57.7. The standard deviation of the raw percent correct scores is approximately 18 for the U.S., so the highest scoring country, Korea, is only about one-sixth of a standard deviation above the U.S. In both these studies, American students who were four years older (13 or 14 years old) were substantially behind the students in most other countries.

2. If GED certificates were counted as diplomas, American secondary school graduation rates would be higher. But the labor market does not view the GED as equivalent to a high school diploma. GED certified high school equivalents are paid 6 percent more than high school dropouts but 8 to 11 percent less than high school graduates. Most GED test takers spend little time preparing for the exam. The median examinee spent 20 hours preparing for the exam and 21 percent did not prepare in any way. Their ASVAB test scores are above those of other high school drop outs but significantly below those of high school graduates who do not go to college. (Cameron and Heckman, 1993). Hence it is not appropriate to count GED certificates along with high school diplomas.

3. Countries such as Sweden, Finland, Norway and Portugal where English language television programs are subtitled in the local language (not dubbed) are exceptions to this generalization. Watching subtitled programs results in children getting lots of practice reading the local language rapidly. In these countries those who watched about 3.5 hours a day had higher reading achievement than those who watched no TV and those who watched over 5 hours a day (Elley, 1992, 72).

4. According to the California Department of Education (1987), the share of the budget going to classroom teachers was 45 percent. The share of school district expenditure that goes for instruction (a category which includes teachers aides, guidance counselors, special instructional personnel and supplies) is 63 percent in California, 56 percent in Milwaukee Wisconsin and 55 percent in the District of Columbia (Fischer 1990; KPMG Peat Marwick, 1989).

5. The very large differentials between college majors found in these data reflect both differences in wage rates and in hours worked per month. If gender was controlled, the differentials would be somewhat smaller.

6. Studies that measure output for different workers in the same job at the same firm, using physical output as a criterion, can be manipulated to produce estimates of the standard deviation of non-transitory output variation across individuals. It averages about .14 in operative jobs, .28 in craft jobs, .34 in technician jobs, .164 in routine clerical jobs and .278 in clerical jobs with decision making responsibilities (Hunter, Schmidt & Judiesch, 1988). Because there are fixed costs to employing an individual (facilities, equipment, light, heat and overhead functions such as hiring and payrolling), the

coefficient of variation of marginal products of individuals is assumed to be 1.5 times the coefficient of variation of productivity. Because about two-thirds of clerical jobs can be classified as routine, the coefficient of variation of marginal productivity for clerical jobs is 30 percent [1.5*(.33*.278+.67*.164)]. Averaging operative jobs in with craft and technical jobs produces a similar 30 percent figure for blue collar jobs. The details and rationale of these calculations are explained in Bishop 1989b.

7. The survey was of a stratified random sample of the NFIB membership. Larger firms had a significantly higher probability of being selected for the study. The response rate to the mail survey was 20 percent and the number of usable responses was 2014.

8. Another possible argument against policies designed to induce employers to reward high school students who study is that poor students will not be considered if an employer learns of this fact. What those who make this argument do not realize is that the policy of providing no information to employers about performance in high school results in no recent graduates (whether good or poor student) getting a job that pays well and offers opportunities for training and promotions. In effect it is being proposed that the interests of the students who do not study and are discipline problems should take precedence over the interests of the students who lived by the schools rules and studied hard. There is nothing unfair about letting high school GPA's influence the allocation of young people to the best jobs. The GPA's are an average which reflects performance on 100's of tests, and the evaluations of over 20 teachers each of which is based on over 180 days of interaction. Selection decisions must be made somehow. If measures of performance in school are not available, the hiring selection will be determined by the chemistry of a job interview and idiosyncratic recommendations of a single previous employer. Since many employers will not request the information, providing information on student performance does not prevent the poorer student from getting a job; it only influences the quality of the job that the student is able to get.

9. The SAT suffers from two very serious limitations: the limited range of the achievements that are evaluated and its multiple choice format. The test was designed to be curriculum free. To the extent that it evaluates the students' understanding of material taught in schools, the material it covers is vocabulary and mathematics. Most of the college preparatory subjects studied in high school--science, social studies, technology, art, literature, music, computers, trigonometry and statistics--are absent from the test. As a result, it fails to generate incentives to take the more demanding courses or to study hard. The newly revised SAT is not a major improvement over the old test. The new version of the ACT test is a definite improvement for it tests science and social science knowledge and attempts to measure problem solving in science. Both tests suffer from the common problems that arise from their multiple choice format. National and provincial exams in Europe are predominantly essay and extended answer examinations. The absence of essays on the SAT and ACT tests contributes to the poor writing skills of American students. The tests advertise themselves as an ability test but are in fact an achievement test measuring a limited range of achievements (Jencks and Crouse, 1982). Jencks and Crouse have recommended that either the SAT evaluate a much broader range of achievements or be dropped in favor of Advanced Placement examinations.

10. The U.K. has an interesting solution to this problem. British universities base their admissions decisions on the GCSE exams taken two years earlier and teacher predictions of the student's grade on the A level exams taken in late spring. Admission offers, however, are conditional on the student actually getting the A exam grades their

teacher predicts. This really puts the pressure on students to study hard right up to the date of the exam.

11. Analysis of data on out of cachement school selections for the Fife LEA found that the Type B school effect estimates (measures of how well each school does compared to others serving pupils of similar ability and social background) are significantly and substantially higher at the schools selected by parents choosing to leave their cachement area. My summary sentence sounds different from Willms and Echols (1993) summary of their own results because they unaccountably base their conclusions on estimates of school effects from models which did not control for the pupil's ability when entering secondary school and which they acknowledge are biased. Luckily they also present results based on correctly specified models with controls for initial ability in Table 3 of the paper.

12. Outstanding academic performance (e.g., high grades or high test scores) would not have to be the only way of defining excellence. Awards could be given for significant improvements in academic performance since the previous year or since the beginning of the school year, for public service in or out of school, for perfect attendance records, and for student of the week (criteria could vary weekly).

13. The reason for the external yardstick is that it helps ensure that students perceive the standard to be absolute rather than relative to others in the class, and it helps create a communality of interest between teacher and student. Teachers need to be perceived as helping the student achieve the student's goals not as judges meting out punishment.

14. The Commission on Workforce Quality and Labor Market Efficiency included in its membership Constance E. Clayton, Superintendent of Schools of Philadelphia, Jose I. Lozano, Publisher of *La Opinion*, William J. Wilson, author of *The Truly Disadvantaged*. The Commission on the Skills of the American Workforce included in its membership Eleanor Holmes Norton, former Chairwoman of the Equal Employment Opportunity Commission, John E. Jacob, President of the National Urban League, Badi Foster, President of AEtna Institute for Corporate Education, Thomas Gonzales, Chancellor of Seattle Community College District VI, Anthony J. Trujillo, Superintendent of Sweetwater Union High School District.

15. A one population standard deviation increase in test scores raises an adult's wage rate by 21 percent (Bishop, 1989, 181, derived by taking the antilog of .19). A population standard deviation is equivalent to about 5 grade level equivalents, so the wage effect is 10.4 percent = antilog(2.6/5)*.19. The mean yearly compensation of adults 18 to 65 years old is about $21,000 in 1992 when the nonemployed are included in the denominator, so the dollar impact is $2184 = .104*$21,000.

16. This estimate of the productivity benefit of a 2.6 grade level equivalent increase in achievement is conservative. College graduation raises the median earnings of males by 60 percent and the median earnings of females by 77 percent. If one were to assume that 3575 hours of additional time spent in elementary and secondary school is equivalent to getting an associates degree, the estimated productivity benefit doubles to $6625 per year. In addition the social costs of going to a 7 hour day and adding 20 days to the school calendar are probably smaller than $34.4 billion, for child care costs will be substantially reduced. Some high school students will be earning less during the summer but this effect is substantially smaller than the savings in child care costs. It should be noted that student leisure time is significantly reduced and that except for the lost work

time of teenagers this is not counted as a cost. This is standard operating procedure when doing benefit cost studies of educational interventions.

17. The present value of the benefits at age 5 of $11.5 billion a year starting at age 18 and running until age 65 is ($11,500,000,000)(25)(.853)(.588) = $144.2 billion. The present value of costs are ($34,400,000,000/13)25(1-.588) = $27.26 billion. If the associates degree equivalent assumption were employed, the benefit cost ratio would be 10.7.

REFERENCES

Adler, M. and G.M. Raab. 1988. Exit choice and loyalty: The impact of parental choice on admissions to secondary schools in Edinburgh and Dundee. *Journal of Educational Policy*. 3: 155-179.

Aigner, D. and G. Cain. 1977. Statistical theories of discrimination in labor markets. *Industrial and Labor Relations Review*, (Jan.): 175-87.

Association of Secondary Teachers of Ireland. 1990. Information sheet opposing changes in examination systems.

Bishop, J. 1985. *Preparing youth for employment*. Columbus: The National Center for Research in Vocational Education, The Ohio State University.

_____ 1987a. The recognition and reward of employee performance. *Journal of Labor Economics* 5 (4, pt 2 October): S36-S56.

Bishop, J. 1987b. Information externalities and the social payoff to academic achievement. Center for Advanced Human Resource Studies Working Paper #87-06, Ithaca, New York: Cornell University.

_____ .1990. Job performance, turnover and wage growth. *Journal of Labor Economics* 8 (3): 363-386.

_____ . 1989a. Is the test score decline responsible for the productivity growth decline. *American Economic Review* 79 (1).

_____ . 1989b. The productivity consequences of what is learned in high school. *Journal of Curriculum Studies*.

_____ . 1992. Impact of academic competencies on wages, unemployment and job performance. *Carnegie-Rochester Conference Series on Public Policy* 37(December): 127-194.

Bishop, J., and S. Carter. 1991. The worsening shortage of college graduate workers. *Educational Evaluation and Policy Analysis* (Fall):.

Bradley, A. 1993. Not making the grade: Teacher firing spurs debate over standards and expectations for students. *Education Week*, (Sept. 13): 1, 19-21.

Bureau of Labor Statistics. 1989. Nearly three-fifths of the high school graduates of 1988 enrolled in college. USDL 89-308, (June), and previous years.

Cain, G., and A. Goldberger. 1983. Public and private schools revisited. *Sociology of Education* 56 (October): 208-218.

California Department of Education. 1987. *The cost of a California school*. Sacramento, California: California Department of Education.

Cameron, S., and J. Heckman. 1993. The determinants and outcomes of post-secondary training: A comparison of high school graduates, dropouts, and high school equivalents. in *Private sector and skill formation: International comparisons,* edited by Lisa Lynch, National Bureau of Economic Research, Chicago: University of Chicago Press.

Carroll, S. 1982. The search for equity in school finance. *financing Education: Overcoming inefficiency and inequity.* edited by Walter McMahon and Terry Geske, Urbana: University of Illinois Press: 237-66.

Clark, W. 1992. *The class of 1986.* Employment and Immigration Canada, Statistics Canada: 1-444.

_____. 1991. *The class of 1982 revisited,* Employment and Immigration Canada, Statistics Canada: 1-233.

College Board. 1988. *AP yearbook 1988.* New York: College Entrance Examination Board.

Commission on Workforce Quality and Labor Market Efficiency. 1989. *Investing in people: A strategy to address America's workforce crisis.* Washington, DC: Dept. of Labor.

Commission on the Skills of the American Workforce. 1990. *America's choice: High skills or low wages!* National Center on Education and the Economy, Rochester, New York (June).

Cooper, H. 1989. *Homework.* White Plains, New York: Longman.

Crain, R., A. Heebner, and Y.P. Si. 1992. *The effectiveness of New York City's career magnet schools: Ninth grade performance using an experimental design.* New York: National Center for Research In Vocational Education, Teachers College, Columbia University: 1-109.

Dalton, P. J., and G.H. Makepeace. 1990. The earnings of economics graduates. *The Economic Journal* 100 (March): 237-250.

Ehrenberg, R., and D. Brewer. 1993. Did teacher's race and verbal ability matter in the 1960's?: *Coleman.* Ithaca, NY: Cornell University, School of Industrial and Labor Relations: 1-57.

Ehrenberg, R., and R. Chaykowski. 1988. On estimating the effects of increased aid to education. *When public sector workers unionize.* edited by Richard Freeman and Casey Ichniowski. Chicago: University of Chicago Press: 245-269.

Elley, W. 1992. *How in the world do students read?* The Hague, The Netherlands: International Association for the Evaluation of Educational Achievement.

Entwisle, D., and K. Alexander. 1989. Issues of inequality and children's transition to full-time schooling. Johns Hopkins University.

Felner, R., and A. Adan. 1988. The school transitional project: An ecological intervention and evaluation. *14 Ounces of Prevention,* edited by Price, Cowan, Lorion and Ramos-McKay, American Psychological Association: 111-122.

Felner, R.D., M.A. Ginter, and J. Primavera. 1982. The impact of school transitions: Social support and environmental structure. *American Journal of Community Psychology* 10: 227-240.

Ferguson, R. 1990. *Racial patterns in how school and teacher quality affect achievement and earnings.* Cambridge, Mass: Kennedy School of Government, Harvard University.

Fischer, M. 1989. *Fiscal accountability in Milwaukee's public elementary schools: where does the money go?* Wisconsin Policy Research Institute Report 3 (4), Milwaukee: The Wisconsin Policy Research Institute: 1-49.

Frank, R. 1984. Are workers paid their marginal product? *American Economic Review* 74 (4): 549-571.

Frederick, W. C. 1977. The use of classroom time in high schools above or below the median reading score. *Urban Education* 11 (4): 459-464.

Frederick, W., H. Walberg, and S. Rasher. 1979. Time, teacher comments, and achievement in urban high schools. *Journal of Educational Research* 73, (2): 63-65.

Freeman, R. 1981. Black economic progress after 1964: Who has gained and why. *Studies in Labor Markets*, edited by Sherwin Rosen, Chicago: University of Chicago Press.

Friedman, T., and E. Williams. 1982. Current use of tests for employment. *Ability testing: uses, consequences, and controversies, part II: Documentation section*, edited by Alexandra K. Wigdor and Wendell R. Gardner. Washington, DC: National Academy Press: 99-169.

Ghiselli, E. 1973. The validity of aptitude tests in personnel selection. *Personnel Psychology* 26: 461-477.

Goodlad, J. *1983. A place called school.* New York: McGraw-Hill.

Graham, A., and T. Husted. Understanding state variation in SAT scores. 1993. *Economics of Education Review,* 12(3): 197-202.

Guthrie, B. 1990. *Graduate starting salaries 1989.* Graduate Careers Council of Australia, University of Sydney. (August).

Hanushek, E. A. 1971. Teacher characteristics and gains in student achievement: estimation using micro-data. *American Economic Review 61*(2): 280-288.

Hashimoto, M., and B. Yu. 1980. Specific capital, employment and wage rigidity. *Bell Journal of Economics* 11 (2): 536-54

Heyns, B. 1986. Summer programs and compensatory education: The future of an idea. Prepared for the Office of Educational Research and Improvement, Chapter One Study Team, Conference on the Effects of Alternative Designs in Compensatory Education Washington, DC. New York University.

Heyns, B. 1987. Schooling and cognitive development: Is there a season for learning. *Child Development* 58 (5):1151-1160.

High School and Beyond. 1982. *Data file users manual.* National Opinion Research Corporation, Chicago, Illinois.

Hollenbeck, K., and B. Smith. 1984. *The influence of applicants' education and skills on employability assessments by employers.* Columbus: The National Center for Research in Vocational Education, The Ohio State University.

Hunter, J., J. Crosson, and D. Friedman. 1985. The validity of the armed services vocational aptitude battery (ASVAB) for civilian and military job performance, Department of Defense, Washington, D.C. (August).

Hunter, J., F. Schmidt, and M. Judiesch. 1988. Individual differences in output as a function of job complexity. Dept. of Industrial Relations and Human Resources, Univ. of Iowa (June).

International Assessment of Educational Progress. 1992a. *Learning science.* Princeton, New Jersey: Educational Testing Service.

International Assessment of Educational Progress. 1992b. *Learning mathematics.* Princeton, New Jersey: Educational Testing Service.

International Association for the Evaluation of Educational Achievement (IAEEA). 1988. *Science achievement in seventeen countries.* New York: Pergamon Press.

James, E., N. Alsalam, J. Conaty, and D. To. 1989. College quality and future earnings: where should you send your child to college? *American Economic Review* (79, 2): 247-252.

Jencks, C., and J. Crouse. 1982. Aptitude vs. achievement: Should we replace the SAT? *The Public Interest.*

Juster, T., and F. Stafford. 1990. The allocation of time: Empirical findings, behavioral models and problems of measurement. Ann Arbor, Mich.: Survey Research Center, Institute for Social Research.

KPMG Peat Marwick. 1989. *Operational review of the District of Columbia public school system.* Washington, D.C.

Karabel, J., and K. McClelland. 1987. Occupational advantage and the impact of college rank on labor market outcomes. *Sociological Inquiry* 57: 323-347.

Katz, L., and K. Murphy. 1990. Changes in relative wages, 1963-1987: Supply and demand factors. *Quarterly Journal of Economics.*

Kominski, R. 1987. What's it worth? Educational background and economic status: Spring 1984. *Current Population Reports,* Series P-70, No. 11, U.S. Government Printing Office, Washington, D.C.

Kominski, R. 1990. What's it worth?, Educational background and economic status: Spring 1987. *Current Population Reports*, P-70, N.o. 21, US. Bureau of the Census.

Kominski, R., and R. Sutterlin. 1992. What's it worth?, Educational background and economic status: Spring 1990. *Current Population Reports,* P-70, No. 32, US Bureau of the Census.

Koretz, D. et.al., 1986. *Trends in educational achievement.* Washington: Congressional Budget Office.

Lapointe, A., N. Mead, and G. Phillips. 1989. *A world of differences.* Educational Testing Service, Princeton: New Jersey.

Lazear, E. 1989. Pay equality and industrial politics. *Journal of Political Economy* 97(June): 561-580.

Longitudinal Survey of American Youth. 1988. *Data file user's manual.* Dekalb, Ill: Public Opinion Laboratory.

MacIver, D. 1991. Helping students who fall behind: Remedial activities in the middle grades. Johns Hopkins University: Center for Research on Effective Schooling for Disadvantaged Students: 2-20.

Maier, M., and F. Grafton. 1981. *Aptitude composites for ASVAB 8, 9 and 10.* Research Report 1308. U.S. Army Research Institute for Behavioral and Social Sciences, Alexandria, Va. (May).

Matthews, J. 1988. *Escalante: The best teacher in America.* New York, NY: Henry Holt.

McKnight, C. et al. 1987. *The underachieving curriculum: Assesing U.S. school mathematics from an international perspective.* A National Report on the Second International Mathematics Study. Stipes Publishing Co.: Champaign, IL (January).

McKinney, F. et al. 1982. *Factors relating to the job placement of former secondary vocational educational students.* Columbus: The National Center for Research in Vocational Education, The Ohio State University.

Ministere de l'Education Nationale et de la Culture. 1992. *Reperes and References Statistiques sur les enseignmements et la formation.* 1992 Edition, (Paris).

Monk, D. 1990. *Educational finance: An economic approach.* New York: McGraw-Hill.

_____. 1992. Subject area preparation of secondary mathematics and science teachers and student achievement. Department of Education, Cornell University: 1-51.

Mueller, R. O. 1988. The impact of college selectivity on income for men and women. *Research in Higher Education* (29): 175-191.

National Assessment of Educational Progress. 1988a. *The science report card.* Princeton, New Jersey: Educational Testing Service.

_____. 1988b. *The mathematics report card.* Princeton,New Jersey: Educational Testing Service.

National Center for Educational Statistics. 1991. *The condition of education: 1991*(1), Washington, D.C.: US Department of Education.

_____. 1992a. *The condition of education: 1992* (1), Washington, D.C.: US Department of Education.

_____. 1992b. *The digest of education statistics: 1992.* Washington, D.C.: US Department of Education.

_____. 1993a. *The condition of education: 1993.* (1), Washington, D.C.: US Department of Education.

National Center for Educational Statistics. *1993b. Occupational and educational outcomes of recent college graduates 1 year after graduation: 1991.* NCES 93-162, Washington, D.C.: US Department of Education.

National Federation of Independent Business. 1987. [Survey of NFIB membership using a questionnaire designed by John Bishop].

Nelson, H. 1990. Memo to Albert Shankar on international comparison of expenditures on administration and teaching compensation. American Federation of Teachers Research Department (March).

Nelson, H., and T. O'Brien. 1993. *How U.S. teachers measure up internationally: A comparative study of teacher pay, training, and conditions of service.* Washington, D.C.: American Federation of Teachers.

New York State United Teachers. 1994. Blowing the whistle on education's 'open secret'. Albany, New York: New York State United Teachers (March 2).

Noah, H.,and M. Eckstein. 1988. Tradeoffs in examination policies: An international perspective. Paper presented at the Annual Meeting of the British Comparative and International Education Society, University of Bristol (September 15-17).

Noll I., U. Beicht, G. Boll, W., Malcher, and S. Wiederhold-Fritz. 1984. Nettakosten der Betrieblichen Ber Ufsbildung Schriften Berufsbildungsforschung, Band 63. Beuth Verlag GMBH, Berlin.

Organization of Economic Co-operation and Development. 1986. *Living conditions in OECD countries: A compendium of social indicators.* Social Policy Studies (3). Paris, France: Organization for Economic Co-operation and Development.

_____. 1992. *Education at a glance.* Paris, France: Organization for Economic Co-operation and Development.

_____. 1993. *Education at a glance*. Paris, France: Organization for Economic Co-operation and Development.

Perry, N. 1989. The new improved vocational school. *Fortune* (June 19): 127-138.

Picus, L. 1993. Estimating the costs of increased learning time. Los Angeles: University of Southern California, Center for Research on Education Finance (March): 1-26.

Postlethwaite, T. Neville and D. Wiley. 1992. *Science achievement in twenty-three countries*. London: Pergammon Press.

Powell, A., E. Farrar, and D. Cohen. 1985. *The shopping mall high school*. New York, New York: Houghton Mifflin.

Public Broadcasting System. 1989. Learning in America. (March 27).

Pressey, S. and F. Robinson. 1944. *Psychology and new education*. New York: Harper and Brothers Publication.

Roper, J. 1989. Technology creates a new physics student. *The Physics Teacher* (January) :26-28.

Rosenbaum, J. 1990. Do school achievements affect the early jobs of high school graduates? Results from the high school and beyond surveys in the US and Japan. Northwestern University: Evanston, Illinois.

Rosenbaum, J. and T. Kariya. 1989. From high school to work: Market and institutional mechanisms in Japan. *American Journal of Sociology* 94(6): 1334-1365.

Sipe, C., J. Grossman, and J. Milliner. 1988. *Summer training and education program: Report on the 1987 experience*. Philadelphia: Public/Private Ventures (April).

Sizer, T. 1984. *Horace's compromise: The dilemma of the American high school*. Boston: Houghton Mifflin.

Slavin, R. 1985. When does cooperative learning increase student achievement? *Psychological Bulletin*.

Solmon, L. 1973. The definition and impact of college quality. in *Does College Matter*, edited by Lewis Solmon and Paul Taubman. New York: Academic Press: 77-102.

Stevenson, H., S.Y. Lee, and J. Stigler. 1986. Mathematics achievement of Chinese, Japanese & American children. *Science* 231 (February): 693-699.

Stiglitz, J. 1974. Risk sharing and incentives in sharecropping. *Review of Economic Studies* 61 (2): 219-256.

Strauss, R.P. and E.A. Sawyer. 1986. Some new evidence on teacher and student competencies. *Economics of Education Review 5*(1): 41-48.

Symonette, H. 1981. Does type of college attended matter?: Decomposing the college-earnings association. Unpublished PhD Dissertation, Department of Sociology, University of Wisconsin, Madison, Wisconsin.

Tim, 1986. Paper for ILR 360, (October): 1-6.

Tsang and H. Levin. The impact of intergovernmental grants on educational expenditure. *Review of Educational Research* 53 (3): 329-367.

Ward. 1994. A day in the life. *N.Y. Teacher*. (Jan.): Albany, N.Y.

Wiley, D. 1976. Another hour, another day: Quantity of schooling, a potent path for policy. In *Schooling achievement in American society*, edited by William H. Sewell, R. Hauser, and D. Featherman. New York: Academic Press.

Wise, D. 1975. Academic achievement and job performance. *American Economic Review* 65. (June)3: 350-366.

CHAPTER 6

THE ECONOMIC RETURN TO SCHOOL QUALITY

David Card

Alan B. Krueger

For the past three decades, education policy in the United States has been guided by the conclusions of the Coleman Report (1966) and subsequent research on test scores and schooling resources. This literature is widely interpreted as showing that increased levels of spending on educational inputs such as lower class size or higher teacher salaries have no significant effect on student achievement. For example, Hanushek's (1986) influential survey of this literature concluded that "there appears to be no strong or systematic relationship between school expenditures and student performance" (p. 1162).

In recent years, the conclusion that schooling inputs don't matter for student achievement has come under renewed investigation for two main reasons. First, there have been advances in the statistical technique of meta-analysis -- a method for quantitatively summarizing a set of studies that address a similar question.[1] In contrast to Hanushek's (1986; 1991) informal summaries, modern meta-analyses have concluded that schooling resources do exert a systematic and positive effect on test scores. Indeed, Hedges (1993) performs a meta-analysis of the same set of studies examined by Hanushek and concludes that "the data are more consistent with a pattern that includes at least some positive relation between dollars spent on education and output, than with a pattern of no effects or negative effects."[2]

Second, and irrespective of the relationship between school resources and test scores, a series of studies have found that increased school spending is significantly associated with improvements in the socioeconomic outcomes of students, including their schooling attainment and their subsequent earnings. Indeed, these studies show remarkably consistent findings, and suggest that a ten percent increase in schooling outlays per student is associated with something like a 1.5 percent increase in earnings *for each year of a student's working life*.

To economic analysts, earnings are a natural focus of study because they reflect the market valuation of skills acquired in school. If better schools impart more or better knowledge, this should be reflected in the higher earnings of students. Furthermore, for many students, the potential earnings gains associated with additional schooling are a primary motivation for attending school. Thus, earnings-based measures of school performance are directly relevant for the students themselves. Many economists also question whether standardized test scores are a reliable indicator of school performance. For example, there is evidence that teachers can coach students to perform well on standardized tests, without any lasting effect on their knowledge. Moreover, a number of studies have found only a weak association between standardized test scores and socioeconomic achievement, once years of schooling are held constant.

This chapter surveys the economics literature on school quality and earnings. Throughout the chapter, we measure school quality by means of indexes of the quantity of resources in the school, for example, by expenditures per student or the pupil-teacher ratio. In Section I we describe the logic and methodology behind the economic approach to the study of school quality, education and earnings. In Section II we present a summary of the literature. Section III concludes the chapter by discussing comparative strengths and weaknesses of the economic approach to school quality and student achievement.

I. ECONOMIC METHODOLOGY

Economic Measures of School Performance

Economists have a strong preference for studying tangible and objectively measured outcomes like income, rather than subjective outcomes like consumer confidence or job satisfaction. In the field of education this has meant that economists typically focus their attention on market-related measures of school performance -- mainly the subsequent earnings of students.[3] In the prototypical economic model of schooling (Becker, 1967) education is viewed as an investment: current resources are spent (or forgone) while the student is in school in anticipation of higher earnings later in life. This framework lends itself naturally to consideration of the costs and benefits of alternative education policies. A reduction in the pupil-teacher ratio, for example, has immediate and readily measured costs. The benefits (if any) are only realized over the lifetimes of the students as they use their improved knowledge to achieve higher pay.

The preference for objective and market-oriented outcome measures has led many economists to eschew other measures of school performance, such as standardized test scores.[4] This approach contrasts sharply with other researchers in the education field, who tend to have more faith in standardized testing. Part of economists' skepticism regarding standardized testing arises because the tests are arbitrarily scaled, and can possibly be manipulated by teachers and test writers. More important, there is no guarantee that standardized tests measure "skills" that are of economic value. A particular outcome measure is only an effective gauge of the economic value of schooling insofar as it is correlated with some aspect of earnings. Standardized test scores typically have a weak relationship with economic outcomes like earnings, once other factors (such as the individual's educational attainment) are held constant.[5]

Finally, many economists have little expertise in conducting or interpreting standardized tests.[6] It is thus not surprising that the large body of research that uses test scores to assess the efficacy of school inputs has been conducted primarily by educational researchers, sociologists, and psychologists; not by economists.

The Relation Between Earnings and Schooling

Although education has many objectives, a major goal of the school system is to raise the productivity and incomes of students. Indeed, an important reason why many students attend school is to improve their labor market prospects. In view of these goals, and economists' relative expertise in using market-related outcome measures, labor economists have focused on models of the relationship between years of education and students' subsequent earnings, and the effect of school inputs on this relationship. A benefit of using earnings as a yardstick of school quality is that it passes a "market test." Economists feel comfortable with the premise that a product or skill is only worth what someone else is willing to pay for it. Earnings, clearly, are a direct measure of the value that the labor market places on individual skills. Of course, there are many other factors that affect individuals' earnings, including geographic location, work amenities, and pure luck. But a worker's wage rate is considered a reliable, if incomplete, indicator of the value of his or her skills.

The economics literature has focused on two main questions concerning education and earnings. First, do individuals with a higher level of education earn more than individuals with a lower level of education? Second, what characteristics of schools affect the relationship between schooling and earnings?

The evidence that earnings tend to be higher for individuals who have higher levels of schooling is undeniable.[7] Figure 6.1 illustrates the strong statistical relationship between hourly wages and years of schooling that is evident in the labor market. The figure simply plots the average of the logarithm of the hourly wage rate of workers at each level of education, using a national sample of data for 1993.[8] It is clear that log wages rise almost linearly with years of education. Furthermore, if we were to fit a line through the points in Figure 6.1 it would be quite steep. Indeed, the data in Figure 6.1 suggest that each additional year of education raises workers' wages by 9.5 percent. The coefficient relating the percentage increase in earnings for an additional year of schooling is referred to as the "rate of return to education." Historically, this rate of return has fluctuated between 5 and 7 percent, although in the 1980s, the return rose significantly (see Levy and Murnane, 1992).

How should we interpret the strong, positive association between earnings and education? Does it mean that we can increase the average wages of people who would normally drop out of high school by forcing them to stay is school longer? Or is it merely a reflection of some omitted factor that is jointly correlated with education and earnings? For example, the parents of children with more education may have better labor-market connections, and these connections may help their children to obtain higher-paying jobs. In this case, we would observe a correlation between wages and schooling, but it would incorrect to conclude that higher schooling *causes* higher wages.

Figure 6.1: Mean Hourly Wages of Adult Male Workers By Level of Schooling

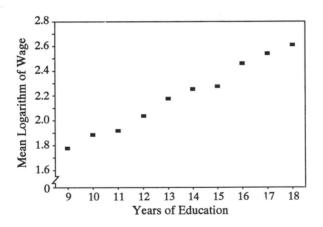

A vast literature in economics has investigated the relationship between earnings and years of schooling with the aim of understanding whether schooling has a causal effect on wages, or only an indirect association. The early wave of these studies tried to control explicitly for individuals' characteristics, such as parental education and IQ (see Griliches, 1977). Essentially, these studies used statistical techniques to create plots like Figure 6.1 for workers who possess similar observed characteristics -- including such characteristics as family background and measured ability. In another set of studies, economists have used data on identical twins, to see whether a twin with higher education earns more than his or her sibling (see Behrman et al., 1980; Ashenfelter and Krueger, 1994). Yet another strand of this literature has taken a different tack, and tried to estimate the gains in schooling and earnings for individuals who obtained higher levels of education for reasons having nothing to do with their innate ability or background. Examples of this approach include Angrist and Krueger (1992), who examine the effect of state-wide compulsory schooling laws, and Card (1993), who examines the effect of growing up in close proximity to a four-year college.

Our interpretation of all three strands of literature is that additional years of schooling do lead to higher earnings, and that this relationship results primarily from the extra schooling itself rather than from extraneous factors.[9] While some economists believe that part of the measured payoff to extra schooling arises from factors other than schooling itself, few doubt that additional schooling leads to at least some increase in the average students' subsequent income.

School Quality and Earnings

How does the quality of schooling affect the relationship between years of schooling and earnings? The most plausible theoretical explanation for a link between school quality and earnings is that -- other things being equal -- students acquire more skills if they attend higher quality schools (i.e., schools with more generous resources). This hypothesis suggests two alternative approaches to modelling the effect of school quality. In the first approach, researchers have assumed that an increase in schooling resources affects the subsequent earnings of all students who attended a particular school (or school system) by an equal amount, regardless of how much schooling they acquired. Specifically, these studies use multivariate regression analysis to relate an individual's earnings at a point in time to their years of schooling and measures of the resources available at the schools they attended. Schooling resources are typically measured by expenditures per student or the number of pupils per teacher in the student's state, school district or school. These studies hold constant several other factors that may be correlated with earnings and the quality of schooling, such as parental education, IQ, and race.

    This approach is illustrated in Figure 6.2 with two levels of school resources: high and low. Notice that average wages at each level of schooling are affected equally by an increase in resources. The figure illustrates a situation in which average earnings are higher for those who attended higher quality schools, although the statistical models that are estimated in the literature allow for the possibility that higher schooling resources increase, decrease, or have no effect on average earnings, depending on the actual patterns in the data.

    The assumption that the earnings differential for those who attend higher quality schools is the same for all levels of education implies that the two lines in Figure 6.2 are parallel. This assumption has the unappealing implication that even students who drop out with low levels of schooling receive the same earnings gains from higher expenditures as those who completed high school. As a practical matter, however, a vast majority of U.S. students complete high school, so this problem is of less significance than might be suspected.

    An alternative approach to modelling the effect of school quality on earnings allows school quality to have a larger impact upon individuals who stay in school longer (Behrman and Birdsall, 1983; Card and Krueger, 1992a; 1992b). Graphically, this approach corresponds to Figure 6.3. Here, the divergence of the two lines for higher levels of schooling means that the earnings premium for attending higher quality schools is *greater* for individuals who stayed in school *longer*. In order to implement this approach, researchers relate an individual's earnings to their years of schooling, with a slope coefficient (i.e., a rate of return to schooling) that depends on school resources. As with the first approach, other factors that may be correlated with earnings are held constant in the analysis.

Figure 6.2: Hypothetical Equal Effect of School Quality

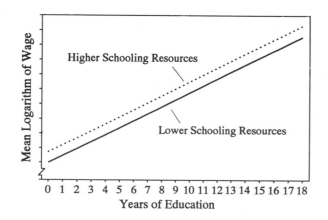

If school quality is measured at the state level, this second approach can be implemented in two steps. First, a separate slope coefficient representing the rate of return to schooling is estimated for individuals educated in each state. Second, these slope coefficients are related to measures of the quality of education in the state at the time the individuals attended school.

There are two important methodological issues that arise in interpreting the measured relation between school quality and earnings. The first is the issue of causality. Schooling resources vary widely across school districts, and parents may choose to live in certain school districts because of the quality of the schools or the level of property taxes used to finance these schools. It is possible that certain family characteristics (such as higher income) lead some families to choose more expensive schools, and also lead their children to earn higher wages. In this case, the measured positive effect of school quality on wages and school quality may be overstated. Researchers attempt to deal with this problem by including controls for family background and other characteristics of the school districts. Some researchers also try to identify differences in school quality that are "exogenously determined" -- such as differences between school quality for black and white students from states that operated segregated schooling systems (Card and Krueger,1992b).

A second methodological issue concerns the unit of observation under study. Some studies of earnings and school quality use microdata on individuals' wages combined with microdata on school resources pertaining to the individuals' school or school district (e.g., Ribich and Murphy, 1975; Link and Ratledge, 1975). Because school level expenditure and staffing data are often noisy (e.g., they vary a lot from year to year for no apparent reason), and because some families may choose their location on the basis of school resources, there are reasons why it may be desirable to aggregate over a larger area (such as a state) to derive average school quality measures. Thus, in other studies, microdata on individual wages are combined with state-level data on the average quality of schooling in a particular state (e.g., Rizzuto and Wachtel, 1980). Finally, some studies have related the average wages of workers from a state to the average school quality in the state when the workers attended school (e.g. Nechyba, 1990).

The advantages and disadvantages of using aggregated versus disaggregated data on earnings and school quality are often misunderstood. Microdata have the advantage of providing greater variation in the explanatory variables. For example, there is a much wider range in expenditures per student across schools within a given state than in the average expenditures per school across states. On the other hand, an important disadvantage of microdata is that the variation is not exogenously determined. Higher-income families may choose to live in a particular suburb in order to send their children to higher-quality schools. Since parental income may exert an independent influence on children's earnings, this is a potentially confounding effect. Another and more extreme example arises if school resources are determined by policies that target increased spending on schools with disadvantaged or low-achieving students. In this case, school resources and student achievement will be negatively correlated, concealing any positive effect of higher resources on student achievement. At the state level, the endogenous determination of school quality is far less of a problem. Fewer families move across state lines to change the quality of schools than move between school districts within a state. The average quality of schools in an entire state gives a balanced picture of the resources available to the average student in the state -- not just the children from high-income families, or those with learning disabilities.

Measurement errors also tend to be a greater problem for studies based on micro-level school quality data. For example, a particular school may appear to have high expenditures in one year because it has high capital expenditures that year, or because its data are misreported. When school-level data are aggregated to the state level, however, mistakes or short-term spending variations tend to average out, leaving a more representative picture of true school quality. As a result, measurement errors are likely to be less important in aggregate data studies than in micro data studies.[10]

School Quality and Educational Attainment

A second way in which higher quality schooling may influence earnings is by encouraging students to stay in school longer. From the students' perspective, schooling may be more pleasant and rewarding in schools with greater resources.[11] Thus higher quality schooling may induce students to attain a higher average level of education.

Any increase in educational attainment due to school quality could also be expected to increase individual earnings. The total effect of school quality can be seen most clearly with the aid of Figure 6.3. An increase in school quality will have two effects. First, at any given level of education, it will push the average worker up from the line for low quality schools to the line for high quality schools. Second, it will push workers to the right along the X-axis of Figure 6.3 (toward higher education), which will also increase earnings because earnings tend to rise with years of education. Note that if improved school resources *only* serve to increase individuals' educational attainment, workers' earnings will still increase as a result of improved school quality because earnings tend to rise with years of education.

Figure 6.3: Hypothetical Unequal Effect of School Quality

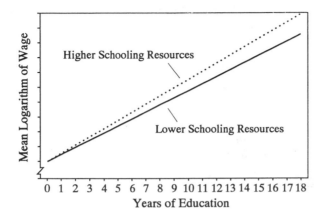

II. REVIEW OF EVIDENCE

School Resources and Earnings

Table 6.1 summarizes published studies of the impact of school resources on students' subsequent labor market income in the U.S.[12] We derived the set of studies in the table by searching the *Journal of Economic Literature*, and by examining citations in known papers and past issues of selected education journals. For each study we report the main estimates in the paper, with separate estimates by race if reported. We were able to find 13 separate studies that are based on eight different data sets on earnings. Table 6.1 reports a total of 25 estimates from these studies.

To place the estimates on comparable footing, we have converted the estimated coefficients in each paper into an "elasticity", representing the percentage gain in earnings for a 1 percent increase in expenditures per pupil. Elasticities are widely used to convey both the sign *and* magnitude of the effect of an independent variable on a dependent variable. For example, an elasticity of 0.10 indicates that a 10 percent increase in expenditures raises an average student's annual earnings by 1 percentage point. Estimates from studies that use the pupil-teacher ratio or the average teacher salary as a school quality measure were converted to estimates of the effect of expenditures per pupil by assuming that teacher salaries represent 60 percent of total expenditures per pupil.

In sharp contrast to the literature on test scores, most of the studies summarized in Table 6.1 suggest that more school resources are associated with higher subsequent income. The arithmetic average of the 25 estimated elasticities is 0.16, and the median value is 0.14. All the estimates are positive, and almost all are statistically significant. Furthermore, although the studies use a variety of data sets and statistical models, the estimated elasticities of earnings with respect to school resources fall in a narrow range.[13] Two-thirds of the estimated elasticities lie between 0.09 and 0.20. The studies in Table 6.1 employ a variety of different statistical methods, samples and controls.[14] Most of the studies control for the worker's education level, so these estimates should be interpreted as the increase in income associated with higher school quality *for a given level of education*. Many of the studies also control for differences in family background by including father's education, family income, or whether the individual grew up on a farm. In addition, to control for interpersonal differences in innate ability, some of the studies include an IQ measure or the Armed Forces Qualifying Test score.

Despite these controls, there is always a chance that the observed correlations between earnings and school quality reflect omitted factors, rather than the true effect of school resources. In our view, the most important omitted variables are likely to be measures of family background characteristics (e.g., family income) that are positively correlated with both school expenditures and students' earnings. The omission of such factors will tend to lead to a spurious over-estimate of the effect of school quality on earnings.

Comparing the estimated elasticities of school spending across studies there is no indication that studies that control for parental background tend to recover lower elasticities. In addition to this fact, another finding in the literature suggests that school resources per se influence students' subsequent earnings. In particular, Card and Krueger (1992a) examine changes in school quality across the states over time. This work essentially compares workers from different birth cohorts who were educated in the same state at different times. For example, over the course of the 20th century school resources in Alabama increased considerably relative to California. Card and Krueger relate the changes in the quality of schooling over time to the differences in the payoff per year of education for men in those cohorts. The results suggest that an increase in school quality within a given state over time leads to a rise in the earnings of people from that state.

Another consideration that arises in interpreting studies of earnings and school quality is that some of the same factors that lead to more generous school resources in a state or area may also lead to better labor market conditions for students after they leave school. For example, if the economy in a certain region is strong, the school authorities may have more revenues to spend on schools. If economic conditions are persistent over time, and if students tend to work in the same area where they attended school, then students' performance in the labor market may be spuriously related to the level of school resources.

Table 6.1: Summary of Studies Estimating the Effect of School Quality on Earnings

Study	Sample	Methodology and Comments	Estimated Elasticity of Earnings w.r.t. $/pupil
1. Morgan and Sirageldin (1968)	1965 SRC Sample Family heads, not self-employed N=1,438	State expenditures (average of 1930, 1940, 1950) matched to individuals by state where they grew up. D.V. = log hourly wage in 1964. Stepwise regression. First step: remove yrs of education, age, sex, race, grew up on farm.	0.29
2. Johnson and Stafford (1973)	1965 SRC Sample White Male non-farm heads; N=1,039	State*decade average expenditures matched to individuals by age/state where they grew up. D.V. = log hourly wage. Other controls: years of education, experience, urban residence/birthplace, father's education.	0.20 (0.05)
3. Morgenstern (1973)	1968 Urban Problems Sample, conducted by ISR. N=1,624 heads of households. Black households oversampled.	State expenditures matched to individuals by state where they grew up. D.V.=average hourly wage last year. Controls include gender, age, place of birth, experience, and parents' education.	Blacks 0.12 (0.04) Whites 0.13 (0.07)
4. Ribich and Murphy (1975)	Project Talent, 1959 9th grade men, re-interviewed in 1968. Blacks and Southerners under-represented. N=8,466.	Expenditures per pupil collected from school survey. D.V.=estimated lifetime earnings, imputed from 1967 earnings (if employed) and education data. Other controls: years of education, AFQT, parental and school-average SES.	0.01 (0.02)
5. Wachtel (1975)	Thorndike-Hagen sample, men age 18-26 in 1943 (army veterans) N=1,812	School-district expenditures matched to individuals by name/location of high school (1936-38 BSE data). D.V. = 1969 earnings. Other controls: yrs of education, experience, hours worked, test score, father's education.	0.20 (0.03)

Table 6.1: Summary of Studies Estimating the Effect of School Quality on Earnings (Continued)

Study	Sample	Methodology and Comments	Estimated Elasticity of Earnings w.r.t. $/pupil
6. Link and Ratledge (1975)	NLS Young Men age 16-26 in 1968, out of school ≥ 1 yr N=1,157	School-district expenditures (for 1968) matched by school district of school attended. D.V.=1968 log annual earnings. Other controls: years of education experience (quadratic), urban residence, IQ, hours worked.	Whites 0.15 (0.05) Blacks 0.55 (0.17)
7. Akin and Garfinkel (1980)	PSID male heads age 30-55 during 1968-72. N=1,049	State*decade average expenditures matched to individuals by state of residence at age 12. D.V.=log average wage 1968-72. Expenditures interacted with years of education. Other controls: IQ, father's income, indicators for family income.	Whites 0.30 (at ed=12) Blacks 0.14 (at ed=10.5)
8. Rizzuto and Wachtel (1980)	1960, 1970 Census white and black men age 14-65 not self employed N=26,204 (1960) N=27,729 (1970)	State expenditure data matched to individuals by state of birth and age interval. D.V.=1959/1969 log earnings. Other controls: years of education, experience, urban residence.	Whites 1960 0.12(0.01) Blacks 1960 0.09(0.03) Whites 1970 0.08(0.01) Blacks 1970 0.11(0.04)
9. Link, Ratledge and Lewis (1980)	NLS Young Men age 19-29 in 1969 N=2,127 PSID male heads as in study 6.	See comments for studies 6 and 7. D.V. for NLS = log average wage in 1971. D.V. for PSID = log average wage 1968-72. Expenditures interacted with years of education. Other controls in NLS: IQ, father's education. Other controls in PSID as in study 7.	NLS Whites 0.13-0.17 NLS Blacks 0.15-0.23 PSID Whites 0.24-0.32 PSID Blacks 0.13-0.15 (at mean ed. for group)
10. Tremblay (1986)	1976 NLS Young men, age 24-34. N=247 Southern, 496 Nonsouthern	See comments for study 6. Expenditures interacted with education. D.V=log monthly income. Other controls include occupation and industry dummies, IQ, race, age, seniority, SMSA, marital status, occupational training dummy, and union status.	High School: South 0.12 Nonsouth 0.04 College: South 0.05 Nonsouth 0.03

Table 6.1: Summary of Studies Estimating the Effect of School Quality on Earnings (Continued)

Study	Sample	Methodology and Comments	Estimated Elasticity of Earnings w.r.t. $/pupil
11. Nechyba (1990)	1950-80 Census black and white males (published median incomes by state, race, and age)	State average teacher salary data by race for selected years matched to individuals living in the state by race and 10-year birth cohort. D.V. = state*cohort* Census black-white relative median income. Other controls: differences in black-white years of education and percentages urban residents, percentages of cotton picked by machine, number of affirmative-action complaints.	0.10 (0.02) (based on effect of relative teacher wages)
12. Card and Krueger (1992a)	1980 Census white men age 31-60, not self employed. N=1,018,477	State average school data for 1926-66 matched to individuals by state of birth and years of school attendance. D.V. = log weekly wage in 1979. Other controls: state of birth and state of residence, experience (quadratic), marital status, urban residence.	0.16 (0.02) (based on effect of pupil-teacher ratio)
13. Card and Krueger (1992b)	1960-80 Census black and white men born in South from 1910-49 N=728,284	State average school data for 1916-66 matched to race* state-of-birth*10-year cohort. D.V. = state*cohort*Census black-white log weekly wage gap. Other controls: cohort dummies, year dummies.	0.15 (0.05) (based on effect of relative pupil-teacher ratio)

Notes: Studies 12 and 13 regress wages (or wage differentials) on pupil-teacher ratios (or pupil-teacher differentials). Estimates are translated into expenditure elasticities assuming teacher salaries represent 60% of total expenditures, and assuming the average pupil teacher ratio is 23 (study 11) or 32 (study 12). D.V. denotes "dependent variable"; AFQT is armed forces qualifying test; SES is a composite socioeconomic status measure.

In Card and Krueger (1992a; 1992b) we attempted to overcome this possible bias by studying groups of workers who were educated in one state, and moved to another state to work. In our 1992b paper, for example, we compared students who were educated in the South and moved to one of nine metropolitan areas outside the South. An intuitive explanation of this line of research is straightforward: consider only high school graduates who work in Chicago. Some of these workers were educated in states with high pupil-teacher ratios, and others were educated in states with low pupil-teacher ratios. Our comparison is based on workers with different school quality backgrounds in the same labor market, providing a stronger test of the "pure" quality effect. Our findings using this type of comparison are very similar to the other findings in the literature.

Finally, and perhaps most persuasively, several studies listed in Table 6.1 have examined the impact of differences in school resources for workers who were educated in the South, where relative school resources for blacks and whites differed dramatically across the states and over time. For example, North Carolina and South Carolina provide a natural contrast that is investigated in Card and Krueger (1992b). In the early part of this century, school resources for blacks in South Carolina were far below those for blacks in North Carolina, while whites in South Carolina had slightly greater school resources than whites in North Carolina.[15] The relative incomes of blacks and whites from the two states mirror these differences in school resources, even when we limit the sample to individuals who were born in North or South Carolina and are observed working in the North. A more extensive comparison involving all 18 states with *de jure* segregated school systems leads to a similar conclusion.

In our view, the remarkable similarity of the estimates from the various approaches used in the studies in Table 6.1 provides strong support for the hypothesis that higher school resources lead to systematically higher earnings for students.

School Resources and Educational Attainment

Several of the studies reviewed in Table 6.1 also report estimates of the effect of school spending (or some component of school spending) on average educational attainment. Table 6.2 presents a summary of the estimated elasticities of schooling attainment with respect to expenditures per pupil from these studies.[16] Like the elasticities of earnings with respect to spending, these elasticities are uniformly positive, although the range of the estimates is wider. The mean and median elasticities are 0.16 and 0.12, respectively. The elasticity based on the black-white differences in educational attainment for Southern-born men from Card and Krueger (1992b) is particularly high. As noted in that study, this estimate implies that virtually all of the convergence in schooling levels between black and whites born earlier (1900-1909) and later (1940-49) in the 20th century can be explained by the relative improvement in black school quality.

In interpreting the estimates in Table 6.2 it is important to recognize that the observed correlation between educational attainment and spending per pupil may give a downward-biased estimate of the "true" effect of per-capita spending on attainment. In other words, the reported estimate may well *understate* the actual effect of increased spending on student attainment. To see this, consider an increase in enrollment in a particular district or state induced by a change in family background or tastes for education. The rise in enrollment will tend to raise the pupil-teacher ratio and depress spending per student, unless school taxes and the number of teachers are increased in proportion to the new enrollment. Thus taste factors or family income changes that lead to increases in enrollment can lead to a decrease in per-student expenditures. In the statistical analyses, this "reverse causation" might partially offset any true positive effect of higher resources on attainment.

We reiterate a point made in reference to Figure 6.1: an extensive and highly sophisticated economics literature suggests that the acquisition of an additional year of schooling leads to a 7-9 percent earnings gain per year throughout an individual's working life. Thus, even if school resources have little effect on the test scores for students who reach a given grade level, more generous resources may still improve students' test scores and incomes by inducing them to stay in school longer. Furthermore, the estimates surveyed in Table 6.2 are consistent with a relatively strong effect of school quality on schooling attainment. This benefit of school resources is ignored in studies that relate the level of test scores (or their growth rate) to resources for students in a given grade level.

Interpreting the Estimates

How do the estimated economic returns to improved school resources compare to the cost of providing these resources? Here we focus on the effect of greater resources *holding constant years of schooling*. Given the evidence in Table 6.2 that years of schooling also rise as school quality rises, and the fact that earnings will rise as a result of this extra education, our estimates should be interpreted as a lower bound.

Recall that the average elasticity of annual earnings with respect to school expenditures for the studies in Table 6.1 is 0.16. The following calculation indicates that an elasticity of this order of magnitude is quite substantial. Consider a school district that currently spends an average of $5,000 per student. Suppose the school district permanently increased its expenditures by 10 percent ($500 per student) to reduce class size, say. Now think about the effect this policy change has on today's kindergarten students. The costs of the policy change are incurred this year and each year until a student leaves school. This future flow of costs must be discounted to present dollars. The present value of

Table 6.2: Summary of Selected Estimates of the Effect of School Quality on Years of Completed Education

Study		Estimated Elasticity of Completed Education w.r.t Expenditures per Pupil
1. Johnson and Stafford (1973)[a]		0.05
		(0.02)
2. Morgenstern (1973)	Blacks	0.15
		(0.03)
	Whites	0.09
		(0.03)
3. Ribich and Murphy (1975)		0.02
		(0.01)
4. Card and Krueger (1992a)		0.19
		(0.01)
5. Card and Krueger (1992b)		0.47
		(0.03)

Notes: See description of studies in Table 6.1. Unless otherwise noted, specifications are similar to the models for wages reported for the same study in Table 6.1. Elasticity estimates assume average education of 12 years. [a]In addition to controls noted in Table 6.1, models for educational attainment include father's education and family size.

the extra spending for a kindergarten student discounted over the next 13 years is $4,977, assuming a real interest rate of 3 percent.

The benefits of this increased spending are the higher earnings that the student will earn over his or her work life. To simplify matters, assume that the student earns $25,000 per year, begins working after leaving high school at age 19, and retires at age 60. If we assume an elasticity of 0.15, the student's earnings will rise by 1.5 percent, or $375, in each year in which he or she works as a result of the 10 percent increase in school expenditures. This future income must also be discounted back to the year in which the child enters kindergarten. Discounting is critical here because the income is earned several decades after the schooling expenditures are made. If we assume a 3 percent real interest rate, the present discounted value of that extra income is $6,052: about 20 percent more than the present discounted value of the costs.

The benefits and costs of educational innovations will be multiplied by the number of students in the school district. For example, if we assume that this school district has 3,000 kindergarten students, the 10 percent increase in expenditures will cost a present value of $15 million, and raise students' subsequent income by $18 million, for a net gain of $3 million. These hypothetical calculations indicate that even modest increases in students' income as a result of increased expenditures can generate large net benefits to society because the benefits accrue each year the students work.

These calculations can be modified to take account of alternative assumptions. For example, a higher discount rate will tend to lead to a less favorable benefit-cost comparison, because the costs of education spending are incurred "up front" whereas the benefits are only accrued over the students' lifetimes. Another modification is to allow for interrupted or shortened career patterns. Some individuals never enter the labor market, enter later in life, or retire early. The direct earnings benefits of higher education spending for these individuals will be lower.

III. CONCLUSION

Our review of the literature reveals a remarkable degree of consistency across studies regarding the effect of school quality on students' subsequent earnings. The studies typically find that a 10 percent increase in school expenditures is associated with a 1 to 2 percent increase in annual earnings for the students later in life. Increases in school resources are also associated with significantly higher educational attainment, although the number of studies of this effect is relatively small and the range of estimates of the effect is wider. Because higher education is strongly positively related to higher earnings, this is an additional economic benefit of higher school spending.

Although one cannot be sure that educational resources and earnings are causally related, many of the studies in the literature control for family background, ability measures, and other factors that might undermine a causal interpretation. Other studies make use of comparisons between workers educated in different states but working in the same labor market, or between black and white workers educated in the South before desegregation. The similarity of the signs and magnitudes of the estimated school quality effects in the literature give us some added confidence that there is a true causal effect of quality on earnings.

A possible criticism of the economics literature on school quality relates to the time lag required to measure earnings effects. Studies of earnings or completed education require data on individuals who have completed their post-secondary education. This poses a significant problem for analysts who need to evaluate a new or on-going education program, and can also introduce biases associated with non-random follow-up of students from better and worse schools. Indeed, one of the advantages of using test scores as a evaluation tool is that tests can be administered easily and cheaply at any time in the education process.

One type of economic indicator of school performance that *is* available early in the life cycle is the high school graduation rate or college matriculation rate. Although some students who drop out of high school may eventually earn a degree or go on to college, most studies suggest that dropping out is associated with a substantially lower level of completed education. An evaluation of the effect of school spending on high school graduation rates (and/or college matriculation rates) can therefore provide useful and timely data on the economic returns to higher or lower spending levels.

As an example of this approach, a recent study by Sander (1993) correlates high school graduation rates by school district with measures of average family background in the district and measures of school spending (the pupil-teacher ratio, average teacher salary, noninstructional spending). Consistent with the studies in Table 6.2, Sander finds that a lower pupil-teacher ratio leads to a significantly higher graduation rate.[17]

Because changes in school resources may have different short-run and long-run effects on student achievement, however, we believe it is important to examine long-term outcomes like educational attainment and earnings. For example, higher quality education may have no short-run effect on test scores, but may influence students' willingness or ability to process and use information decades later. We are unaware of any study that relates working-age individuals' standardized test scores to their past school resources. But this is precisely the kind of evaluation (albeit using earnings) that is attempted in the economic literature. For these reasons, we recommend that educators devote at least some attention to evaluation of schools based on long-term outcomes, such as students' subsequent income and educational attainment.

NOTES

1. See Glass, McGaw, and Smith (1981) and Hedges and Olkin (1985) for general introductions to the techniques of meta-analysis. A meta-analysis is (loosely) a statistical analysis of the estimates from a series of related papers. Meta-analysis methods can be used to adjust the estimates from different studies to a common basis, making it easier to identify common factors in a diverse body of research.

2. Meta-analyses by Glass and Smith (1978); McGiverin, Gilman and Tillitski (1989); Hedges and Stock (1983) also conclude that children assigned to smaller classes have higher academic achievement.

3. Haveman and Wolfe (1984) catalog a variety of outcomes, unrelated to markets, that may be influenced by education (e.g. criminal participation).

4. See Johnson and Stafford (1973) for example.

5. For example, the addition of test score information to the earnings models reported by Griliches and Mason (1972; Table 3) improves the explanatory power of their models by less than one-half of a percentage point. Research on the GED test suggests that simply passing the test has no significant effect on labor market outcomes (Heckman and Cameron, 1993). These findings underscore the importance of directly examining labor market outcomes.

6. Notable exceptions are researchers in the field of economics education, e.g. Walstad and Becker (1994); and Becker, Greene and Rosen (1990).

7. Of course, some individuals with a high level of education may have low earnings. The literature focuses on central tendencies, as measured by average wages at each level of education.

8. It is common in economic studies of wages to study the distribution of the natural logarithm (log) of wages. There are two reasons for this. First, simple plots show that the log of wages is approximately normally distributed (i.e., a graph of the frequency distribution of log wages looks like the familiar "bell-shaped" curve). Second, many standard economic theories predict a linear relationship between the log of wages and years of education (see Mincer, 1974; Willis, 1986). Heckman and Polachek (1974) find that earnings and schooling have an approximately log-linear relationship.

9. In a classic article, Griliches (1977) reaches much the same conclusion. See Card (1995) for a survey of the most recent literature that investigates the causal effect of schooling.

10. See Malinvaud,1980; pp. 416-419 for a general analysis of the benefits of averaging in the presence of measurement errors.

11. Higher-expenditure school districts may establish enrichment programs or special interest programs (sports, music, drama) that keep students interested in school.

12. The table is limited to studies of U.S. data. See Behrman and Birdsall (1983) for a seminal article on the effect of school quality on students' subsequent income in Brazil. Note that if an author published more that one article using the same data set to estimate a similar empirical specification, we report results from only one of the articles in Table 6.1.

13. One explanation for the low estimates by Tremblay (1986) is that she controls for the workers' occupation and industry. Since higher quality education may raise individuals' earnings by enabling them to enter a higher paying occupation or industry, we would not consider this an appropriate variable to hold constant.

14. The studies focus primarily on male workers, because female workers historically had a much lower labor force participation rate.

15. For example, in the early 1920s the black schools in South Carolina had over 60 students per teacher, while black schools in North Carolina had 45-50 students per teacher. White schools in South Carolina had about 30 students per teacher, while white schools in North Carolina had about 35 students per teacher.

16. We have not attempted an exhaustive study of the literature on the effect of school quality on schooling attainment.

17. Assuming that a high school graduate will eventually complete 2 more years of schooling than a high school drop out, Sander's estimates imply an elasticity of 0.04 (standard error 0.01) of completed education with respect to spending.

REFERENCES

Akin, J. and I. Garfinkel. 1980. The quality of education and cohort variation in black-white earnings differentials: Comment. *American Economic Review* 70 (March): 186-191.

Angrist, J. and A. Krueger. 1991. Does compulsory schooling affect schooling and earnings? *Quarterly Journal of Economics* 106 (November): 979-1014.

Ashenfelter, O. and A. Krueger. 1994. Estimates of the economic return to schooling for a new sample of twins. *American Economic Review*, forthcoming.

Becker, G. 1967. *Human capital and the personal distribution of income.* Ann Arbor: University of Michigan Press.

Becker, W., W. Greene, and S. Rosen. 1990. Research on high school economic education. *American Economic Review* 80 (May): 14-22.

Behrman, J. and N. Birdsall. 1983. The quality of schooling: Quantity alone is misleading. *American Economic Review* 73 (December):928-946.

Behrman, J., A. Hrubec; P. Taubman, and T. Wales. 1980. *Socioeconomic success: A study of the effects of genetic endowments, family environment, and schooling.* Amsterdam: North Holland Publishing Co.

Cameron, S. and J. Heckman. 1993. The nonequivalence of high school equivalents. *Journal of Labor Economics* 11 (January, Part 1): 1-47.

Card, D. 1993. Using geographic variation in college proximity to estimate the return to schooling. National Bureau of Economic Research Working Paper 4483, October 1994.

Card, D. 1995. Schooling, earnings and ability revisited. In Solomon Polachek, editor. *Research in labor economics*, forthcoming.

Card, D. and A. Krueger. 1992a. Does school quality matter? Returns to education and the characteristics of public schools in the United States. *Journal of Political Economy* 100 (February): 1-40.

Card, D. and A. Krueger. 1992b. School quality and black-white relative earnings: A direct assessment. *Quarterly Journal of Economics* 107 (February): 151-200.

Coleman, J., et al., 1966. *Equality of educational opportunity.* Washington: GPO.

Glass, G. and M.L. Smith. 1978. *Meta-analysis of research on the relationships of class-size and achievement.* ERIC Document Reproduction Service No. ED 168 129.

Glass, G., B. McGaw, and M.L. Smith. 1981. *Meta-analysis in social research.* Beverly Hills, California: Sage Publications.

Griliches, Z. 1977. Estimating the returns to schooling: Some econometric problems. *Econometrica* 45 (January): 1-22.

Griliches, Z. and W. Mason. 1972. Education, income, and ability. *Journal of Political Economy* 80 (May, Part II): S74-S103.

Hanushek, E. 1986. The economics of schooling: Production and efficiency in public schools. *Journal of Economic Literature* 24 (September): 1141-1177.

Hanushek, E. 1991. When school finance 'reform' may not be good policy. *Harvard Journal on Legislation* 28 (Summer): 423-464.

Haveman, R. and B. Wolfe. 1984. Schooling and economic well-being: The role of nonmarket factors. *Journal of Human Resources* 19 (Summer): 377-407.

Heckman, J. and S. Polachek. 1974. Empirical evidence on the functional form of the earnings-schooling relationship. *Journal of the American Statistical Association* 69 (June): 350-354.

Hedges, L.V. 1993. Does money matter? Unpublished Working Paper, University of Chicago.

Hedges, L.V. and W. Stock. 1983. The effects of class size: An examination of rival hypotheses. *American Educational Research Journal*, 20 (Spring): 63-65.

Hedges, L.V. and I. Olkin. 1985. *Statistical methods for meta-analysis.* Orlando, Florida: Academic Press.

Johnson, G. and F. Stafford. 1973. Social returns to quantity and quality of schooling. *Journal of Human Resources* 8 (Spring): 139-155.

Johnson, S. 1984. Preparing black students for the SAT: Does it make a difference? Mimeo., Howard University, Washington, DC.

Levy, F. and R. Murnane. 1992. U.S. earnings levels and earnings inequality: A review of recent trends and proposed explanations. *Journal of Economic Literature* 30 (September): 1333-1381.

Link, C. and E. Ratledge. 1975. Social returns to quantity and quality of education: A further statement. *Journal of Human Resources* 10 (Spring): 78-89.

Link, C., E. Ratledge, and K. Lewis. 1976. Black-white differences in returns to schooling: Some new evidence. *American Economic Review* 66 (March): 221-223.

Malinvaud, E. 1980. *Statistical methods of econometrics*. Amsterdam: North Holland Publishing Co.

McGiverin, J, D. Gilman and C. Tillitski. 1989. A meta-analysis of the relation between class size and achievement. *The Elementary School Journal* 90 (September): 47-56.

Mincer, J. 1974. *Schooling, experience, and earnings*. New York: National Bureau of Economic Research.

Morgan, J. and I. Sirageldin. 1968. A note on the quality dimension in education. *Journal of Political Economy* 76 (September/October): 1069-1077.

Morgenstern, R. 1973. Direct and indirect effects on earnings of schooling and socio-economic background. *Review of Economics and Statistics* 55 (May): 225-233.

Nechyba, T. 1990. The southern wage gap, human capital, and the quality of education. *Southern Economic Journal* 57 (October): 308-322.

Ribich, T. and J. Murphy. 1975. The economic returns to increased educational spending. *Journal of Human Resources* 10 (Spring): 56-77.

Rizzuto, R. and P. Wachtel. 1980. Further evidence on the returns to school quality. *Journal of Human Resources* 15 (Spring): 240-254.

Sander, W. 1993. Expenditures and student achievement in Illinois. *Journal of Public Economics* 52 (October): 403-416.

Tremblay, C. 1986. The impact of school and college expenditures on the wages of southern and non-southern workers. *Journal of Labor Research* 7 (No. 2): 201-211.

Wachtel, P. 1975. The returns to investment in higher education: Another view. In F. Thomas Juster, editor. *Education, income, and human behavior*. New York: McGraw Hill.

Walstad, W. and W. Becker. 1994. Achievement differences on multiple-choice and essay tests in economics. *American Economic Review* 84 (May): 193-196.

CHAPTER 7

THE VALUE OF REPEAT DATA FOR INDIVIDUAL STUDENTS

Charles R. Link

James G. Mulligan

The general unavailability of experimental data has contributed to economists' development of a wide array of statistical methods to cope with problems inherent to historical data and not usually encountered when using experimental data. In this chapter we explain how analysts of educational issues can proceed when they are fortunate enough to have information for each student in multiple time periods, for example, for two or more years. We show the advantages of such data and indicate how they can be analyzed. An actual application using three years of standardized test score data is given and its results are reported.

Bishop (Chapter 5) and Card and Krueger (Chapter 6) provide detailed discussions of the advantages and disadvantages of using standardized test scores to measure academic success. As Bishop argues, standardized test scores may be the only measurable means for stimulating student learning. While Card and Krueger employ earnings of students after the students have left school as their indicator of success, a long time interval is usually required to measure the effect of educational programs. While Card and Krueger offer alternative measures of success, such as graduation rates and college matriculation rates, educators continue to emphasize standardized test scores as a relatively low-cost and quickly-obtained measure of performance.

In this chapter we describe a statistical technique for analyzing the true impact of the school, class, or teacher on test scores by controlling for those factors likely to confound the results, such as motivation and ability level of the student and the turnover of students among different schools. The technique makes better use of the type of student and teacher background data that are usually at the disposal of educators. While we focus on the statistical approach, we also illustrate its usefulness by reporting results of a study using data from the Sustaining Effects Study (SES), a national sample of elementary school students involving three years of repeated testing of the same students. At the end we provide a discussion of possible extensions of this work plus an outline of practical uses of this approach for school administrators.

The theoretical basis for our approach is the educational production function or input-output model, which is discussed in more detail in the first two chapters of this book. In this model, output, such as student test scores, depends on school, family, peer group and other inputs, along with the ability and motivation of the student.

In Section I we provide a detailed description of the statistical technique, called *panel analysis*, which has been used in the economics of labor markets literature but to date, has had limited use in educational studies. In Section II we describe the nature of the SES data used in our study of mathematics and reading achievement. In Sections III and IV we present and interpret our statistical results and relate these results to those found in earlier research.

Section V outlines the advantages of the panel analysis approach for a wide range of issues facing school, district, state, and national education officials. For example, we show how the approach can be used to isolate the effect of individual teachers, school or school districts on students' test scores. The approach would also be useful in determining the impact of unionization, the racial composition of the classroom, pay scales based on seniority and teacher's educational attainment as opposed to merit, cost effectiveness of new technology, tracking by ability, and the length of the school day and year. The schools that are having a greater impact on learning will be better able to present their case to the public when competing for students, while those that are underperforming can see what actually works.

This chapter presents new empirical results that differ in many ways from earlier findings of both us and other researchers. The value of this chapter, however, is the introduction of a technique that could be used easily by educators who have access to repeated test results and classroom and personal data for each student. The technique is more powerful than those utilized to date to isolate the impact of educational inputs under the control of policy makers. This is so, because it allows the researcher to account for unobservable characteristics of the student, which are likely to confound estimates obtained in analyses based on cross-sectional data sets.

I. STATISTICAL ANALYSIS OF PANEL DATA

The main objective in a production function or input-output model is a better understanding of the factors affecting educational performance or output. Most studies in this literature employ standardized tests to measure performance. However, some studies have used output measures such as college continuance rates, student attitudes, and attendance rates (see Hanushek, 1986). One could argue that what we really want is a measure of how an individual performs in the market after the formal educational process is completed. Some researchers have attempted to analyze this issue by looking at factors that affect individual earnings (See Card and Krueger, this volume).

While we recognize the importance of each of the above as legitimate outputs of the school system, administrators, policy makers, and parents are clearly interested in test scores. While we focus on test scores as our output measure (that is, the measure of achievement whose determinants are to be estimated statistically), the approach permits the use of other measures of output such as earnings or attitudes. However, the method works only if between successive dates on which output quantities such as test scores are reported, there are changes in the variables hypothesized to influence the output quantities. For example, there must be variation over time in factors such as the length of school day, class size, composition of the classroom, etc. These are called the "educational inputs."

The most common statistical approach, called a cross-section analysis, involves observations of the characteristics of a large number of students at the same point in time. To the extent that the variation among students in these characteristics is correlated with variations in outputs, such as test scores, the researcher might conclude that increases in a certain input, such as hours of instruction, may be responsible for a change in test scores.

More specifically, the conceptual model underlying a typical cross-section study of the determinants of achievement is illustrated by the following equation

$$(1) \quad Y_{it} = b_0 + b_1 X_{i1t} + b_2 X_{i2t} + b_3 X_{i3t} + b_4 Z_{it} + \in_{it}.$$

where for the ith student at time period t, Y_{it} is a standardized math or reading posttest score, X_{i1t} is a vector (that is, a set) of variables measuring the attributes of the student's classmates, X_{i2t} is a vector of school related instructional inputs, X_{i3t} is a set of family background characteristics, Z_{it} denotes innate ability, and $\in_{it}$ is a normally distributed error term with a mean of 0 and a constant variance σ^2. The coefficients, b_1 through b_4, indicate the change in achievement test scores associated with a one unit change in the independent variable of interest.

Many difficulties typically beset statistical analysis of a cross-sectional relationship such as equation (1). We will note two such problems of particular importance:

Absence of pertinent data from the past:

There is general agreement that the inputs in equation (1) should apply to the individual student and also reflect cumulative effects up to the time the particular test is administered. Cumulative effects must be considered because current as well as past inputs can influence current achievement. Most data sets provide only contemporaneous information on the explanatory variables. For instance, in a cross section, information on school inputs usually applies only to the inputs received by each student during the year the tests were administered.

Missing variables

Three of the most important variables influencing achievement undoubtedly include innate ability, motivation, and family background or home environment. In most studies, due to data limitations, these variables are likely to be measured imperfectly or not be available at all. In the case of a cross-section data set, omitting an important determinant of achievement, such as motivation, is likely to bias the estimated coefficients of the achievement equation. The size of the bias is determined by the correlation between the omitted variable and the other variables in the equation as well as the size of the direct effect on achievement of the omitted variable. If, for instance, socioeconomic status of the student's parents is included as an independent variable but this happens to be correlated with the omitted innate ability variable, the statistical estimation will credit the influences of innate ability to the socioeconomic status variable and the impact of socioeconomic status will be overestimated.

The availability of data, such as those in the Sustaining Effects Study (SES), where there are repeated measurements on the same individuals over time, provides the researcher with a way of handling the omitted variable problem in cases where the unobserved (omitted) variable does not change over time. This method of adjusting for unobserved variables that do not change over the observed time period can be illustrated in the two period case by differencing the data, that is, by considering not the magnitudes of the variables at any particular point in time, but instead examining how their values change from one period to the next and examining the effect of these changes on the changes in the output variable (test score performance). One obtains the magnitudes of those variable changes by taking the magnitude of each variable in some given period, t, and subtracting from it the value of the same variable in the previous period, t-1. Equation (2) shows the achievement equation for period t-1.

(2) $Y_{it-1} = b_0 + b_1 X_{i1t-1} + b_2 X_{i2t-1} + b_3 X_{i3t-1} + b_4 Z_{i4t-1}$

$$+ \ldots + b_{ikt-1} + \in_{it-1}$$

The equation and the variables are exactly the same as in equation (1) except that each variable now refers to observations in period t-1. For the ith student, Z_{it} denotes innate ability and is likely to be unobservable (at least it is unknown to the researcher). If the innate ability variable is omitted because it is unobservable, the other coefficients will be biased. But the innate ability of the ith student is likely to be constant over time, $Z_{it} = Z_{it-1} = Z_{it-2} = \ldots = Z_i$. Thus, when equation (2) is subtracted from equation (1), factors that are invariant for an individual student but vary between students over time (that is, the fixed inputs) are eliminated from the equation by subtraction, since an unchanged variable subtracted from its value in the next period will cancel itself out (meaning the *change* in its value is, by definition, zero). This subtraction process yields equation (3).

$$(3)\ Y_{it} - Y_{it-1} = b_1(X_{i1t} - X_{i1t-1}) + b_2(X_{i2t} - X_{i2t-1}) +$$

$$b_3(X_{i3t} - X_{i3t-1}) + (\in_{it} - \in_{it-1})$$

Since equation (3) has exactly the same coefficients as equation (1), the statistical evaluation of the coefficients of (3) are the same as those that would have been estimated from (1) if ability had been an observable variable. This procedure can be generalized when more than two time periods are involved. A software routine created by William Greene of New York University, called LIMDEP, is available for calculating the estimated coefficients.[1]

An example will bring out the importance of the methods just described. There has long been concern in cross-sectional studies over whether or not a pretest score should be included as an explanatory variable in an achievement model. In the cross-sectional studies on educational production functions most researchers have used a student's later test (posttest) performance as the dependent variable (the output variable that is to be explained statistically) and have used as one of the explanatory variables the student's score on an earlier test (the pretest). The basic argument for inclusion of the pretest score as an explanatory variable in the achievement equation is that it allows the researcher to control for influences that have occurred before the current year (i.e., the year of the posttest). That is, the pretest can provide information encompassing influences such as student ability or resources devoted to the student in previous years, whether these resources are school or home related.

As Becker, Greene, and Rosen (1990) note, the issue is a crucial one and the key problem arises because the pretest score may well be correlated with the posttest results (and, therefore, with the error term in the achievement equation). To the extent that such a correlation is present, the estimated coefficients in the achievement equation are subject to bias, as was just explained. Gilby, Link, and Mulligan (1995) provide a detailed discussion of this issue and empirical and theoretical support for omitting the pretest score in a panel analysis.

The SES and its panel format allow us to avoid the problem associated with including or excluding a pretest variable. In our panel we do not have to include the pretest score as an explanatory variable because we can follow each student for three consecutive years. The panel techniques thereby allow us, without use of the pretest results, to control for the unobserved characteristics of each student that vary among students but are constant for each student over time. Since our data cover only a three-year period, it seems reasonable to assume that such unobservables as a student's motivation and ability are relatively constant over such a short period. Family background characteristics are also likely to be stable.

In the next two sections we illustrate the value of the approach just described by providing results derived from a panel analysis of the SES data. Section II describes the data while Section III reports the results. Appendix 7.A presents a more technical discussion of certain aspects of this technique and considers two assumptions about the way in which omitted factors that do not vary over the time period affect achievement.

II. DATA FROM THE SUSTAINING EFFECTS STUDY

The data employed in our past and ongoing research were obtained from the Sustaining Effects Study (SES). In the fall of 1976, the first year of the SES study, data were collected from approximately 118,000 public elementary school students in 328 public schools in the United States. Most production function studies have been based on small and/or specialized samples from one or a few schools in a particular locality. With the exception of the Coleman Report in 1966, our study is one of the few production function (input-output) studies that are based on a large random sample from the U.S. population.[2] As a result, our findings are more likely to be generalizable to the population of public elementary students, schools, and school districts in the United States than are studies based on a single class, school or district.[3] It is, therefore, a prototype for the kind of studies possible if individual states or the entire country were to initiate frequent standardized testing programs.

The original purpose of the SES was to analyze compensatory education in the U.S. Both the design of the methods underlying the sampling procedures and the actual data collection for the SES were undertaken by the System Development Corporation for the U.S. Office of Education. The SES provides researchers with a wealth of information on a host of issues related to student achievement in the United States. Literally hundreds of pieces of information were collected for each of approximately 118,000 students in the fall of 1976. Examples of information collected about each student include scores on standardized mathematics and reading achievement tests, detailed characteristics of classmates and teachers along with descriptions of the instructional programs in reading and mathematics classes, and information related to learning opportunities in the home.

Separate questionnaires were sent to principals and superintendents who provided information about the individual schools and school districts respectively. Data acquired from the principals included such information as enrollment, length of school year, various dimensions of parent-teacher interaction, extent of busing for various reasons, including integration, methods of assigning pupils to different levels of instruction, and socioeconomic characteristics of families of students attending the school. District data included items ranging from school expenditures, teacher unionization and contract characteristics, to matters related to teacher autonomy and parent involvement in the classrooms. The preceding list of variables only scratches the surface of the information included in the SES.[4] Data of the type collected for this study are generally available at school districts. With more frequent standardized testing, school officials can use these data to replicate and expand upon the type of study reported here.

Given the recent interest at all levels of government in improving the quality of education for minorities, the oversampling of minority students in the SES provides a unique opportunity to analyze educational inputs and their effects on achievement of blacks and Hispanic students. The results of the analyses can help to determine the best ways of utilizing resources to enhance academic advancement. Particularly important here is the extent to which it becomes possible to test what allocations of resources, if any, affect members of minority groups differently from others. Sample sizes are large enough for separate analyses for whites, blacks, and Hispanics.

The most important feature of the SES study, however, is the panel nature of the data. Panel data provide repeated observations on each student at different points in time. One of the objectives of the SES was an assessment of educational achievement using pre-and posttests in the fall and spring, respectively, for three consecutive years. In particular, the SES contains data about individual students who were in grades one to six in the fall of 1976. Each student in grades one to four in 1976 was followed for three years. It should be emphasized that for each student, data giving characteristics of the instructional programs, other school inputs and peer inputs are available for each of the three years.

In order to measure students' achievement over time as they learned new material and improved their mastery of earlier skills, repeated testing was conducted using examinations of varying levels of difficulty and including items covering different materials. However, direct comparison of the number of test questions answered correctly would not have yielded meaningful quantitative measurements of students' improvement over time, because the actual tests differed.[5]

In the Sustaining Effects Study, the sample design and scheme of giving two different tests within a few weeks of one another were selected in order to enable the conversion of raw scores into rescaled scores. This conversion allowed for the measurement of changes in achievement over time, and facilitated the interpretation of the scores by providing empirically based national percentile norms. The test scores, nonlinearly rescaled into different units of measurement and mapped onto a commonly based scale, were referred to as "Vertically Scaled Scores."[6] The process of creating reliable vertically scaled test scores is crucial with repeated testing over a long time period. The vertical scaling reduces concerns about ceiling and floor effects that are associated with repeated use of the same test.

As already noted, the ability to follow the same student over time provides important advantages compared to the typical cross-sectional data set that underlies most previous production function (input-output) analyses. Thus, the SES data used in the study constitute a rare opportunity for the analysis of student achievement. Moreover, its replication and extension is well within the capability of school districts and states given the technological advances that have occurred in management information systems and data collection.

III. GENERAL COMMENTS ON THE RESULTS

The results of the study illustrate the insights that can be provided by the methods just described. A few points should be reemphasized before discussing the results. The Sustaining Effects Study provides a unique opportunity for the educational researcher to analyze the effects on achievement of a host of key individual student inputs, classroom inputs, and student classmate effects within the context of a panel analysis. The main advantage of the estimation procedure is that it allows us to eliminate the distorting influence of a host of unobservables, such as motivation and innate ability, for which researchers using cross-sectional information simply have not been able to control.

Our results, summarized in Appendix 7.B and described below, show the potential problem of relying on results from cross-sectional data sets, since our results are not completely consistent with those found in earlier cross-sectional studies. We have also been able to add new insights because of the richness of the data and our ability to take into account the characteristics of each individual who is in the student's class. As Hanushek (1986) has emphasized, the individual student is the appropriate unit of analysis. The unit of observation for our analysis of the SES data is the individual student, whether the data refer to hours spent in mathematics instruction, number of students in the class, etc. In our earlier cross-sectional studies based on the SES, we also employed data focussed upon the individual student.

We report the results for reading and mathematics achievement separately for whites, blacks, and Hispanics for different grade cohorts. The first cohort includes students who were third graders in 1976. They were followed during the third, fourth and fifth grades. The second cohort includes students who were fourth graders in 1976 and were followed in grades five and six. Thus, we have three years of data for each student in each particular cohort.

IV. THE RESULTS

Appendix 7.C presents the means and standard deviations of each of the variables included in the model of the production function. There is separate information for each cohort and for both mathematics and reading. Appendix 7.C shows annual averages over the entire three-year period for each cohort. While Appendix 7.B provides detailed listings of the regression results, we summarize them here and then compare them to our earlier results. Our estimates of the effects of class size, racial composition of the classroom, ability of a student's classmates, hours of instruction per week, and the tracking (or grouping) of students are not generally consistent with our earlier results using a cross-section analysis of the data from the first year of the sample period. In the next section we discuss possible extensions of this approach.

Hours of Instruction

A variable to which our earlier research attributed great importance is the number of hours per week of mathematics and reading instruction received by each student. This variable is of obvious interest since our coefficient estimates provide information about the incremental impact on achievement of changing the number of hours of instruction within the current institutional rules, including the usual current school day length, holding other factors constant.

For blacks and whites, the coefficients derived from our 1991 study were not statistically significant for either the third or fourth grade cohorts in mathematics. (Throughout the rest of the chapter we refer to the third through fifth grade cohort as "the third grade" and the fourth through sixth grade cohort as "the fourth grade.") The incremental effects of mathematics instruction were negative for fourth grade Hispanics and insignificant for third grade Hispanics. In contrast, the panel analysis indicates that the coefficients for mathematics instruction are positive for fourth grade Hispanics and whites and significant at the 5 percent level, and for third grade Hispanics and whites at the 10 percent level. The coefficients for blacks, however, are statistically insignificant. Note that these are marginal effects calculated at the mean values of the data and do not necessarily indicate the effect of a large change in a variable.

While the coefficients are statistically significant, the marginal effects are relatively small. For example, the test score gain associated with an additional hour of mathematics instruction per week is only 1.96 for third-grade whites, 5.27 for fourth-grade whites, and 4.45 for third-grade Hispanics.[7]

It is noteworthy that the marginal gain from additional instructional hours of mathematics is lowest for blacks. Interestingly, the data reveal that blacks received more hours of instruction than whites. Third-grade whites received 4.90 hours per week and improved their test scores on average by 60 points per year, compared to 4.83 hours of instruction and a 51 point average annual gain in test scores for fourth-grade whites. Blacks had a 5.56 and 5.43 hours per week and 52 and 41 point improvement, respectively. Hispanics received 5.24 and 4.99 hours of instruction and improved by 56 and 59 points, on average, each year.

Additional hours of math instruction may help explain why the gap in mathematics test scores between blacks and whites has narrowed over time even though the gap remains large. The additional instruction received by blacks within the current length of the school year seems to have reached the point where still further increases in hours of instruction per week are not likely to raise test scores.

The number of hours of reading instruction per week received by each student in the panel exhibited effects similar to those we found in our cross-sectional work (1991). The pattern for blacks entailed a negative coefficient of the linear hours term and a positive coefficient of the quadratic term. This suggests that one obtains a curve that is U-shaped when plotting achievement against hours of instruction. With the exception of the squared term for third grade whites, the effects for Hispanics and whites were not statistically significant.

When evaluated at the mean number of hours of instruction for each cohort, the incremental effects of reading instruction were close to zero for blacks. In addition, the marginal contribution of reading instruction hours, as for mathematics, is lowest for blacks. It should be emphasized that this low estimate is based on small changes from the mean value for each cohort. If there were large changes in hours of instruction and if there were increasing returns to achievement from extra hours of instruction, large differences in achievement might be possible. Unfortunately, that would involve using values that are not within the range of the data in our study.

The data reveal that blacks and Hispanics receive more hours of reading instruction than whites. Third-grade whites received 6.14 hours per week and improved their test scores, on average, by 31 points per year, compared to 5.51 hours of instruction and a 28 point average increase in test scores for fourth-grade whites. Blacks had a 7.00 and 6.86 hours and 28 and 25 point improvement respectively. Hispanics received 6.69 and 6.18 hours of instruction and improved annually by 27 and 30 points, on average.

We are obviously talking about changing the number of hours per week in a given school year and not about changing the length of the school year. While the statistical approach is capable of studying the effect of lengthening the school year, the lack of variability in the length of the school year at the time of the SES study limited our ability to study the effects of variation in this figure. Recent changes taking place in states such as California that spread out annual instruction over a longer time period will eventually generate data that can be used to test the importance of changes in the structure and length of the school year.

Tracking

Tracking means different things to different people. While often used interchangeably with "ability grouping", the term usually refers to the organization of students into groups of similar ability either within a classroom or in separate classes. However defined, tracking has recently received considerable criticism. While few statistical results have favored tracking, a majority of students at all levels through high school receive instruction in groups or classes grouped by ability.[8]

Although most earlier studies of tracking have been experimental in nature, the richness of the SES data allowed us to construct a measure of heterogeneity in ability of each student's classmates, providing an operational measure of tracking. The heterogeneity variable used is the standard deviation of the pretest scores for the classmates of each student. Larger standard deviations imply that the classroom exhibits greater heterogeneity in ability--that there is less tracking. Despite obvious differences in within-class grouping between math and reading instruction, it is noteworthy that the results are similar for math and reading. In both cases more homogeneous classes do not outperform more heterogeneous classes. A significant negative coefficient would indicate that more heterogeneity lowers test scores, which is not the case here.

The coefficients for whites based on the panel data are never statistically significant. The coefficient of the ability dispersion variable is statistically significant and negative for blacks in third grade reading, but it is positive for fourth grade reading and third grade mathematics. In our 1991 results based on a cross section for black students the coefficient was positive and statistically significant for third grade reading and third and fourth grade math. It was also positive and statistically significant for whites in third and fourth grade reading. Otherwise, it was not statistically significant.

In the current study, the ability dispersion coefficient for whites and Hispanics was never statistically significant. In the one case (third grade reading for black students) where the coefficient is negative and statistically significant, the size of the coefficient is small. For example, an increase in the dispersion variable (that is, the standard deviation of the class pretest) by 1 percent would decrease a student's test score by 0.0014 percent. These results suggest that homogeneous grouping of students by ability does not contribute to higher test scores.

Class Size

The impact of class size on reading achievement for third grade blacks is statistically significant and negative although small (that is, an increase in class size impedes reading achievement). The coefficient for third grade blacks (reading) is -0.17, indicating that a one student increase in class size reduces reading test scores by a mere -0.17 points. The average pretest score for third grade blacks is 479.16.

Whites, however, exhibit small statistically significant positive coefficients for class size in reading (0.08 and 0.09). Reading achievement of Hispanics is unaffected by class size. Class size was not significant for mathematics instruction.

These results are in contrast to those reported in our 1991 study using the cross-section data. In that study the coefficient was negative and statistically significant for Hispanics in third grade reading and fourth grade math and for blacks in third grade mathematics.

Busing

The coefficient of the variable "percentage bused for racial purposes" entered into the mathematics achievement equation negatively and significantly only for fourth grade blacks and third grade whites. A negative coefficient indicates that more busing hinders achievement. In both cases, however, the coefficients were small.

These results are in sharp contrast to those reported in our 1991 study where the coefficient was positive and statistically significant for third grade whites (reading) and Hispanics (third grade reading and fourth grade math) and negative and statistically significant for blacks (third and fourth grade reading and third grade math), Hispanics (third grade reading and math), and whites (fourth grade math).

It should be emphasized that the percentage of students bused for the purpose of racial balance was, on average, extremely small, ranging from 1.01 percent for third grade whites to 1.59 percent for fourth grade whites. Comparable numbers for third and fourth grade blacks are 1.07 and 1.19 percent.

Racial Composition of the Classroom

In our earlier research (1991) we addressed the issue of the lack of evidence in the education literature that busing of black students had resulted in a significant improvement in black student test scores during the 1970s and 1980s. We hypothesized that changes in the classroom environment are likely to have at least two opposing effects on achievement. While being placed in a classroom with more able classmates might improve one's test scores, being placed in a classroom with fewer students of one's own racial group might reduce achievement. The variable of interest here measures the percentage of the student's classmates who are of the same race as the student. Our emphasis of this variable results from the concern over minority student achievement.

Based on cross-sectional data, we found a significant and positive coefficient for this variable for blacks in third and fourth grade reading and fourth grade mathematics. That is, blacks performed better on achievement tests when a larger percentage of the student's classmates were black. The coefficient of this variable was negative and statistically significant for third-grade reading for Hispanics. In this case the results suggested that Hispanic third graders scored higher on reading achievement tests as the percentage of Hispanic students in the class decreased.

In contrast, the coefficients estimated from the panel data for minorities revealed no statistically significant effects of variations in the racial composition of the class (at the 5 percent level) on achievement.

V. CONCLUSION

In this chapter we have introduced a statistical approach especially suited to the analysis of data with repeated observations of standardized test scores for individual students. When matched with demographic and instructional data, the panel approach permits more effective ways of dealing with some of the impediments to statistical analysis of educational data.

We have illustrated a statistical method called *panel analysis* using data from the Sustaining Effects Study. To date, we have used this approach to investigate the effect on individual student achievement of class size, classmates' ability, tracking of students, racial composition of the classroom, and hours of instruction. The results have been briefly reported here to illustrate what the method can achieve.

The approach described and illustrated here can easily be extended to quantitative analyses of particular problems facing a school, district, or state. As noted, the panel regression analysis approach isolates the effect on achievement of a variable that changes during the periods of repeated observations. For example, variations in the hours of instruction received by a student at different times during the entire time a student is in school can help to isolate the effect of changes in the number of these hours on student achievement as measured either by test scores or other yardsticks. The approach is not limited, however, to hours of instruction or the other influences discussed earlier. Any input that does not remain constant during the observation period can be entered into the postulated production function if it is suspected to be an important determinant of achievement or of some other educational output.

An important extension concerns the role of teachers. To date, cross-section studies have identified specific teacher characteristics that one may perhaps suspect to be correlated with higher student test scores. Hanushek (1986) reports that teacher experience has been the only measurable teacher-related variable that is positively correlated with test scores. In our 1986 paper we confirmed the earlier findings surveyed by Hanushek showing that teacher education and other such plausible influences are not statistically important. More recently, results by Bosshardt and Watts (1991) using a variation of the panel analysis approach described here for teachers of economics at the college, high school, and elementary school levels showed that teachers do make a difference in student achievement, even if the difference is not correlated with traditional measures of teacher inputs.

With a panel, the contribution of individual teachers to student achievement can be determined as long as a student does not have the same teacher during each of the time intervals between tests. Teacher effects are found by including for each teacher his or her own identifying variable, referred to as a 0-1 covariate or a "dummy variable." The estimated equation determines the impact of each teacher on achievement. The determinants of the magnitude of that effect can then be studied statistically by means of an ordinary least squares regression, using each of the teacher characteristics as an explanatory variable.

This approach can be valuable to administrators at different levels. At the most local level the researcher can identify teachers who have an effect on student test scores. Administrators can use this information to reward these teachers. At the state and national level, education officials can determine and influence these teacher characteristics that are important to student learning. Examples include education and training.

In another extension (Gilby, Link, and Mulligan, 1995), we have used a panel analysis of these data to show that achievement levels tend to be highest in schools with collective bargaining agreements, despite earlier contrary results by others, such as Eberts and Stone (1986). For example, Eberts and Stone used the cross-section data from the first year of the Sustaining Effects Study but evaluated them in aggregate form without taking account of the student and classroom characteristics controlled for in our study. We found that white and black students showed considerably more improvement in schools with collective bargaining agreements, whereas there was no effect upon Hispanic students. The improvement for black students was as much as 47 percent on average (fourth-grade cohort for math).

Use of the panel approach to study the effects of other educational inputs will be possible only if suitable information is available to the researcher. Educators, however, have access to a wealth of information about the characteristics of their teachers, their students, and their students' families. By employing panel analysis, they would be able to interpret these data more effectively.

Appendix 7.A: Panel Analysis

This appendix provides a technical discussion of the theoretical justification for the statistical procedures advocated in the text.   This is a summary of a more detailed discussion that can be found in Greene (1990), among others.

The general form for modelling unobservable individual effects in a panel analysis is

$$Y_{it} = \mu_i + \beta' x_{it} + \epsilon_{it}$$

where the μ_i's are the unobservable individual effects, the β's are the coefficients to be estimated, and the ϵ_{it} is a classical disturbance term with $E[\epsilon_{it}] = 0$ and $Var[\epsilon_{it}] = \sigma_\epsilon^2$.

When the individual intercept terms, the μ_i's, are treated as random variables, this is called a random effects specification of the educational production model.   The μ_i's are assumed to be independent of the residuals, the ϵ_{it}'s, such that the covariance between the intercepts and the error terms, $Cov[\mu_i, \epsilon_{it}]$, equals 0.   Students are assumed to be independent of one another in a statistical sense, so the $Cov[\mu_i, \mu_j] = 0$ for i not equal to j, and constant among students, so that $Var[\mu_i] = \sigma_\mu^2$.   Thus, the error term for each student, v_{it}, is comprised of two components:

$$v_{it} = \mu_i + \epsilon_{it}.$$

The variance of each individual's error term, $Var[v_{it}]$, equals $\sigma_\epsilon^2 + \sigma_\mu^2$. For a given student, but in different time periods, the disturbances are correlated as a result of their common error component, so that $Corr[\epsilon_{it} + \mu_i, \epsilon_{is} + \mu_i] = \sigma_\mu^2 / \sigma_v^2$.

The efficient estimator is generalized least squares (GLS). The model is estimated using a two-step procedure. The variance components are estimated from OLS residuals.   Feasible GLS estimates are then computed using the estimated variances.

If the μ_i's are viewed as separate constant terms for each individual, the model becomes the fixed effects model discussed in the body of the chapter, which may be estimated within the classical regression framework by including a separate dummy variable for each individual (least squares with dummy variables or LSDV). The consistency of the LSDV estimates depend upon the size of T (that is, the number of time periods of observation), whereas the consistency of the random effects estimates do not.

The LSDV model can be expressed as a special case of the random-effects GLS estimator.   The GLS estimator may be expressed as a matrix weighted average of the between and within group variation. The weight, θ, is defined as

$$\sigma_\epsilon^2/(\sigma_\epsilon^2 + T \sigma_\mu^2).$$

If $\theta = 1$, then $\beta GLS = \beta OLS$ and $\sigma_\mu^2 = 0$. In other words, if there is no difference in students' ability and motivation, then the GLS estimator is identical to the OLS estimator.[9] If $\theta = 0$, then $\beta GLS = \beta LSDV$ and either $\sigma_\epsilon^2 = 0$ or T approaches infinity. Thus, if T is large or the variation of the individual error component, σ_μ^2, is large relative to the variation of the random error term, then the GLS estimator approaches the LSDV estimate.

Another advantage of panel data is an increase in the efficiency of the estimated coefficients. Estimates of θ reveal the inefficiency of the OLS estimates relative to the GLS estimates. See Greene (1990), Judge et al. (1985) and Hsaio (1986) for a rigorous description of the model, its implications, and a more detailed discussion of the advantages and disadvantages of the estimating techniques.

Breusch and Pagan (1980) have developed a Lagrangian multiplier test for the importance of individual effects in the learning model based on testing the null hypothesis that σ_μ^2 equals zero. If the null hypothesis is rejected, one would be included to accept the presence of individual effects. Appendix 7.B presents the results of the Lagrangian multiplier test which indicates that the presence of individual effects is appropriate for each cohort.

Hausman (1978) proposed a test of the null hypothesis that the individual effects are uncorrelated with the other regressors in the model. Failure to reject this hypothesis is evidence favoring the random effects specification over the fixed-effects model. As a result of the Hausman test shown in Appendix 7.B, we can rule out the possibility that the random-effects model is superior to the fixed-effects model.

Appendix 7.B: Statistical Results

This appendix provides detailed estimates of the regression coefficients for the fixed effects specification of the educational production function described in Appendix 7.A and test statistics indicating that for all cohorts individual effects are important and the fixed effects specification is statistically superior the random effects specification for these data. Results are presented for both mathematics and reading performance by cohort.

Table 7.B-1: Regression Results for Blacks (Reading)

Variable	Third to Fifth Grade Cohort[a]	Fourth to Sixth Grade Cohort[b]
Percent Own Race	-16.57** (8.81)	12.71 (10.97)
Class Size	-0.17* (0.05)	0.02 (0.06)
Class Average Pretest	0.10* (0.02)	0.15* (0.03)
Standard Deviation of Class Pretest	-0.15* (0.05)	0.04* (0.05)
Hours of Instruction per Week	-4.94* (1.07)	-3.21* (1.41)
Hours Squared	0.31* (0.06)	0.17* (0.08)
Percent Bused for Racial Balance	-0.23 (0.17)	-0.21 (0.17)
Time Period 2 Dummy	23.26* (1.42)	19.29* (1.59)
Time Period 3 Dummy	45.19* (2.00)	40.75* (2.12)
Adjusted R-Squared	0.82	0.84
Lagrangian Multiplier Test Statistic[c] With 2 D.F.	1,301	1,268
Hausman Test[c] With 7 D.F.	565	402

a 3,708 observations   b 3,075 observations
c See Appendix 7.A for a discussion of these test statistics
*   Coefficient significant at 5 percent level
**   Coefficient significant at 10 percent level
Figures in parentheses are standard errors.

Table 7.B-2: Regression Results for Hispanics (Reading)

Variable	Third to Fifth Grade Cohort[a]	Fourth to Sixth Grade Cohort[b]
Percent Own Race	14.96** (8.04)	0.04 (9.57)
Class Size	0.11 (0.10)	-0.25 (0.11)
Class Average Pretest	0.13* (0.05)	0.08** (0.04)
Standard Deviation of Class Pretest	0.05 (0.08)	-0.07 (0.08)
Hours of Instruction per Week	0.75 (2.23)	-1.07 (2.80)
Hours Squared	- 0.03 (0.15)	0.11 (0.18)
Percent Bused for Racial Balance	0.17 (0.23)	0.36 (1.45)
Time Period 2 Dummy	26.91* (2.77)	25.67* (3.09)
Time Period 3 Dummy	46.98* (4.06)	53.50* (4.13)
Adjusted R-Squared	0.85	0.84
Lagrangian Multiplier Test Statistic[c] With 2 D.F.	492	365
Hausman Test[c] With 7 D.F.	55	129

a 1,011 observations   b 915 observations
c See Appendix 7.A for a discussion of these test statistics
*   Coefficient significant at 5 percent level
**   Coefficient significant at 10 percent level
Figures in parenthesis are standard errors.

Table 7.B-3: Regression Results for Whites (Reading)

Variable	Third to Fifth Grade Cohort[a]	Fourth to Sixth Grade Cohort[b]
Percent Own Race	0.13 (5.12)	-7.94 (5.66)
Class Size	0.08* (0.04)	-0.05 (0.04)
Class Average Pretest	0.09* (0.02)	0.09* (0.02)
Standard Deviation of Class Pretest	0.00 (0.03)	-0.01 (0.03)
Hours of Instruction per Week	-0.94 (0.78)	1.09 (1.04)
Hours Squared	0.09** (0.05)	0.01 (0.07)
Percent Bused for Racial Balance	0.00 (0.12)	0.01 (0.08)
Time Period 2 Dummy	28.27* (1.03)	33.32* (1.05)
Time Period 3 Dummy	58.95* (1.41)	59.51* (1.52)
Adjusted R-Squared	0.86	0.88
Lagrangian Multiplier Test Statistic[c] With 2 D.F.	4,997	4,147
Hausman Test[c] With 7 D.F.	1,113	905

a 8,721 observations   b 7,782 observations
c See Appendix 7.A for a discussion of these test statistics
*   Coefficient significant at 5 percent level
**   Coefficient significant at 10 percent level
Figures in parentheses are standard errors.

Table 7.B-4: Regression Results for Blacks (Mathematics)

Variable	Third to Fifth Grade Cohort[a]	Fourth to Sixth Grade Cohort[b]
Percent Own Race	-11.56 (13.96)	-5.51 (20.00)
Class Size	-0.16 (0.12)	0.07 (0.16)
Class Average Pretest	0.11[*] (0.04)	0.14[*] (0.04)
Standard Deviation of Class Pretest	0.30[*] (0.06)	-0.07 (0.05)
Hours of Instruction per Week	-0.17 (1.95)	0.06 (2.85)
Hours Squared	0.06 (0.13)	-0.02 (0.17)
Percent Bused for Racial Balance	-0.21 (0.24)	-1.09 (0.29)
Time Period 2 Dummy	34.49[*] (2.74)	20.58[*] (3.03)
Time Period 3 Dummy	61.59[*] (4.31)	61.74[*] (4.65)
Adjusted R-Squared	0.71	0.66
Lagrangian Multiplier Test Statistic[c] With 2 D.F.	844	725
Hausman Test[c] With 7 D.F.	285	223

a 3,708 observations   b 3,075 observations
c See Appendix 7.A for a discussion of these test statistics
*   Coefficient significant at 5 percent level
**   Coefficient significant at 10 percent level
Figures in parentheses are standard errors.

Table 7.B-5: Regression Results for Hispanics (Mathematics)

Variable	Third to Fifth Grade Cohort[a]	Fourth to Sixth Grade Cohort[b]
Percent Own Race	21.30 (14.22)	21.59 (25.47)
Class Size	0.14 (0.25)	-0.21 (0.42)
Class Average Pretest	0.26[*] (0.08)	0.25[*] (0.09)
Standard Deviation of Class Pretest	-0.18 (0.11)	-0.02 (0.11)
Hours of Instruction per Week	11.65[**] (6.67)	3.46 (8.79)
Hours Squared	-0.72 (0.55)	-0.23 (0.64)
Percent Bused for Racial Balance	0.53 (0.41)	-0.22 (4.10)
Time Period 2 Dummy	31.95[*] (5.59)	12.84 (8.75)
Time Period 3 Dummy	59.39[*] (9.59)	39.61[*] (11.52)
Adjusted R-Squared	0.67	0.43
Lagrangian Multiplier Test Statistic[c] With 1 D.F.	204	68
Hausman Test[c] With 7 D.F.	41	14

a 3,708 observations   b 3,075 observations
c See Appendix 7.A for a discussion of these test statistics
*   Coefficient significant at 5 percent level
**   Coefficient significant at 10 percent level
Figures in parentheses are standard errors.

Table 7.B-6: Regression Results for Whites (Mathematics)

Variable	Third to Fifth Grade Cohort[a]	Fourth to Sixth Grade Cohort[b]
Percent Own Race	-4.47 (8.54)	-6.33 (12.65)
Class Size	-0.03 (0.09)	0.04 (0.12)
Class Average Pretest	0.18* (0.03)	0.04 (0.03)
Standard Deviation of Class Pretest	0.05 (0.04)	-0.05 (0.03)
Hours of Instruction per Week	3.63** (1.94)	10.10* (2.54)
Hours Squared	-0.17 (0.16)	-0.50 (0.21)
Percent Bused for Racial Balance	-0.46 (0.21)	0.01 (0.16)
Time Period 2 Dummy	35.79* (2.11)	38.96* (2.22)
Time Period 3 Dummy	68.84* (3.46)	71.43* (3.22)
Adjusted R-Squared	0.69	0.63
Lagrangian Multiplier Test Statistic[c] With 2 D.F.	1,856	1,486
Hausman Test[c] With 7 D.F.	564	493

a 3,708 observations   b 3,075 observations
c See Appendix 7.A for a discussion of these test statistics
*   Coefficient significant at 5 percent level
**   Coefficient significant at 10 percent level
Figures in parentheses are standard errors.

Appendix 7.C-1: Three-Year Sample Means And Standard Deviations (Mathematics)

	Third to Fifth Grade Cohorts			Fourth to Sixth Grade Cohorts		
	Blacks	Hispanics	Whites	Blacks	Hispanics	Whites
Student Posttest	530.88 (67.72)	544.24 (69.62)	572.46 (73.94)	563.35 (74.57)	578.87 (78.87)	613.23 (78.30)
Student Pretest	479.16 (70.73)	488.12 (76.18)	512.98 (73.53)	522.06 (79.41)	520.49 (87.84)	562.08 (85.74)
Own Race Ratio	0.78 (0.31)	0.52 (0.29)	0.87 (0.18)	0.83 (0.29)	0.50 (0.28)	0.88 (0.16)
Class Size	24.93 (6.71)	25.81 (6.58)	24.54 (6.37)	25.40 (6.35)	24.91 (6.40)	24.32 (6.34)
Class Pretest Average	481.53 (55.80)	489.82 (54.41)	510.04 (55.43)	524.12 (53.63)	523.74 (66.32)	559.20 (55.51)
Class Pretest Standard Deviation	44.84 (15.90)	49.19 (16.36)	48.28 (17.53)	57.15 (23.17)	56.41 (24.70)	64.07 (23.59)
Hours of Instruction	5.56 (1.66)	4.99 (1.11)	4.90 (1.04)	5.43 (1.46)	5.24 (1.28)	4.83 (0.91)
Hours of Instruction Squared	33.70 (24.26)	26.16 (13.19)	25.08 (12.44)	31.60 (23.33)	29.15 (17.56)	24.15 (10.92)
Percent of Students Bused for Racial Balance	3.07 (10.58)	1.17 (6.68)	1.59 (7.21)	0.75 (4.07)	0.20 (0.77)	0.82 (4.86)

Appendix 7.C-2: Three-Year Sample Means And Standard Deviations (Reading)

	Third to Fifth Grade Cohorts			Fourth to Sixth Grade Cohorts		
	Blacks	Hispanics	Whites	Blacks	Hispanics	Whites
Student Posttest	500.14 (56.19)	507.71 (60.88)	549.71 (63.37)	521.18 (61.16)	525.82 (58.52)	581.40 (67.10)
Student Pretest	471.69 (57.79)	480.63 (62.86)	519.47 (65.89)	495.71 (60.92)	496.27 (63.61)	553.48 (69.72)
Own Race Ratio	0.79 (0.31)	0.51 (0.29)	0.87 (0.17)	0.83 (0.29)	0.50 (0.28)	0.89 (0.16)
Class Size	21.42 (9.60)	20.17 (9.63)	21.04 (9.12)	22.34 (9.19)	22.13 (9.61)	22.10 (8.67)
Class Pretest Average	475.83 (43.86)	486.90 (42.62)	514.79 (45.48)	498.43 (45.00)	507.18 (50.75)	548.62 (47.11)
Class Pretest Standard Deviation	41.63 (13.10)	49.55 (14.23)	48.39 (13.13)	44.29 (13.69)	48.21 (16.45)	52.52 (14.96)
Hours of Instruction	6.95 (2.50)	6.69 (2.09)	6.14 (1.96)	6.86 (2.22)	6.18 (1.79)	5.52 (1.52)
Hours of Instruction Squared	54.53 (43.82)	49.08 (32.27)	41.60 (29.78)	52.02 (37.96)	41.42 (27.37)	32.75 (21.24)
Percent of Students Bused for Racial Balance	2.64 (10.04)	1.45 (7.64)	1.61 (7.31)	0.72 (3.85)	0.25 (0.88)	0.79 (4.77)

NOTES

1. The researcher must enter each unit of data for each individual at each point in time. The implicit differencing is accounted for in the more general specification by adding dummy variables for each time period. Probably the most convenient aspect of this technique for the researcher is that the coefficients are interpreted in the same way as those from an ordinary least squares (OLS) cross-section regression.

2. Others, such as Eberts and Stone (1986), have used subsamples of the SES data, but no one else has attempted to use the SES data to determine the effects of classroom-level inputs on student achievement.

3. While we are somewhat surprised that few researchers have attempted to employ the SES data, the task of matching and merging data spread across 240 separate files is a time consuming task.

4. See Hemenway et al. (1978) for a detailed discussion.

5. For example, the tests could have had different numbers of questions, questions of different form, questions covering different material, or questions differing in levels of difficulty. Even if the tests were identical, practice effects would have made direct comparisons of raw scores difficult to interpret.

6. For a more detailed discussion see Hemenway et al. (1978).

7. The incremental effect is equal to the derivative of the educational production equation with respect to hours of instruction. Since hours of instruction is in the equation as both hours and hours squared, the incremental effect of one hour of instruction equals the coefficient of the hours variable plus two times the coefficient of the hours squared variable times the mean value of hours of instruction.

8. Tracking has also received attention in the press. For a recent summary of some of the arguments see Laura Mansnerus (1992).

9. In our case, the OLS estimator is similar to that in a model that does not include a pretest score or other proxy for student ability or motivation. There are, however, repeated observations of the posttest score.

REFERENCES

Becker, W., W. Greene, and S. Rosen. 1990. Research on high school economic education. *Journal of Economic Education*, Vol. 21 (Summer):231-245.

Becker, W. and W. Walstad. 1990. Data loss from pretest to posttest as a sample selection problem. *Review of Economics and Statistics*, Vol. 72 (February):184-188.

Bosshardt, W. and M. Watts. 1990. Instructor effects and their determination in precollege economic education. *Journal of Economic Education*, Vol. 21 (Summer):265-276.

Breusch, T. and Pagan, A. 1979. A Simple test for heteroscedasticity and random coefficient variation. *Econometrica*, 47: 1287-1294.

Card, D. and A. Krueger, this volume.

Eberts, R.W. and J.A. Stone. 1986. Teacher unions and the cost of public education. *Economic Inquiry*, XXIV (October): 631-43.

Gilby, E., C. Link, and J. Mulligan. 1993. A Cost-benefit analysis of collective bargaining agreements for elementary school teachers. University of Delaware Working Paper, (1).

Gilby, E., C. Link, and J. Mulligan. 1995. Flow versus stock models of learning: A Panel analysis. University of Delaware Working Paper. (2).

Greene, W.H. 1990. Econometric analysis. New York: Macmillan Publishing Co.

Hanushek, E. 1986. The economics of schooling. *Journal of Economic Literature*, 24 (September): 1141-1177.

Hausmann, J. 1978. Specification tests in economics. *Econometrica*, 46: 69-85.

Hemenway, J.A. et al., 1978. Report #9: The Measures and variables in the sustaining effects study. Prepared for the Office of evaluation and dissemination, U.S. Office of Education, by System Development Corporation, Santa Monica, CA, December.

Hsiao, C. 1986. *Analysis of panel data*. Cambridge: Cambridge University Press.

Judge, G.G., W.E. Griffiths, R.C. Hill, H. Lutkepohl, T.Lee. 1985. *The theory and practice of econometrics*. New York: Wiley.

Link, C. and J. Mulligan. 1991. Classmates' effects on black student achievement in public school classrooms. *Economics of Education Review*, 10, (4) (December): 297-310.

_____ . 1986. The Merits of a longer school day. *Economics of Education Review*, 5, (4) (December): 373-381.

Mansnerus, L. 1992. Should tracking be derailed?. *The New York Times*, Section 4A, November 1: 14-16.

Walstad, W. 1990. Research on high school economic education: comment. *Journal of Economic Education*, 21 (Summer): 248-253.

CHAPTER 8

METHODS OF TEACHER
REMUNERATION:
MERIT PAY AND CAREER
LADDERS

Elchanan Cohn

A remarkable resurgence of interest in and concern about the nation's teaching force has been witnessed during the past few years. Concerns about U.S. competitiveness, declining SAT scores, increased violence and substance abuse in the nation's schools, teenage pregnancy, and the spread of the HIV virus among young people, among others, have rekindled interest in the quality and efficacy of American schools. A common assumption is that the quality of the teaching force is directly connected to the quality of the schools. If improvement in the payment mechanism can help recruit and retain better teachers, then such improvements would lead to improvement in the quality of schools.

The typical argument is that teacher salaries, in general, are too low, that they are subject to low ceilings, and that they are paid without regard to performance or field of expertise. Generally low salaries discourage high-ability and high-achieving students from enrolling in colleges of education. Low salary ceilings discourage some people from entering the profession and others from remaining in the field; they encourage some teachers to pursue other positions in education (e.g., administration), or to leave education for other (public or private) industries.   Furthermore, payments that are not connected to performance discourage high productivity and retention, while not taking field of expertise into account is likely to create shortages in some teaching areas (e.g., science, math, special education, foreign languages, and some vocational education; see Ginsberg et al., 1989, 34).

The predominant payment mechanism for teachers in the United States is the single salary schedule.   Although a number of variants exist, the basic principle is that teachers receive a base salary if they have a B.A. degree and no teaching experience, with supplements provided for additional education and years of experience.   Other supplements are commonly provided for extra work, to persons such as department heads and coaches, and for extracurricular activity and summer teaching.

The single salary schedule has had its critics for many years.   One of the best-known critiques of the single salary schedule was provided by Kershaw and McKean (1962), invoking the lack of differentiation in pay by discipline and by performance (though devoting virtually all of their effort to the former).   Others have argued for "payment by results," also known as merit pay, which is primarily designed to increase the range of teachers' salaries (e.g., Lieberman, 1959), or differentiated staffing, which is intended to "professionalize" the teaching force, with concomitant improvements in both the average and range of teachers' salaries (e.g., Benson, 1974; Carnegie Forum, 1986).

Labor economics provides a framework for analyzing competing claims about the "ideal" pay structure in education, and a considerable body of evidence has been gathered both in the education arena and in other areas concerning the effect of various payment mechanisms.   The purpose of this chapter is to discuss the various approaches, their pros and cons, and some of the relevant statistical evidence.

I. ARE TEACHERS' SALARIES TOO LOW?

It is frequently asserted that teachers' salaries are too low to recruit top-notch persons into the teaching profession or to retain the best teachers.   The Carnegie Forum (1986) compared teachers' salaries with those of accountants and other professionals, and concluded that teachers are severely underpaid. The problem is especially severe for highly experienced, "lead" teachers, because of the compression in salaries. This may help to explain why colleges of education are only able to recruit low-ability students (as indicated by SAT and GRE scores) to become teachers. Studies show that the SAT scores of education majors are lower than those of any other major for which data are available (Carnegie Forum, 1986). Similar results have also been found for GRE scores of education majors (McCauley, 1992).

Table 8.1 provides data on teacher salaries for the period 1950-1991. Average classroom teacher salaries are provided in nominal (col. 1) and "real" terms (adjusted for inflation; see col. 3), showing improvements in the purchasing power of salaries over time, with the exception of the period 1970 to 1980. Relative to U.S. per-capita income, teachers' salaries improved between 1950 and 1960, and then worsened up to 1980, when a reversal took place (see col. 5). Still, in 1993, teachers' salaries relative to per-capita income were at a level much lower than in 1960, a substantial worsening of the relative economic position of teachers. More encouraging results for teachers appear in col. 7, showing the ratio of teachers' salaries relative to annual earnings by workers in private industry. Teachers' salaries have increased much faster than earnings in private industry during the '80s.

Salaries of faculty in institutions of higher education have been, on average, 27 to 45 percent higher than teachers' salaries (col. 9). Although we cannot draw strong conclusions on the trend in relative wages of the two groups, because data sources for the four years shown in the table are diverse and may not be fully consistent (AAUP data are less comprehensive than data provided by the National Center for Education Statistics), the data for 1970 - 1993 are based on similar samples, so that it appears that teachers' salaries have improved relative to faculty salaries during that period.[1] Also, data provided by the National Research Council (1991) indicate that median salaries of doctorates in educational institutions were $51,000 in 1989, and that median salaries in 4-year colleges ($51,300) exceeded salaries in other educational institutions ($46,300).

Although **starting** salaries for teachers may be competitive with salaries for other college graduates,[2] taking into account the fact that teachers work for only nine months, **maximum** salaries tend to be relatively low. It is true that salaries in a few school districts are excellent (e.g., Radnor Township, PA, with average salaries of $48,138 in 1991). But such salaries are atypical. Data for Pennsylvania indicate that only 6.1 percent of classroom teachers earned more than $50,000 in 1991, only 7/100 of one percent earned over $60,000, and just one high school teacher earned $70,000 or more (*Public Schools Professional Personnel, 1990-91*, 1991). In contrast, the dispersion of salaries in higher education and in many non-teaching occupations (such as accountancy) is much more pronounced, allowing outstanding professionals to obtain substantial salary increments without having to leave the profession.

In conclusion, although teachers' salaries improved in real terms and relative to private industry earnings during the '80s, both the average and dispersion of salaries remain too low to attract some of the best college students to teaching. As the Carnegie report (1986) shows, one of the major changes contributing to the decline of the teaching profession has been the shift of women away from teaching and into other fields, especially business. With new and expanded opportunities open to women in business, law, medicine, and university teaching, the best select better paying occupations outside K-12 teaching. A reversal of the trend would seem to require a substantial revision in the structure of teachers' salaries.

Table 8.1: Average Classroom Teachers' Salaries in Relation to Per-Capita Income, Average Annual Earnings in the Private Sector, and Average Faculty Salaries in Institutions of Higher Education (IHEs)

Academic Year Ending	Average Classroom Teachers' Salaries (current dollars)	Consumer Price Index (1982-84 =100)	Average Classroom Teachers' Salaries (constant dollars)	Per-Capita Personal Income (current dollars)	Ratio of Teachers' Salaries to Per-Capita Income	Average Annual Earnings in Private Industry (current dollars)	Ratio of Teachers' Salaries to Private Earnings	Average Salary of Faculty in IHEs (current dollars)	Ratio of Faculty to Teachers' Salaries
	1	2	3	4	5	6	7	8	9
1950	$3,010	24.1	12,490	1,500	2.01	2,657	1.13	NA	NA
1960	4,995	29.6	16,875	2,264	2.21	4,034	1.24	NA	NA
1970	8,635	38.8	22,255	4,052	2.13	5,992	1.44	12,511	1.45
1980	15,970	82.4	19,381	9,948	1.61	11,755	1.35	21,348	1.34
1990	31,391	130.7	24,018	18,699	1.68	17,268	1.82	40,133	1.28
1993	35,334	144.5	24,453	20,861	1.69	18,682[P]	1.89	44,714	1.27

Notes: Col. 3 = (Col. 1 / Col. 2) * 100; Col. 5 = Col. 1 / Col. 4; Col. 7 = Col. 1/Col. 6; Col. 9 = Col. 8 / Col. 1.
[P]Based on preliminary data.
Sources: Col. 1, from National Center of Educational Statistics, *Digest of Educational Statistics* (Washington: Government Printing office), various editions; Cols. 2, 4, and 6, from *Economic Report of the President*, 1991 and 1992 editions (Washington: Government Printing office, 1991, 1992), Tables B-23, B-31, and B-44 (1991 edition), and Tables B-16, B-28, B-45, and B-59 (1994 edition); Col. 8 from AAUP data and the *Digest*.

II. PROPOSALS TO REFORM THE TEACHERS' PAY STRUCTURE

As noted above, there are a number of problems in K-12 education that are said to be connected to the teachers' pay structure. Among them one can identify the following:

- Low average and little dispersion of salaries inhibit recruitment and retention of high-ability students to teaching.
- The Single Salary Schedule fails to discriminate among subject-matter areas and does not provide a reward for superior performance.

Numerous solutions have been proposed for these problems. Solutions include the following:

- Across-the-board increases in teachers' salaries.
- Merit pay: pay for performance.
- Differentiated staffing: career ladders; differential pay by subject-matter area; lead teachers.
- Efficiency wages: pay teachers salaries exceeding market-clearing wages.[3]
- Non-wage improvements: better teaching climate; less paperwork; treatment of teachers as professionals.

In the present analysis, the main focus will be on merit pay, incorporating differentiated staffing and efficiency wages into merit pay.

Across the Board Raises

The idea of increasing wages across the board has gained momentum in recent years, as shown in Table 8.1. But in these times of budgetary difficulties at all levels of government, it is doubtful that it is possible to increase average salaries so much that teacher pay would successfully compete with compensation in such areas as accounting, law, engineering and chemistry. For example, in 1980-81 "the average public school teacher in the United States earned $17,364; the average salary was $24,215 for accountants, $35,891 for attorneys in salaried positions, $31,820 for engineers, [and] $35,983 for chemists" (Ward, 1983: 165). The situation in 1985 was no better: average teachers' salaries ($23,500) did not compare well with average salaries of mail carriers ($24,232), accountants ($31,300), engineers ($39,500), or attorneys ($51,400) (Carnegie Forum 1986: 37). It would be far more difficult for teachers to compete with the medical profession. Still, increasing average pay should be helpful in reducing pay disparities between teaching and alternative occupations within and without the education industry, and should therefore contribute to increasing the overall quality of the teaching profession.

It would be possible to increase substantially average teachers' salaries if we abandoned the notion that a small class size is necessarily superior to a larger class.   Recent research offers inconsistent evidence on the relation between scholastic achievement and class size (see, e.g., Glass, et al., 1982 and Tomlinson, 1988), suggesting that increases in class size might not adversely affect achievement. Following Hanushek (1986), it is necessary to point out, however, that changes in class size must not be drastic, since effectiveness data are derived only from the observed region of production. For example, it is not known what the effect on achievement would be of reducing class size to two or increasing it to three hundred (Cohn, 1990).   If average class size were to increase, the number of required teachers would decrease, and the same school budget could be used to increase average teacher pay.

A major problem with across-the-board increases is that such increases benefit not only good but also bad teachers, and not only future recruits but also those already in the system. It has been argued that teachers already in the system are doing their best. Also, it has been argued that salaries are not extremely important determinants of either recruitment or retention, since teachers are, as a group, very conservative, and they tend to seek primarily non-monetary benefits, such as job security and good working conditions (e.g., improved student discipline), as long as average pay is adequate (see, e.g., Johnson, 1983; Mickler, 1987; and Bobbitt, et al., 1991). If these two arguments are valid, then across-the-board increases are inefficient. The funds used for such raises might more efficiently be used to improve the school climate, or, perhaps, to recruit exceptionally able and motivated persons into the teaching profession.

Merit Pay Systems

• Individual Incentive Pay

This brings us to the merit pay controversy. In principle, economic theory suggests that all pay should be merit pay. If all teachers are identical, the marginal productivity theory of income distribution suggests that for each firm (school district), teachers' pay be equated to the value of the marginal product (VMP) of the last teacher hired.[4] If teachers are heterogeneous, then wages would be paid according to the same principle for each group of identical teachers. In the limiting case, where each teacher is different from all others, each teacher's pay should be set individually so that the value of each teacher's marginal product is equal to her/his wage.

This last case is similar to a pay structure known as "piece-rate pay," under which a worker receives payment on the basis of the output s/he produces (Ehrenberg and Smith, 1991, 413-416). Piece-rate pay was particularly popular in the textile industry, where a worker's output could easily be identified and measured. As U.S. industry moved away from individualized work stations into assembly lines and team work, the incidence of piece-rate pay has greatly diminished, and only a small fraction of employees are paid according to this scheme.

Payment of commissions and tips are two other examples of individualized merit pay. Although in both cases the typical worker receives a base pay, the base is quite low and is supplemented by commissions and/or tips. Commissions or tips are generally directly related to performance. Both are designed to encourage more output (higher sales, better service). Another form of merit pay is in the form of bonuses, either to individual workers or to management (or both), as a reward for outstanding performance. Such bonuses may be large or small; sometimes they are exceedingly large, as in the case of executives who receive substantial bonuses. Frequently, however, bonuses are only a small fraction of salaries, so that while compensation is a function of merit, it cannot be characterized as a wage that is remotely equal to VMP[5]. Since it is extremely difficult to evaluate teachers' VMP, it would be very difficult to devise an ideal piece-rate teacher pay plan. Two alternative approaches are described in Appendix 8.A.

• Group Incentive Pay

An alternative plan would take into account the nature of modern production where team work is stressed (e.g., assembly-line operations). Group incentive pay is quite common in private business, and its purpose is to counter problems associated with individual piece-rate pay (for example, workers might pursue selfish interests, ignoring complementarities among workers in production; lack of incentive by workers to spend time on equipment maintenance). As Ehrenberg and Smith (1991) point out, group incentive plans take different forms. One genre includes plans that "tie at least a portion of pay to some component of profits (group productivity, product quality, cost reductions) or they may directly link pay with the firm's overall profit level" (p. 416). Most commonly, group incentive pay is given to executives, and in many cases such plans are tied to long-run rather than short-run profits, in order to discourage opportunistic behavior. A merit-pay proposal incorporating both piece-rate and group incentives for teachers is illustrated in Appendix 8.B.

• Efficiency Wages

Under efficiency wages, employees receive wages higher than what is required to recruit and retain them. The basic idea is that such higher wages promote productivity, and reduce turnover, absenteeism and shirking. Ultimately, in private industry, the higher wages are expected to result in higher profits (Ehrenberg and Smith, 1991, 422-4). Similarly, in education, higher wages might reduce turnover, promote teacher morale and motivation, and assist in the recruitment of outstanding teachers. Efficiency wages might be particularly helpful for districts in distressed areas or where image building is necessary to improve adverse conditions.

III. MERIT PAY IN EDUCATION

Some History

Merit pay was the rule of the day in American education until the mid-twenties: "In 1918-1919, less than one-half of the cities had salary schedules. But by 1922-1923 approximately sixty-five percent of the city schools studied by the National Education Association had schedules for salary payments to instructional personnel. ...By 1956-1957, ninety-seven percent of the city school districts had developed and used salary schedules" (Knezevich and Fowlkes, 1963, 400). Merit pay, based on merit ratings by principals, was abandoned primarily because it was considered to be arbitrary and capricious, harmful to the recruitment, retention and development of a high-quality professional workforce (op. cit., p. 401). Strangely, some of the same arguments that were raised in favor of the single salary schedule during the early part of this century have more recently been cited as reasons for the introduction of merit pay.

The Recent Experience

In recent years, merit pay plans have been introduced in many states and districts (see Murnane and Cohen, 1986). Some are essentially equivalent to an across-the-board bonus, since eligibility criteria are so weak that virtually any teacher can obtain the bonus. Other plans provide bonuses to a select number of teachers. Bonuses tend to be relatively small. Murnane and Cohen (1986) point out that most merit-pay plans have been short-lived. Likewise, Mickler (1987) argues that "...by the early seventies, only about five percent of school districts paid their teachers according to merit" (pp. 137-8).

Mickler (1987) mentions three merit-pay plans that have been successful over the years: Ladue School District, MO, Dalton County, GA, and Lake Forest, IL. In the Ladue district, teachers participate in the performance evaluation, and the evaluation system is used, at least in part, to determine salary increases. In Dalton, too, teachers are involved in the evaluation process, and merit pay, which may be substantial, is also determined to an extent by the teacher evaluation procedure, although, as Mickler points out, merit raises are given to all teachers "who are performing up to expectations" (p. 139). Mickler argues (and others, such as Brandt, 1990, agree) that an important ingredient in a successful implementation of merit pay is the active participation and involvement of teachers in the evaluation process.

The South Carolina Teacher Incentive Program

The South Carolina Teacher Incentive Program (TIP) provides two models from which districts can select. The first is the bonus model, under which teachers may apply for a bonus ranging from $2,000 to $3,000 The second is the campus/individual model, under which teachers may receive a share of the bonus given to the entire school (a variation on the group incentive pay method) and/or an individual bonus patterned after the bonus model just described. The amount of the total bonus given to any teacher cannot exceed $3,000 per year. In either case (where individual bonuses are awarded), specific eligibility requirements are set forth, including attendance, performance evaluation, self-improvement, and student achievement. Each school district (or a consortium of districts) must set up a TIP committee, composed primarily of teachers, which makes awards on the basis of the following standard criteria:

> *Attendance* - Candidates must have an attendance record with no more than ten days of absence (out of 190-day contract year) during the year of consideration.

> *Performance Evaluation* - Candidates must be evaluated with the aid of a district instrument and obtain a rating determined through an appropriate standard-setting procedure to represent superior performance. It is also important that individual teacher performance must be "evaluated with a school district instrument which meets state criteria established by the State Board of Education for instruments used to evaluate Annual and Continuing Contract Teachers."

> *Self-Improvement* - Candidates must provide evidence of self-improvement through advanced training. As a result, candidates are required to complete at least one self-improvement activity from the list of approved advanced training options.

> *Student Achievement* - All candidates are required to be evaluated for teaching performance in relation to improved student learning and development.

As Brandt (1990) points out, "the use of student gain scores as the most important criterion for determining superior teaching and productivity is quite distinctive" (p. 32). It creates special problems and concerns, but it may prove to be an important feature of any merit pay plan that succeeds in improving educational productivity.[6]

Career Ladders and Differentiated Staffing

"Career-ladder" and other differentiated staffing plans have become quite popular in recent years. Most of these plans have a strong merit-pay element, since criteria for promotion within the career ladder are frequently couched in terms quite similar to those found in bonus and other merit-pay structures. An early advocate of career ladders, Benson (1978) proposed the arrangement in order to reduce attrition from teaching into administration and to raise the status of the teaching profession. The idea has been recommended by several commission reports, including the Carnegie Forum (1986) and the Holmes Group (1986). It has also been adopted by Tennessee at the urging of former Governor Lamar Alexander, and a successful implementation of such a plan in Orange County, Virginia is described in Brandt (1987, 1990).

The basic structure of a career-ladder model is borrowed from higher education. A teacher begins her career at a base level, and can move up the career ladder (to such positions as Master Teacher I, Master Teacher II, and Lead Teacher) in response to specific professional-growth activities and performance evaluation. Substantial salary increments have been proposed to accompany promotion.[7] The Holmes group recommended a five-stage teacher certification process which proceeded hierarchically from "teacher candidate" to "intern teacher" to "novice teacher" to "career teacher" and ultimately to "professional career teacher."

It has also been proposed to pay salary differentials by subject-matter area. Kershaw and McKean (1962), for example, recommend salary differentials from eight to fifteen percent higher than what the normal salary schedule would provide for persons teaching in subject-matter areas where shortages exist. The differentials depend on the specific subject matter and whether the teacher has a major or a minor in that area. Kershaw and McKean recommend that information be gathered about wages offered, say, to mathematicians in competing jobs in the area, so that salary differentials for mathematics teachers can be based on market wages. Although there are objections to the Kershaw-McKean plan (e.g., Benson, 1973), it may serve to reduce shortages in key areas (such as mathematics, natural sciences, and foreign languages). The fact is that in higher education a similar principle has been followed successfully - though admittedly not without rancor from those in subject matter areas that receive lower pay.[8]

IV. MERIT PAY - CRITIQUE

Opportunistic Behavior

One criticism of merit pay for teachers (and other workers) that is based on the piece-rate pay concept is that pay for performance ignores the interaction among teachers. It might encourage "opportunistic" behavior, that is, behavior that benefits the individual teacher at the expense of others (Murnane and Cohen, 1986). The feeling is that in a school where teachers are paid according to merit, each teacher is on her/his own. Cooperation is shunned, while competition is encouraged. As Johnson (1984) points out, "schooling is a very interdependent process. Teachers rely on those who instruct other grades or subject levels to do their work well so that the final product of this educational assembly line is a well-educated student" (p. 183). Johnson concludes that "the introduction of merit pay into schools would likely obstruct rather than advance efforts to promote collegiality and cooperation among teachers" (p. 184). In the same vein, Murnane and Cohen (1986) argue that "the nature of the work in schools" is such that teachers must "work as a team" (p. 6).

As noted earlier, the importance of team work has not escaped the scrutiny of private enterprise. Similar plans may be formulated for education, with teachers in a given grade or building sharing bonuses based on their team's performance, or principals and superintendents receiving bonus pay for outstanding performance in their schools or districts, respectively. The Campus portion of the Campus/Individual model of the South Carolina TIP program, described above, is a case in point.

Performance Evaluation

Another argument against merit pay in schools is the enormous difficulty besetting evaluation of teaching performance. Before standardized tests were common, merit pay was based on "merit ratings" by administrators, opening the door to nepotism, arbitrariness, and discrimination. Such merit systems often were responsible for serious morale problems, and strong pressure by the National Education Association had all but eliminated merit pay by the 1930s. The resurgence of merit pay in recent years has also faced severe hostility from teacher unions and associations. Such opposition is not limited to the issue of evaluation. It is a natural defense of the core of the power base of teacher unions whose influence might wane if merit pay becomes a significant component of teacher pay.

Murnane and Cohen (1986, 7) argue that an acceptable merit-pay system must at least provide to each teacher an answer to the following questions:

1. Why does worker X get merit pay and I don't?
2. What can I do to get merit pay?

They claim that the merit-pay plans they examined either do not provide reasonable answers to these questions, and hence have disappeared (or are bound to disappear soon), or else they are not really merit-pay plans. For example, one merit-pay plan that has survived over time allows most of the teachers to receive bonuses, hence question (1) is moot while the answer to question (2) is simple - just apply. In that case, merit pay is essentially equivalent to an across-the-board pay raise.

A merit-pay plan can be devised that will provide answers to the two questions. An example is the South Carolina Teacher Incentive Program (TIP), described earlier. The answer to question (1) is: Worker X got the award because she met the criteria and you didn't. And the answer to question (2) is: if you, too, will work to meet the criteria, e.g., attendance or self-improvement, then you, too, will receive an award.

Role of Student Achievement

A major bone of contention is the use of student achievement data. For example, Berk (1990) argues that since there are so many factors that influence student achievement, it is practically impossible to attribute students' achievement gains to the performance of any individual teacher. Similar arguments are raised about the entire performance-evaluation format: While principals might know who the good teachers are, they frequently cannot tell you **why** they are good teachers. Objective indicators of teaching performance are difficult to generate, but they are necessary for an impartial and effective merit-pay system.

Although one must recognize the limitations of test scores, it is difficult to deny the importance of such data in the evaluation process. If test scores are used, it is necessary to guard against "teaching for the test," cheating, and teachers ignoring other important educational outputs. This can be done by broadening the evaluation process to include teachers' portfolios, direct classroom observations, and parental and student input. Moreover, data should be collected on variables that might affect test scores, other than the contribution of the teacher (see, e.g. Hanushek, 1986; Cohn with Millman, 1975).

Other Arguments

Other arguments against merit pay include the following:

1. There is little agreement among educators about educational goals (Johnson, 1984: 181). Absent such agreement, it is impossible to define and measure the product of teachers. Neither rational piece-rate nor rational group-performance pay structures can, therefore, be devised.
2. "Merit pay is not an effective incentive for all people" (Johnson, 1984, 183).
3. Merit pay "may well interfere with efforts to improve schools" (Johnson, 1984, 183). Mickler (1987) adds that merit plans do not solve old problems, and may create new ones.

Resolution of these problems may be difficult but not impossible. Agreement on educational goals can be reached by involving teachers, parents and other members of the community in the goal-setting process (Brandt, 1990). The

Pennsylvania Plan (Beers, 1970), which includes ten goals of education, is an example of how common goals can be formulated, even for an entire state (and so much more so for a single school district).

While "merit pay is [clearly] not an effective incentive for **all** people" (emphasis added), Murnane and Cohen (1986) admit that incentive pay **does** influence behavior. Moreover, it is not necessary to influence **all** people to generate an effective merit-pay system, as long as one can have an effect on **many** people. In addition, statements to the effect that teachers really care little about money are based on surveys of practicing (and sometimes former) teachers, responding to a battery of questions about job satisfaction and the like. It is easy to misinterpret survey results, as is the case of a recent publication by the U.S. Department of Education (Bobbitt, et al., 1991). The data described in the report are for a follow-up survey of 56,242 public and 11,529 private school teachers selected from all fifty states. Since the follow-up survey (1988-89) derived from an earlier survey (1987-88), it was possible to investigate changes in employment (whether a teacher remained in a position, moved to another teaching position in a public or private school, moved to other positions within the school system, found employment outside the school system, retired, chose to stay at home, became unemployed, attended a college or university, or other). Current and former teachers were administered separate questionnaires. For leavers, information is provided on reasons for leaving. For both groups, opinions about the most effective steps that may be taken by schools to reduce turnover were solicited. Various variables are also available regarding the characteristics of sample respondents and their schools (for movers, before and after the move).

Bobbitt, et al. (1991) drew the following conclusions about the role of salaries. Approximately two-thirds of current teachers (in 1988-89) selected higher salaries and fringe benefits as the best policy to reduce teacher turnover. "However, among former public school teachers who cited 'dissatisfaction with the teaching as a career' as one of their main reasons for leaving the profession, 7.3 percent cited 'poor salary' as their main area of dissatisfaction, while 26.4 percent cited 'inadequate support from the administration' as their main area of dissatisfaction" (p. iii).

It must be noted that all of the preceding conclusions are based entirely on cross tabulations and no controls are provided for intervening variables. One must be particularly concerned about the second sentence in the conclusion relating to the effect of "poor salary" vs. "inadequate support from the administration" on the attrition decision. First, as shown in Table 8 of the report, only 8.9 percent of leavers selected "dissatisfied with teaching as a career" as the main reason for leaving. In contrast, 13.4 percent left "to pursue another career," 4.5 percent "for better salary or benefits," and many others for a variety of reasons that may be connected with compensation (e.g., retirement, further education, or even becoming a homemaker - implying that foregone earnings may not be especially high). Simple calculations, based on the statistics provided, suggest that more than twice as many teachers left for salary reasons (5.1 percent) as for "inadequate support from the administration"(2.3 percent).

Other surveys also frequently stress non-salary factors as the primary reason for attrition, though frequently salary is also a very important reason. Perhaps more important, none of the studies that I have examined asked **potential** teachers about the role of salary in occupational decisions. An informal survey of undergraduate students in my introductory economics class during April 1992 was quite revealing: (1) None of the students chose education as a major; they preferred to major in business, pharmacy, and other areas. (2) In response to the question, "Would you consider entering the teaching profession if salaries were competitive to those in your chosen major?," nearly one-half of the students expressed such an interest. While not a scientifically-valid study, the experiment suggests that available published surveys may provide misleading information.

Finally, the argument that merit pay may be counterproductive (see, e.g., Murnane and Cohen, 1986; Mickler, 1987) rests on the proposition that opportunistic behavior by teachers, jealousy by those not receiving the merit bonus, and effect of merit pay on administrators' evaluations may have harmful effects on the school climate and the rigor with which administrators pursue teacher evaluation. Since "school climate" is frequently cited as one of the characteristics of an effective school, merit-pay systems that hinder the cooperative school climate can reduce school effectiveness. While such detrimental consequences may occur, there is no reason why careful planning cannot eliminate much of the problem (e.g., group incentive plan combined with individual merit pay and greater participation by teachers in the development and implementation of the plan). Moreover, to the extent that the beneficial effects of merit pay outweigh the detrimental consequences, the merit-pay plan may prove to be effective. To the best of my knowledge, there is no evidence to support the contention that a carefully planned and executed merit-pay structure leads, on balance, to negative results.

V. STATISTICAL EVIDENCE ON MERIT PAY

A Review of Statistical Methods

The following paragraphs provide a very brief review of statistical methods relevant to the merit-pay issue. Since it is impossible to provide a detailed description in the context of this chapter, readers who are interested in conducting analyses on their own, or who are interested in improving their understanding of statistical methods, should consult the sources indicated below or other texts covering statistical analysis for social and behavioral research. It is assumed that the reader is familiar with basic statistics, including sample selection and descriptive statistics (means, standard deviations, etc.).

The choice of the statistical model (or models) for analysis obviously depends on the hypotheses one wishes to test. For example, one might wish to test the hypothesis that teachers receiving merit pay outperform other teachers who do not receive merit pay, **other things equal**. Suppose that we could obtain a sample of teachers, half of whom receive merit pay while the other half do not receive merit pay. Moreover, assume that the two groups are otherwise identical (they have, on average, equal talents, years of schooling and experience, and similar student characteristics and educational climates). Then we may conduct a statistical test of differences between means, which will indicate whether or not the hypothesis of no differences between the two groups is accepted. (see, e.g., Hays, 1981, 280-287; Levin, 1987, 397-410). Alternatively, one could calculate the correlation coefficient between the variables Y (student performance) and X ($=1$, for teachers receiving merit pay and $= 0$, otherwise), and test the null hypothesis that the correlation coefficient is equal to zero (i.e., no correlation exists) against the alternative hypothesis of a positive correlation between Y and X. If the test (described in Hays, 1981, 464-467) indicates that the null hypothesis should be rejected, then one could argue that receipt of merit pay is associated with improved student performance.

A major problem with the preceding analyses is that it is virtually impossible to obtain a sample of two groups of teachers for which the only difference between the two groups is merit pay. It is, therefore, necessary to collect data on teacher and student characteristics, educational climate, and other intervening data, so that we may be able to control for variables other than merit pay that are likely to influence student performance. A multi-variate model may be specified and estimated. Economists generally prefer to use some variant of the multiple-regression model of the following type:

$$Y_j = a + b_1X_{1j} + b_2X_{2j} + ... + b_kX_{kj} + e_j,$$

where a and the b's are coefficients to be estimated, the X's are k explanatory (independent) variables, Y is the dependent variable (to be explained or predicted), and e is an error term (the subscript j represents the subject or individual in the sample, $j = 1,2,...,n$). For the case just described, Y_j is average student performance for teacher j, $X_{1j} = 1$ if teacher j receives merit pay and $= 0$ otherwise, and the other X's represent other influences on student performance.

The most common method of estimating the relevant coefficients is ordinary least squares (see, for example, Hays, 1981, 327-329 and 474-480; Levin, 1987, 568-580). The method provides estimates of a and the b's. For statistical inference, it is also necessary to examine whether the coefficients are statistically significant (tests of statistical significance for the multiple regression model are described, for example, in Hays, 1981, 483-486, or Levin, 1987, 584-592). If, for example, the estimate of $b_1 = 2$, and if the standard error of b_1 is sufficiently low that we can reject the hypothesis that $b_1 = 0$, then one might conclude that merit pay is associated with an increase in student performance, and that the best estimate of the magnitude of the difference is 2 points in the performance scale, **when all other factors included in the model are held constant**. One can also test whether the increase in Y associated with merit pay is significantly greater than some specific value other than 0. For example, we can test the null hypothesis H_0: $b_1 = 1$, against the alternative hypothesis H_a: $b_1 > 1$.

The requirement that other factors must be held constant is, however, difficult to achieve in practice. Failure to include all relevant factors in the model could bias the estimated coefficients to such an extent that they might be totally meaningless. More advanced econometric methods have been devised to reduce the force of this criticism (see, for example, Greene, 1993; Maddala, 1983, 1992), though it must be recognized that no statistical analysis, however sophisticated, can totally account for **all** relevant influences.

Evidence from Private Industry

Although it is difficult to measure individual productivity even in private industry, one finds a "widespread use of formal performance appraisal [by] employers ... [to] rate the productivity of their employees" (Bishop, 1987, $\underline{S}$37). Bishop (1987) provides some evidence that wages respond (weakly) to performance (see Appendix 8.C). Using data from the 1982 National Center for Research in Vocational Education Employer Survey, he concludes that "while starting wages are based on background characteristics and credentials, later wage rates increasingly depend on actual job performance" (p. $\underline{S}$47). His research indicates that the effect of productivity on wages is limited to small (less than 100 workers) and non-union medium-sized firms (100 - 400 workers).

Blakemore, et al. (1987) use the Panel Study of Income Dynamics (1970-81) to study the effect of increases in base salary vs. bonuses on voluntary job turnover. Their results indicate that bonuses have a much stronger effect on turnover than base wages. For bonuses, "a $1,000 increase in average bonus pay lowers the probability of quitting by more than two percentage points in the natural log specifications and more than 3.5 percentage points in the linear equations. This compares to effects of 0.02 and 1.3 percentage points, respectively, for $1,000 increases in base wages" (p. $\underline{S}$134). Leonard (1987) also finds that "higher wages are ... associated with lower turnover rates," but argues "that the reductions in turnover achieved are not sufficient to establish the profitability of wage bonuses" (p. $\underline{S}$150).

Ehrenberg and Smith (1991) provide a summary of the effects of pay for performance (and other pay structures). In regard to executive compensation, they conclude that "virtually all studies find a strong positive correlation between compensation changes and firm performance" (p. 418).

Milkovich and Wigdor (1991) provide a brief survey of psychological literature on tests of, among others, expectancy and goal-setting theories in relation to incentive pay structure (see Appendix 8.D). Results of the survey strongly suggest a link between incentives and performance.

Marriott (1971) provides evidence from a variety of sources indicating that pay incentives are associated with higher productivity. In some cases, implementation of a merit pay system was associated with increases in production exceeding 100 percent. He is careful to caution, however, that, increases in productivity may level off over time, and, moreover, that frequently introduction of merit pay systems are coupled with managerial changes, and it may be the latter that is really responsible for the rise in productivity. Similar conclusions are provided by Isaac (1967), who examined incentive-wage structures in Australia.

There is also some evidence on the effect of group performance pay plans, such as profit sharing. For example, Kruse (1992) concludes from a survey of earlier studies that there exists a positive relation between profit sharing and productivity. Using data on 2,976 U.S. firms during the period 1971-85, Kruse concludes that "adoption of profit sharing is associated with 2.8-3.5% productivity increase for manufacturing companies, and a 2.5-4.2% increase for non-manufacturing companies. The effect nearly triples when "profit sharing is measured as proportion of employees covered" (p. 35).

There are also some findings about the effect of "efficiency wages," that is, wages that are set above the rate at which the labor market would clear. As Weiss (1990) points out, "the positive effect of high wages on performance has been traced at least as far back as ... 1734" (p. 55n), and high wages have been found in recent studies to correlate, among others, with high profit rates and a highly qualified labor force (p. 100). Also, Raff and Summers (1987) discuss Henry Ford's decision to double wages in 1914, which, they argue, were clearly above the market rate. The higher wage led to increased output and profits for the Ford Motor Company. Ehrenberg and Smith (1991) note, however, that "while initial increases in pay may well serve to increase the profits of the firm, after a point the costs to the employer of further increases may well exceed the benefits" (p. 423).

Evidence from the Public Sector

Two studies on merit pay in the public sector will be mentioned here. The first is a study of wage incentive systems in Israel (Shwinger, 1975). Like Marriott and Isaac, Shwinger stresses the need to disentangle the effect of incentive wages from the effect of improved management. Thus he shows that while the apparent effect of introducing a wage incentive system (WIS) in Israel resulted in output increases of sixty-five percent, that latter figure is reduced to only twenty-five percent after adjustment is made for "improved methods in the plan" (p. xv). Although "the productivity changes from month to month after the introduction of WIS were much less stable than before," Shwinger finds - contrary to Marriott - that "in every period after WIS was introduced the level of productivity is higher than before the WIS was introduced" (p. 162). The study also provides attitudinal data from surveys of employees, supervisors, and others, generally suggesting that workers and managers have been pleased with the wage incentive plan and that, by and large, it had positive outcomes.

The second study was prepared by the National Research Council at the request of the Office of Personnel Management (Milkovich and Wigdor, 1991). The main question is whether a merit pay plan for the U.S. federal civil service would increase productivity. In addition to an examination of the federal Performance Management and Recognition System, research on performance pay in the private sector was also utilized. The report concludes that "merit pay can have positive effects on individual job performance." Although it is recognized that problems may arise, the authors "believe the direction of effects is nonetheless toward enhanced performance" (p. 4).

Evidence from Education

Most of the research on merit pay in education is based on case studies (e.g., Murnane and Cohen, 1986) or survey data (e.g., Brandt, 1987, 1990). Surveys typically ask teachers and administrators their opinion about merit pay and whether it had an effect on morale, teaching methods, retention, and other variables. Teachers often react with hostility toward merit pay, though as Brandt points out, opposition to merit pay is much stronger among experienced teachers.

An evaluation of career-ladder programs (Brandt, 1990) provides a few clues about the likely effects of merit pay. For example, career-ladder programs result in more frequent and effective teacher evaluations. Classroom visitations by administrators and colleagues have become much more numerous, and teachers must react to the increased emphasis on good teaching practices. Also teachers serving as evaluators learn from those whom they evaluate, and absenteeism has been reduced in many districts in South Carolina after teacher absences have been included in the TIP criteria.

What about student learning? Data from North Carolina indicate that students in districts piloting a career-ladder program had higher gains in achievement for two consecutive years than those not in pilot districts (Brandt, 1990, 209). Likewise in Arizona, students in career-ladder districts performed above expectations while the reverse was true for those in non-career ladder districts, and average achievement rose during the three years in which the career-ladder program was in effect (pp. 209-210).

Two studies were conducted in South Carolina. An earlier study by MGT (1989) did not find "an appreciable correlation ... between the percentage of teachers in a school receiving individual teaching awards and the school gain index" (Brandt, 1990, 210), despite earlier claims by the State Department of Education that there were improvements in achievement test scores since TIP was instituted.

The second study was conducted by the University of South Carolina for the SC Department of Education (See Cohn and Teel, 1992). Using a multi-level stratified random sampling technique, more than five hundred teachers from twenty-two school districts were surveyed. The experimental group consisted of teachers receiving a TIP award from the bonus or the campus/individual plans, whereas the control group consisted of teachers in the same districts, matched on the basis of grade taught, age, sex, education, and experience, who did not participate in the program. After controlling for teacher and classroom characteristics, and confining the inquiry to grades 1-6, it was shown that receiving an award had a significant impact on both average and median gain scores in reading and math. The results for median gain scores are summarized in Table 8.2. Although one must interpret results such as these with a great deal of caution, the study suggests that TIP awards are positively linked to gains in student achievement. At the very least, the results suggest that the student achievement criterion is effective - that is, better teachers (defined as those whose students show higher gain scores) are more likely to receive a TIP reward. This result is contrary to widespread feelings among teachers in South Carolina that many good teachers are not rewarded, perhaps because they don't feel that the hassle of applying for a TIP award is worthwhile.

VI. CONCLUSION

Teacher pay has been and will probably always be a contentious issue. The self interest of various constituencies guarantees conflict. Those who are well served by the single salary schedule - including a large segment of the current teaching force - can only be expected (as, indeed, they do) to oppose structural changes in teachers' pay. They will, however, undoubtedly continue to lobby for across-the-board increases. Judging by historical trends, they have been modestly successful. On the other hand, those who find the single salary schedule unsatisfactory - because of shortages in certain subject matter areas or because of efficiency considerations - can be expected (as they have) to lobby for structural changes in pay. That group, too, has had some success, in the form of the introduction of merit pay or career ladder plans in some areas, though this success has been extremely limited in scope. It is clear that the politics and economics of teacher pay must be considered simultaneously, if significant progress is to be made. One possible solution would be to provide a choice to teachers already in the system between the existing structure and alternative ones, making reforms mandatory only for new teachers. Support for this notion comes from a study by Brandt (1990) showing that recently-hired teachers are much less likely to oppose a career-ladder plan than older, more experienced teachers. But there is reason to believe that the structure of teacher pay must ultimately be reformed, if significant improvements in the educational system are to be achieved.

Additional research is needed to provide answers to the following questions, among others: (1) To what extent can the educational system recruit better teachers if salaries are increased across the board? Are such salary increases cost effective? (2) Is the concept of efficiency wages relevant to education, and under what circumstances is it cost-effective? (3) Is there a causal link between merit pay (or differentiated staffing plans) and school improvement? Which plans are cost-effective? (4) Finally, what non-salary alternatives are available to recruit and retain better teachers, and ultimately to improve student performance, and which of these are cost-effective?[9]

Table 8.2:   Estimated Partial Regression Coefficients (b) and t Statistics for Median Gain Scores in Reading and Math

Independent Variables	Reading		Math	
	b	t	b	t
Intercept	5.12	1.89[b]	3.13	1.03
B	2.21	3.67[a]	2.71	4.01[a]
C	2.35	3.81[a]	2.26	3.26[a]
Sex	-.89	-.41	.42	.17
Race	1.45	1.64	-1.23	-1.24
EXP	-.02	-.56	-.06	-1.24
BA	-2.76	-2.93[a]	.97	.92
BAPLUS	-1.41	-1.31	1.51	1.27
MA	-1.00	-1.18	1.49	1.57
CSize	-.01	-.37	-.06	-1.66[b]
Grade	-.29	-1.71[b]	-.09	-.48
PCTFemale	3.08	1.44	1.19	.50
PCTFRL	-8.55	-8.28[a]	-5.61	-4.82[a]
R^2		0.26		0.14
F		10.15[a]		4.82[a]
N		364		364

NOTES: [a] Statistically significant at the 5 percent level, two-tailed test. [b] Statistically significant at the 10 percent level, two-tailed test.

Definitions of Independent Variables
B = 1 for award winners in the bonus model and 0 otherwise;
C = 1 for award winners in the campus/individual model and 0 otherwise;
SEX = 1 for female teachers and 0 otherwise;
RACE = 1 for black teachers and 0 otherwise;
EXP = number of years of teaching experience;
BA = 1 for teachers with a Bachelor's degree only and 0 otherwise;
BAPLUS = 1 for teachers with BA plus 18 semester hours and zero otherwise;
MA = 1 for teachers with a Master's degree and 0 otherwise;
GRADE = grade taught by teacher;
CSIZE = number of students in the class;
PCTFEMALE = percentage of students in class who are female;
PCTFRL = percentage of students in class who are eligible to receive either free or reduced-fee lunch.

Appendix 8.A: Piece-Rate Pay Plans

Assume that the marginal value product (VMP_i) of teacher i (i = 1,2,...,n) is measurable and known. Then, ideally, the piece-rate pay for teacher i, given by w_i, is given by: $w_i = VMP_i$. The problem, however, is that VMP is difficult to measure. Since the correlation between VMP and the marginal product (MP) is very high, and MP is more easily obtained than VMP, one alternative is to use Equation (1) as a guide for a piece-rate pay plan:

(1) $$w_i = S_i + f(MP_i),$$

where S_i is "base salary," calculated from a variant of the single-salary schedule (may be determined on the basis of educational preparation and years of experience as well as other pertinent variables, such as subject-matter taught), and $f(MP_i)$ is a schedule of bonuses or penalties associated with the teacher's level of marginal productivity, such that:

$$f(MP_i) \quad < 0, \text{ for } MP_i < \overline{MP},$$

$$= 0, \text{ for } MP_i = \overline{MP}, \text{ and}$$

$$> 0, \text{ for } MP_i > \overline{MP},$$

where $\overline{MP} = \sum_{i=1}^{n} MP_i / n.$

Under this system, the single salary schedule will continue in use, although a teacher's salary will also be influenced by measured productivity, so that teachers whose MP exceeds the average will receive a reward while those whose productivity is below average MP will be penalized. Such a pay plan may be attractive because it recognizes the difficulties in measuring MP precisely, yet it provides rewards and penalties that are directly related to measured productivity. Clearly, the greater the penalty and rewards, relative to S_i, the closer one gets to the ideal pay system. This is shown in Fig. 8.1(a), where S_i is assumed to be invariant with respect to MP_i, $w_i < S_i$ for teachers whose marginal productivity is less than the average, and $w_i > S_i$ for teachers whose marginal productivity exceeds the average.

A second alternative is very similar to the first but has the appearance of providing no penalties. The purpose of this alternative is to make the plan politically more attractive.

Let the bonus associated with productivity be $g(MP_i)$ such that $g(MP_i) = f(MP_i) - \min f(MP_i) + C$, where C is any scalar. $g(MP_i) = C$ for teachers with the lowest MPs, and greater than C for all others. Also, let $S^*_i = S_i - [\Sigma g(MP_i)] / n$. Then the alternative salary schedule is given by Equation (2):

(2) $w_i = S^*_i + g(MP_i)$

The value of C can be selected such that the total salary cost of alternative (2) will be identical to that of alternative (1). Note that under this plan, too, teachers receive an award when their marginal productivity exceeds the average MP and are penalized when the reverse is true. But this fact is hidden by the substitution of S^*_i for S_i. This may be shown graphically by comparing Fig. 1(b) with Fig. 1(a). Notice that the schedule $w_i = S^*_i + g(MP_i)$ in panel (b) is equivalent to the schedule $w_i = S_i + f(MP_i)$ in panel (a), though in panel (b) it appears that while a reward is provided for increased productivity, there is no explicit penalty associated with lower productivity. Such a plan may be easier to sell to school boards, city and county councils, or legislatures.

Choice between alternatives (1) and (2) depends on which issue is more important: teacher morale or strong signalling of teachers' productivity. In the former case, alternative (2) may be more appropriate. The reverse would be the case if it is deemed more important to clearly signal to teachers that high productivity results in a reward, and, especially, that low productivity will result in a penalty.

Figure 8.A-1: Alternative Teachers' Salary Schedules Including Reward for Performance

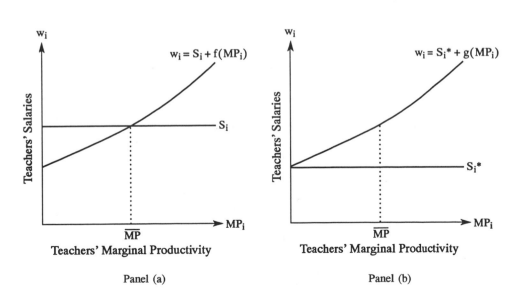

Appendix 8.B: Team Incentive Pay Plans

Assume that the marginal productivity for an individual teacher depends on the effort of the entire team, and that the VMP for the team (VMP_T) is measurable and known. If all teachers are treated equally, then $w_i = (1/n) VMP_T$, where n is the number of teachers hired.

Again, VMP is difficult to measure. Moreover, all teachers are not alike. Therefore, a new pay plan could be devised to provide bonuses and/or penalties on the basis of both individual and group merit. Define S_i, S^*_i, $f(MP_i)$, and $g(MP_i)$ as in Appendix 8.A above. Also, let $h(MP_T)$ represent a function of the team's contribution to production. Then two alternative salary plans (analogous to the two piece-rate plans described in Appendix 8.A) are given below:

(3) $w_i = S_i + f(MP_i) + [h(MP_T)]/n$, and

(4) $w_i = S^*_i + g(MP_i) + [h(MP_T)]/n$.

One could vary $f(MP_i)$ and C so that the salary cost of the team pay plan would equal the salary cost of the piece-rate plan.

Note that the South Carolina Campus/Individual plan is a variant of (4), though it does not go far enough in distinguishing differences in MP among teachers or teams.

Appendix 8.C: Bishop's Methodology

Consider n pairs of workers. Each pair consists of 2 persons doing the same job. The jth pair is denoted by the subscript j. You obtain data on the workers' wages (W), productivity (P), and other attributes (X - a vector of k variables).

Let the symbol "Δ" represent the difference between the two workers for each pair. For example, ΔlnW_j is the difference in the natural logarithm of wages for pair j between worker 1 and worker 2. If a and b_1 are scalars (numbers) and B a vector of scalars (i.e., sets of numbers, all to be estimated statistically), and if u_{1j} and u_{2j} are individual-specific error terms, then we may form the following model:

(5) $\Delta lnW_j = a + b_1 \Delta P_j + B \Delta X + u_{1j} - u_{2j}$.

Bishop employs a regression technique based on a fixed-effects model to estimate the coefficients in Equation (5), making use of the Employer Survey conducted by the National Center for Research in Vocational Education. Of greatest interest at this point is the estimate for b_1, which represents the effect of productivity differentials on wages.

Note that Bishop measures wages at two points: "Starting Wage," and "Latest Wage." Also, the measure of productivity is derived from employers' perceptions, and is measured at three points: (1) after the second week of employment; (2) between 3 and 12 weeks of employment; and (3) at the time of interview or separation from employment (whichever comes first).

Appendix 8.D: Expectancy and Goal-Setting Theories

Expectancy theory (Vroom, 1964) postulates improved employee motivation and the increased likelihood of desired job performance when employers implement pay-for-performance schemes. Several conditions must, however, be satisfied, including the following:

(1) Employers understand the plan's performance goals and view them as 'doable' given their own abilities, skills, and the restrictions posed by task structure and other aspects of organization context;

(2) There is a clear link between performance and pay increases that is consistently communicated and followed through; and

(3) Employees value pay increases and view the pay increases associated with a plan as meaningful (that is, large enough to justify the effort required to achieve plan performance goals) (Milkovich and Wigdor, 1991, 80-81).

Goal-setting theory (Locke, 1968) is a complement to expectancy theory, stressing the importance of the practicality (doability) of performance pay plans in linking pay and performance. "The goal-setting process is most likely to improve employee performance when goals are specific, moderately challenging, and accepted by employees. In addition, feedback, supervisory support, and a pay-for-performance plan making pay increases - particularly 'meaningful increases' - contingent on goal attainment appear to increase the likelihood that employees will achieve performance goals" (Milkovich and Wigdor, 1991, 81).

NOTES

I thank McKinley L. Blackburn, Sharon Cohn, B.F. Kiker and the Editors for helpful comments on earlier drafts of this manuscript. The usual caveats apply.

1. Similar conclusions are obtained by using another data source (NCES, 1992), providing the ratio of faculty salaries in IHEs to teachers' salaries for 1976, 1980 and 1990. The respective ratios are: 1.38, 1.40, and 1.28. These data strongly suggest an improvement during the '80s in teachers' salaries relative to salaries in IHEs.

2. Data on starting salaries are reported by the American Federation of Teachers and reproduced in NCES (1992). For the years 1976, 1980, and 1990, beginning salaries, in 1990 prices were, respectively, $19,024, $17,433, and $20,476. Also, Murnane, Singer and Willett (1988), using a sample of teachers in Michigan, found that 10-month starting salaries for teachers in 1972 and 1973 "were only slightly below twelve-month starting pay for college graduates in all specialties except chemistry, physics and mathematics" (Brandt, 1990, 221).

3. As far as I know, the idea of efficiency wages has never been discussed in reference to teachers' salaries.

4. Let TP = the total product produced by teachers, T = the number of teachers employed, and MP = the marginal product of the last teacher hired, given by $d(TP)/dT$ (i.e., the extra output produced by the last teacher hired). Also, let VMP = p x MP, where p = the price (or social value) per unit of the total product produced by teachers. If the number of teachers hired (T) is predetermined (perhaps because of legislation mandating certain class sizes), and if it is desired to maximize the net value provided by teachers, then each teacher should receive a wage, W, equal to VMP. This wage meets the objective of "efficiency," because it is designed to maximize the net value produced by teachers. The wage might also be considered equitable, because teachers receive a compensation that is commensurate with their contribution to society.

5. The foregoing analysis is based on the assumption of perfectly competitive markets. While the existence of non-competitive markets would require adjustments in the analysis, the essence of the argument is not sensitive to the competitive assumption. For some evidence on the effect of monopsony on teacher salaries see Landon and Baird (1971). Thornton (1975), and, most recently, Borland and Howsen (1992).

6. South Carolina also has a program to reward principals (PIP), and a school incentive reward system, which provides extra funds for schools exceeding their expected achievement outcomes. In the latter program, however, funds cannot be used to supplement staff salaries. See Richards and Sheu (1992).

7. An early example of a career-ladder plan is the Harvard Plan developed in 1959 for the Concord (MA) public school district (Harvard Center, 1963). A more recent proposal is provided by the Carnegie Forum (1986). See also Cohn (1988) for a proposed salary schedule for lead teachers in Orangeburg, S.C., which was based on wage data for persons outside the K-12 education system with educational credentials and responsibilities similar to those proposed for lead teachers. The proposed schedule was developed in response to a request from the district's superintendent, but the concept of lead teachers was never adopted by the district.

8. Issues concerning problems of implementation of merit-pay systems have also been discussed in Barr (1963) and Lerman (1990). Lieberman (1959) offered an

interesting proposal on the evaluation issue, suggesting a self-supporting national foundation that would certify teachers on the basis of qualifications determined by the foundation. Teachers earning a certificate can then command higher salaries.

9. In a recent book, Murnane, et al. (1991) argue that some strategies don't work, including merit pay, requiring teachers to obtain master's degrees, or rewarding teachers for earning such degrees. On the other hand, they believe that other strategies do work, including across the board increases in teachers' salaries, salaries that are consistent with market conditions, improved working conditions, and improved practices in teacher recruitment. Although they do not recommend merit pay, they favor rewarding current teachers for "meaningful" professional development.

REFERENCES

Barr, A.S. 1963. Problems in the measurement and prediction of teacher effectiveness. In *Perspectives on the economics of education*, ed. Charles S. Benson, pp. 412-418. Boston: Houghton Mifflin.

Beers, J.S. 1970. *The ten goals of quality education: Rationale and measurement.* Harrisburg: PA Department of Education.

Benson, C.S. 1978. *The economics of public education*, 3rd ed. Boston: Houghton Mifflin.

_____. 1974. The money we spend and what happens to it. In *The employment of teachers: Some analytical views*, ed. Donald Gerwin, pp. 134-140. Berkeley: McCutchan.

Berk, R.A. 1990. Limitations of using student-achievement data for career-ladder promotions and merit-pay decisions. In *Assessment of teaching purposes, practices, and implications for the profession*, ed. J.V. Mitchel, Jr., S.L. Wise, and B.S. Plake, pp. 261-306. Hillsdale, NJ: Lawrence Erlbaum.

Bishop, J.H. 1987. The recognition and reward of employee performance. *Journal of Labor Economics* 5 (4, pt. 2): S36-56.

Blakemore, A.E., S.A. Low, and M.B. Ormiston. 1987. Employment bonuses and labor turnover. *Journal of Labor Economics* 5 (4, pt. 2): S124-135.

Bobbitt, S.A., E. Faupel, and S. Burns. 1991. *Characteristics of stayers, movers, and leavers: Results from the teacher followup survey, 1988-89.* E.D. Tabs, NCES 91-128. Washington, D.C.: National Center for Education Statistics, U.S. Department of Education.

Borland, M.V. and R.M. Howsen. 1992. Student academic achievement and the degree of market concentration in education. *Economics of Education Review* 11 (1): 31-39.

Brandt, R.M. 1990. *Incentive pay and career ladders for today's teachers: A study of current programs and practices.* Albany: State University of New York Press.

_____. 1987. An ethnography of career ladder planning and implementation. Paper presented at the annual meeting of the American Educational Research Association, April 20-24, 1987. (EDRS No. Ed.300.891)

Carnegie Forum on Education and the Economy. 1986. *A nation prepared: Teachers for the 21st century.* New York: Carnegie Corporation.

Cohn, E. 1990. School management and efficiency. In *The International encyclopedia of education, supplementary volume two*, ed. T. Husen and T.N. Postlethwaite, pp. 531-539. Oxford: Pergamon.

_____. 1988. Estimating lead-teacher salaries from survey data: The 1987 Orangeburg Survey. In *Compensating lead teachers: A design for the teaching profession of Orangeburg (S.C.) School District Five*, ed. B. Berry and K. Stevenson. Columbia, S.C.: Center for Educational Policy, University of South Carolina.

Cohn, E. and T.G. Geske. 1990. *The economics of education*, 3rd ed. Oxford: Pergamon.

Cohn, E. with S.D. Millman. 1975. *Input-output analysis in public education*. Cambridge, MA: Ballinger.

Cohn, E. and S.J. Teel. 1992. Participation in a teacher incentive program and student achievement in reading and math. *1991 proceedings of the Business and Economic Statistics Section, American Statistical Association*. Alexandria, VA: American Statistical Association.

Ehrenberg, R.G. and R.S. Smith. 1991. *Modern labor economics: Theory and public policy*. New York: Harper Collins.

Ginsberg, R., E. Cohn, C.G. Williams, S.T. Pritchett, and T. Smith. 1989. *Teaching in South Carolina: A retirement initiative*. Columbia, S.C.: University of South Carolina, College of Education, Education Policy Center.

Glass, G.V., L.S. Cahan, M.L. Smith, and N.N. Filby. 1982. *School class size: Research and policy*. Beverly Hills, CA: Sage.

Greene, W. 1993. *Econometric analysis*, 2nd ed. New York: Macmillan.

Hanushek, E.A. 1986. The economics of schooling: Production and efficiency in the public schools. *Journal of Economic Literature* 24 (September): 1141-1177.

Harvard Center for Field Studies. 1963. A salary plan. In *Perspectives on the economics of education*, ed. Charles S. Benson, pp. 427-433. Boston: Houghton Mifflin.

Hays, W.L. 1981. *Statistics*, 3rd ed. New York: Holt, Rinehart & Winston.

Holmes Group. 1986. *Tomorrow's teacher*. East Lansing, MI: Holmes Group.

Isaac, J.E. 1967. *Wages and productivity*. Melbourne: F.W. Cheshire.

Johnson, S.M. 1984. Merit pay for teachers: A poor prescription for reform. *Harvard Education Review* 54 (May): 175-185.

Kershaw, J.A. and R.N. McKean. 1962. *Teacher shortages and salary schedules*. New York: McGraw-Hill.

Knezevich, S.J. and J.G. Fowlkes. 1963. Salary schedules. In *Perspectives on the economics of education*, ed. Charles S. Benson, pp. 400-406. Boston: Houghton Mifflin.

Kruse, D.L. 1992. Profit sharing and productivity: Microeconomic evidence from the United States. *Economic Journal* 102 (January): 24-36.

Landon, J.H. and R.N. Baird. 1971. Monopsony in the market for public school teachers. *American Economic Review* 61 (December): 966-71.

Lerman, J.L. 1990. Merit pay and career ladders: Part of the problem or part of the solution? In *Advances in research and theories of school management*, vol. 1, ed. S.B. Bacharach and S.C. Conley, pp. 95-122. Greenwich, CT: JAI Press.

Leonard, J.S. Carrots and sticks: Pay, supervision and turnover. *Journal of Labor Economics* 5 (4, pt. 2): S136-152.

Levin, R.I. 1987. *Statistics for management,* 4th ed. Engelwood Cliffs, NJ: Prentice-Hall.

Lieberman, M. 1959. A foundation approach to merit pay. *Phi Delta Kappan* XLI (December): 118-122.

Locke, E. 1968. Toward a theory of task motivation and incentives. *Organizational Behavior and Human Performance 3* :157-189.

Maddala, G.S. 1991. *Introduction to econometrics,* 2nd ed. New York: Macmillan.

_____. 1983. *Limited dependent and qualitative variables in econometrics.* New York: Cambridge University Press.

Marriott, R. 1971. *Incentive payment systems: A review of research and opinion,* 4th ed. London: Staples Press.

McCauley, C. 1992. What to do about declining SATS. Bryn Mawr, PA: Department of Psychology, Bryn Mawr College (unpublished manuscript).

_____. 1991. How to attract good people to teaching. *Wall Street Journal* 218 (November 7): A14.

Mickler, M.L. 1987. Merit pay: Boon or boondoggle? *The Clearing House* 61 (November): 137-141.

Milkovich, G.T. and A.K. Wigdor, eds. 1991. *Pay for performance: Evaluating performance appraisal and merit pay.* Washington: National Academy Press.

MGT of America. 1989. An evaluation of the teacher incentive program 1987-88 pilot-testing following the payment of incentive awards. Report submitted to the South Carolina Department of Education. Tallahassee, FL: author.

Murnane, R.J. and D.K. Cohen. 1986. Merit pay and the evaluation problem: Why most merit pay plans fail and a few survive. *Harvard Education Review* 56 (February): 1-17.

Murnane, R.J., S.D. Singer, and J.B. Willett. 1988. The career paths of teachers: Implications for teacher supply and methodological lessons for research. *Educational Researcher* 17 (6): 22-30.

_____, J.J. Kemple, and R.J. Olsen. 1991. *Who will teach? Policies that matter.* Cambridge: Harvard University Press.

National Center for Educational Statistics. 1992. *American education at a glance.* NCES 92-696. Washington, D.C.: U.S. Department of Education.

National Research Council. 1991. *Survey of doctorate recipients.* Washington, D.C.: author.

Public Schools Professional Personnel 1990-91. 1991. Harrisburg: Pennsylvania Department of Education.

Raff, D.M.G., and L.H. Summers. 1987. Did Henry Ford pay efficiency wages? *Journal of Labor Economics* 5 (4, pt. 2): S57-86.

Richards, C.E. and T.M. Sheu. 1992. The South Carolina school incentive reward program: A policy analysis. *Economics of Education Review* 11 (1): 71-86.

Shwinger, P. 1975. *Wage incentive systems.* New York: Wiley.

Thornton, R.J. 1975. Monopsony and teachers' salaries: Some contrary evidence: Comment. *Industrial and Labor Relations Review* 28 (July): 574-5.

Tomlinson, T.M. 1988. *Class size and public policy: Politics and panaceas.* Washington, D.C.: Office of Educational Research and Improvement, U.S. Department of Education.

Vroom, V. 1964. *Work and motivation.* New York: Wiley.

Ward, J.G. 1983. On teacher quality. In *School finance and school improvement linkages for the 1980s*, ed. Allan Odden and L. Dean Weber, pp. 163-170. Fourth Annual Yearbook of the American Education Finance Association. Cambridge, MA: Ballinger.

Weiss, A. 1990. *Efficiency wages: Models of unemployment, layoffs, and wage dispersion*. Princeton: Princeton University Press.

CHAPTER 9

TEACHING SALARIES AND TEACHER RETENTION

Peter Dolton

Wilbert van der Klaauw

Those who argue for parsimony in school budgets often imply that an increase in educational expenditure constitutes "throwing money at the problem" and suggest that such a rise in outlay has little effect. This study provides strong evidence to the contrary. It demonstrates the use of hazard models in the analysis of duration and shows that increases in salaries can induce qualified teachers to remain in the profession considerably longer, and induce more former teachers to return to the profession.

The turnover of teachers is determined by the rate at which existing teachers leave and the rate at which ex-teachers return to the profession. The empirical analysis of the decision to leave and the decision to return to teaching has been relatively neglected in the recent economics literature. This paper aims to partially rectify this omission by the study of pertinent cohort data.

The issue has recently grown in importance in the United Kingdom as the pattern of supply and demand for teachers changed. The situation is best described with the aid of the aggregate time series in the U.K. over the period 1964-1986, illustrated in Figure 9.1. It shows that the number of new teachers under 25 years old who enter the profession has been falling dramatically since the mid-1970s from around 27,000 per annum in 1975 to 10,000 per annum in 1981 and less than 7,000 in 1986. This fall in the supply of teachers was made up in the 1980s by the rise in the number of female ex-teachers who re-entered the profession and a small decline in the number of female teachers who left it. Over the same period the numbers of male teachers leaving and re-entering the profession remained roughly constant. This is a dramatic change in the composition of the supply flow of teachers in the U.K. with re-entrants from the "pool of inactive teachers" to the job becoming a more important component of supply than new recruits after 1982. It is therefore important to study in more detail the timing of the decisions of teachers to quit and re-enter teaching.[1]

Overall, the market for teachers in the U.K. has been characterized by persistent shortages of skilled teachers in certain subjects and geographic regions. There has also been concern about a perceived fall in the overall quality of the teaching force, which has increased interest in policies aimed not only at attracting promising college graduates to the profession, but also at retaining effective current teachers and attracting back the best former teachers.

Exactly what influences a teacher's propensity to leave teaching for a different career or for a non-labor market alternative, and what influences his or her decision to return? The extent to which teacher salaries and potential earnings in alternative occupations influence these decisions is of considerable importance and constitutes the primary issue in this research. A better understanding of teacher turnover can help in identifying and evaluating policies and conditions that are effective in retaining and attracting back to teaching the most able teachers as well as teachers in shortage subjects and geographic areas. It would also help educational authorities improve their predictions of both future teacher attrition and the supply behavior of teachers in the reserve pool, which in turn will lead

Figure 9.1: U.K. Teacher Entrants and Leavers 1964-1986

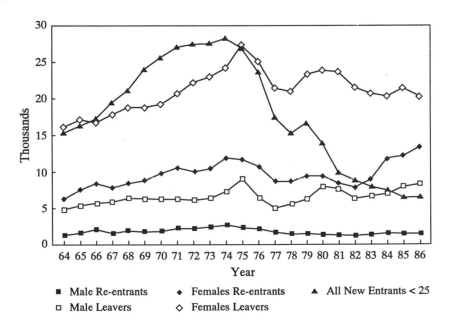

to better forecasts of teacher supply and demand. These forecasts are important in determining the number of new trainees to admit to teacher training programs. Given the rising costs of teacher training, it has become increasingly important to learn which (future) teachers are most likely to leave and least likely to return to teaching.

In this paper we analyze the early careers of a national sample of 1980 U.K. graduates who chose to become full time primary or secondary school teachers in their first job. Given that both teacher exit and re-entry rates are highest for teachers at the beginning of their careers, this sample is ideally suited for a study of these aspects of teaching careers.

To characterize this teacher turnover behavior, this study employs proportional hazard models that relate the propensity to leave or return to teaching to a number of individual and job specific characteristics, such as the individual's (expected) wage earnings in the teaching and nonteaching sector, regional labor market conditions and the teacher's education and social background. In our analysis of teacher attrition we will distinguish between different exit types: by destination states and reasons for leaving. This distinction is important because teacher salaries and opportunity wages (salaries offered in other professions) are likely to have an effect on the propensity to leave for a nonteaching job different from that on the propensity to stop working altogether. The latter is particularly common for female teachers, who represent a majority of teachers, and differentiating by type of exit permits a more informative analysis of the importance of earnings and other characteristics on teacher attrition and on the decision to leave the labor force.

Our results show that teacher salaries and opportunity wages are important determinants of the decision to leave teaching and that their effects differ for different types of exit. These findings exemplify the insight gained by distinguishing between multiple destinations or exit types in teacher attrition studies. Our empirical analysis of re-entry decisions shows that earnings also have a strong influence on the decision to return to teaching and that re-entry rates into teaching from the different destination states vary substantially.

The next section provides some brief background material on the teacher market in the U.K. and on related economic research on the supply and career choices of teachers. This is followed, in Section II, with a discussion of some theoretical modelling considerations. A description of the data used in this study is given in Section III and Section IV discusses the specification and estimation of our empirical models. Section V presents our empirical findings.

I. THE MARKET FOR U.K. TEACHERS

The U.K. market for teachers appears to be in (almost) continuous disequilibrium. For most of the post-war period up to the early 1970s the imbalance in the supply and demand has been characterized by a shortage of teachers. Since then a sharp fall in the number of pupils in schools has led to a small excess supply of teachers (see Zabalza, et al.,1979; Dolton, 1992, for a description of the market for teachers in the U.K. during the 1960-1986 period). Superimposed on the problems of aggregate teacher supply and demand are the specific market differences found within each subject and region of the country. This leads to the current position where the small aggregate excess supply of teachers coexists with a shortage of teachers in certain subjects, primarily in mathematics, physics and the sciences, and in certain areas of the country, most markedly in the greater London area. In addition, teaching appears to fail increasingly in attracting and retaining the academically most able college graduates, reinforcing the general view of the teaching profession as a low-status, low-salary occupation only chosen by those with no better options.

Low teacher salaries are often cited as the main cause of teacher shortages. Since the mid 1960s the teaching profession in the U.K. has sustained a considerable decline in relative earnings. Although the average real earnings of teachers has been rising over nearly the whole post war period, when compared to all workers and nonmanual workers over the 1965-1988 period, their relative salaries have fallen. With the exception of a couple of sharp pay raises in 1974/75 and 1980/81 (after the Houghton Report and Clegg Commission respectively) teachers' pay has been restricted, both in terms of starting salaries and increment scales. As a result, teachers' relative pay (compared to the nonmanual earnings index) was some 10-13 percent lower in the 1980s than in the 1960s.[2]

This decline in relative earnings, combined with a fall in the demand for teachers, has led to a steady decline in the proportion of university graduates who choose teaching as a career[3] and a doubling since 1960 of the proportion of teachers leaving the profession within the first six years of teaching to 37 percent in 1980. The resulting shortage in teachers has serious short- and long-term policy implications, not least of which is the threat of deleterious effects on the quality of recruitment and retention in teaching, and the consequences for the standards of education in the U.K.

The existence and persistence of teacher shortages is closely related to the organizational structure of the teacher market and in particular to the structure of teacher salary schedules. The public sector in the U.K. is a near monopolistic supplier of education and a near monopsonistic buyer of teacher services. Hence both the supply and demand for teachers is politically manipulable. Since the government sets guidelines for pupil/teacher ratios and maximum class sizes, and determines the size and funding of teacher training courses it has direct control over most of the major determinants of teacher supply and demand. More overtly, since the government decides on the overall level of public expenditures on education as well as the average level of teacher salaries, it has a pervasive influence over the market. One additional complication for the analysis of demand is that uses of these instruments under the control of the government are usually determined in isolation from each other and are subject to different pressures.

There are also two factors, largely outside the control of the government that are important elements in a complex problem. The first, on the demand side, is the demographic changes in the birth rate and its regional geographical variation. To a large degree the government should be able to predict these changes but it has only limited influence over them. Large changes in this rate or its geographical disparities can cause wild swings in the demand for teachers. The second, on the supply side, is the changes in the other labor markets that attract potential teachers away from the profession. The government has only limited control over the relative pay and conditions in the other (private sector) occupations and therefore may exercise only indirect influence on the recruitment, retention and wastage of teachers.

While in the U.S. teacher salary scales are set locally by each school district, in the U.K. uniform salary scales are set by the government (in negotiations with teacher unions) and apply throughout the country, leaving local authorities only limited control over individual teachers' salaries. The existence of a uniform salary structure could create imbalances within the teaching profession if differences among teachers were valued differently in external markets. While salary levels are fixed for all teachers of a particular grade or post (eg. head teacher) with a particular level of qualification and experience, local authorities have some flexibility in appointing and promoting teachers to higher posts. There is some evidence that teachers in shortage subjects, skills and areas are in fact paid more than others with the same experience and qualifications, but the difference is very small (see Zabalza, et al., 1979; Dolton, 1992).

The relative insensitivity of teachers' compensation explains the difficulty in hiring and retaining teachers in the mathematics and science fields because college graduates trained in these subjects can command much higher salaries in business and industry. A similar argument can be made to explain shortages in the greater London area as well as problems in attracting and retaining the academically most able.

The problems of teacher supply have been studied by many researchers over the years. In the U.K. Thomas and Deaton (1977), Zabalza (1979), Zabalza, Turnbull and Williams (1979), Blackstone and Crispin (1982), Dolton (1990), Dolton and Makepeace (1993) and Dolton and Mavromaras (1994) were all concerned with the problems of teacher supply in the modern era of "shortage". Studies such as those by Zarkin (1985) and Manski (1987) considered the supply and market for teachers in the U.S. Most of these studies are concerned primarily with the supply of new entrants to the profession and find that earnings have a strong influence on this supply.Research on teacher turnover, on the other hand, has been confined to studies of teachers in the U.S.. Most notably the work of Murnane and Olsen (1989, 1990) and Murnane et al., (1989), has explicitly modelled the effects of salaries and opportunity wages on the length of stay in teaching for teachers in North Carolina and Michigan. These studies found both earnings measures to have a strong influence on teacher attrition. In this paper we build on their approach to study both exit and re-entry decisions of U.K. teachers.

II. THEORETICAL MODELLING CONSIDERATIONS

Teacher attrition can be either voluntary or involuntary. Reasons for voluntary exits include higher income and better working conditions in alternative employment, more leisure time or more time to spend at home rearing children. Reasons for involuntary attrition can be poor performance on the job, cuts in overall employment, mandatory retirement and illness.

The voluntary decision to leave for economic reasons can best be explained with the aid of economic theories of job turnover, on-the-job search and occupational choice and mobility. Occupational choice theories postulate that individuals choose from among the options open to them, the alternative that provides the highest expected net pecuniary and nonpecuniary benefits. The monetary benefits include the expected stream of earnings and retirement benefits in a given profession. The nonpecuniary benefits include working conditions, prestige, job security, working hours, holidays and its complimentarily with family responsibilities. The cost of entering an occupation consists primarily of the cost of preparing for an occupation or of retraining (schooling and foregone earnings) for another one.

Once an individual has entered the occupation that maximizes the net expected returns, it may become optimal for the individual to change occupation at some time. There are three main reasons for such mobility. First, the individual may be using the current occupation as a "stepping stone" to build experience that will ease transition to jobs in which such experience will be highly rewarded. In the case of teaching, such mobility occurs to other jobs in the education field, such as teaching in further or higher education, central or local government educational administration and jobs in the human service occupations such as social work, psychology and law. This type of exit is a particularly likely one for career minded teachers and teachers of higher ability.

A second reason for job attrition is imperfect information. At the time the initial occupational choice decision is made, individuals have incomplete information about the characteristics of the chosen occupation and about those of possible alternatives. As such knowledge becomes available, either through learning by experience or through on-the-job search for alternative jobs, it may become optimal to change to another occupation with a higher expected return when such an opportunity arises.

Beginning teachers often find that teaching is more stressful and difficult than they had expected. Learning about such, previously unknown, nonpecuniary characteristics as well as learning about the pecuniary ones, is likely to predominate in the first few years in teaching. Those teachers with better options and higher expected earnings outside teaching are especially sensitive to this new information because these teachers, on average, are more likely to have had atypically high and unrealistic expectations about the nonpecuniary benefits in teaching (Murnane and Olsen, 1990). They are also more likely to have received atypically low offers outside teaching when the initial decision to enter teaching was made. The correspondingly high attrition rate of teachers with stronger credentials and academic ability is an issue of great concern to policy makers attempting to improve the quality of entering teachers.

A third reason for departure from teaching is the result not of the uncertainty and incomplete information about the available options but rather of changes in the options themselves. Changes in market conditions can make other occupations more attractive relative to teaching. If at any point in a teacher's career the present value of benefits in an alternative occupation exceeds the sum of benefits in teaching plus the cost of changing occupations, the teacher will have an inducement to leave the profession for a job in the preferred occupation when it materializes.

While job experience accumulated in teaching may facilitate promotion or transitions to certain attractive jobs outside of the classroom, it generally reduces the probability of exit to most other professions. According to human capital theory, as long as an individual stays in the profession, he/she accumulates occupation-specific human capital that translates into wage premiums that are available as long as the individual works within that profession. This explains why most occupational movement occurs during the early years in a career.

Like experience, education and training also can have an occupational-specific character. Teachers whose training is directly oriented towards teaching are, relatively speaking, likely to have considerably higher productivity in teaching than outside teaching, and the relative wages they will be able to obtain in the profession compared to other professions will be greater than for those with a more general training. We therefore expect those with a bachelor's degree in education to be less likely to leave teaching than teachers with a mathematics or other science degree, whose background and skills are more easily transferred to other, possibly better-paying jobs, in other professions.

Not all voluntary exits are made solely for career reasons. Life cycle events such as marriage, the births of children, migration and retirement are all strong influences on teacher attrition. The employment status and career decisions of the spouse are also important. These may cause the individual to reevaluate the current position and may lead to exit from teaching if an alternative job or withdrawal from the labor force seems preferable to the current teaching job. These factors are especially important for the majority of teachers, who are women. Many women leave teaching temporarily for family related reasons and re-enter the teacher force once the value of domestic work declines.

In addition to voluntary exit, some teachers may leave the profession unwillingly. All new teachers in the U.K. face a period of at least one year's probation after which they may either be confirmed or not confirmed in their appointment. Some teachers are only appointed to fixed-term temporary contracts and are often compelled to leave when financial or school conditions dictate unavailability of a permanent job for them. Such temporary contracts are often occasioned by maternity leave of other teachers and usually last for only one or two terms. In rare circumstances teachers may be fired or transferred to other duties within a local education authority. Teachers who have exited from their job involuntarily may find employment in another school or another occupational sector, or may spend some time unemployed, looking for new jobs, or out of the labor force, rearing children.

From this discussion it is clear that full understanding of teacher exit and re-entry decisions requires a study within the context of both career and life cycle decisions, such as fertility, marriage and household migration choices. In this study, instead of formulating and estimating an economic model that explicitly incorporates all these life cycle choices, we will focus on the empirical relationship between the underlying economic and socioeconomic determinants of these career and life cycle choices and teacher turnover.[4] Economic variables, such as the current salary received, are known to have an important influence not only on career and work decisions but also on migration decisions as well as fertility and marriage decisions (van der Klaauw, 1993). Estimates of our model's parameters will measure the combined direct (given all other decisions) and indirect (through other decisions) effects of economic variables on teacher attrition. In addition, in our analysis of teacher attrition, differentiation between the different reasons for leaving and the different destination states will provide information about the importance of wages and other teacher characteristics on the different motivations and life-cycle choices leading to teacher attrition. Furthermore, our analysis of the corresponding re-entry patterns of former teachers will help to identify which exit types and which determinants of attrition are more likely to lead to permanent rather than temporary exit from teaching. In interpreting attrition data for policy purposes, it clearly is of interest to know the actual rate of return to teaching. Attrition of high quality teachers may only be a real concern if their departures from teaching are permanent or of long duration.

Before turning to the specification of models that can be estimated statistically and that incorporate these theoretical attributes of teacher exit and re-entry decisions, we will first discuss the data used in this study because their nature will affect both the model specification and its estimation.

III. THE DATA SET

The data analyzed in this study were obtained from a U.K. survey undertaken in 1987. The survey covered one out of every six individuals who graduated from universities and other institutions of higher education in 1980 and provides information about the 1980-1987 period in their early career. There are 3978 male and 3163 female graduates in our original sample. This sample size is reduced by omitting individuals from the sample who did not respond to key questions relating to earnings, occupational choices or other variables used in the econometric investigation. The usable sample contains 6098 graduates of whom 3484 were men and 2614 were women. In this sample 923 individuals were full-time school teachers in their first job.

A full description of the survey is contained in Dolton and Makepeace (1992). The variables used in this study can be grouped into: i) social and personal variables; including the social class of the parents as measured by their occupations; ii) educational variables; type of teacher training and education obtained, degree class (a measure related to GPA rank), postgraduate qualifications; iii) work and wage information; the complete work and unemployment history from 1980 to 1987, including, for each job held: sector and type of employment, occupation, starting salary and regional location of job.

One advantage of using this data set is that it contains a relatively large national sample of teachers whose complete early teaching careers were observed even when it involved switching between teaching jobs and migration to other parts of the country. A second attractive feature of these data is that observations on earnings are available for the individuals in the sample at several points in their career. We use the information on teacher salaries to predict the experience-earnings profile for each teacher in the sample and use data on starting wages for those who entered the nonteaching sector to predict each teacher's opportunity wage at each level of teaching experience.

A drawback of the survey is that it only covers the early work history of graduates. Observing individuals in the labor force for six and a half years at a maximum, implied that our analysis of teacher attrition had to be restricted to the first exit out of teaching and that our analysis of teacher re-entry patterns had to be restricted to those teachers who had left teaching within that period. For almost all cases where more than one spell in teaching was observed, the second spell had only just started by the time of the 1987 interview and contains therefore little information about subsequent decisions to leave teaching.

Variable means for the total sample of 923 teachers are reported in the first column of Table 9.1. Of the 923 corresponding spells in teaching, 340 (37 percent) ended with exit from teaching with all other spells "right censored" (CENSOR) at the survey date in 1987.[5] The typical teacher in our sample is female, received a bachelor's degree from a polytechnic (UNIV=0) rather than from a university (UNIV=1), had attended a public high school (SCHTYPE=0), rather than an independent one (SCHTYPE=1), had no postgraduate qualifications (ACA=0, NACA=0) and experienced about three months of unemployment (UNBJ1) before accepting the teaching job.

Of all teachers 71.5 percent are female, 7.5 percent obtained a certificate of education (CERT), 41 percent have a bachelor's in education (BED) and 38 percent a postgraduate certificate of education (DPGCOE). Thus, of a total of 923 teachers, 124 (13 percent) have no teaching qualifications, i.e., neither a bachelor's in education, nor a postgraduate teaching certificate nor a nondegree teaching certificate. Secondary school teachers (SECONDARY) outnumber primary school teachers 83.5 percent to 16.5 percent. Further, 6 percent of teachers obtained a postgraduate academic qualification (ACA) while 4 percent received a nonacademic professional qualification (NACA). Almost 10 percent of the teachers in our sample reported that they had started their first job rather reluctantly (RELC), mainly because they could not find anything better or more suitable at the time, and 13 percent taught in the greater London area (LONDON).

Table 9.1: Sample Means

Variable	Total Sample	Stayers	Movers
DURAT	54.12	67.39	31.37
CENSOR	0.632	1.0000	0.000
SECONDARY	0.835	0.847	0.815
CERT	0.075	0.069	0.085
BED	0.414	0.441	0.368
DPGCOE	0.382	0.374	0.397
SCIENG	0.148	0.142	0.159
DEGCLASS	4.556	4.580	4.515
UNIV	0.412	0.386	0.456
ACA	0.062	0.053	0.076
NACA	0.040	0.019	0.076
MALE	0.285	0.316	0.232
UNBJ1	2.970	2.921	3.053
SCHTYPE	0.063	0.045	0.094
RELC	0.099	0.079	0.132
SCLASS	4.506	4.412	4.668
LONDON	0.127	0.122	0.135
PRE80EXP	0.735	0.740	0.725
UNEM(1)	8.960	9.336	8.314
SWAGE	2488	2517	2438
FWAGE[1]	----	2754	---
NUMBER OF OBS.	923	583	340

[1] Calculated for nonmissing wage observations only. All wages are deflated into 1976 pounds.

In columns 2 and 3 those who were still teaching in 1987 are compared to those who had left teaching sometime before 1987. On average, male teachers, teachers with a bachelor's degree in education, with high starting salaries (SWAGE) and teachers who started their first jobs in regions with relatively high unemployment rates (UNEM(1)) are more likely to continue teaching. Movers are more likely to be teachers with postgraduate academic or nonacademic qualifications, graduates with a university degree, teachers who went to an independent high school, who live in the greater London area and those belonging to a higher social class (SCLASS).[6] Movers are also more likely to have started in their first teaching job reluctantly.

Table 9.2 gives variable means by type of exit: distinguishing first between those who left teaching for a nonteaching job (column 2) and those who left for the nonemployment state (column 3). In total, 25 percent of those who exit from teaching leave for a nonteaching job with all others leaving employment altogether. In our sample 22 percent of the teachers who left for a nonteaching job found other employment in the education sector (as university teacher or in administration), 31 percent found work in the legal, welfare and health sectors or found jobs as social scientists, 14 percent found jobs in business or management and 7 percent were employed as engineers or technicians.

Comparing these two types of movers, we find that those leaving for a nonteaching job are more likely to be male, less likely to have a bachelor's degree in education and more likely to have a postgraduate certificate of education or postgraduate academic qualifications than those who stop working. They also have higher average degree levels (DEGCLASS, ranked from eight (first degree) to two (pass) and one for nondegree holders), are more likely to have gone to an independent secondary school, live in the greater London area and have more pre-1980 work experience (PRE80EXP). Teachers who were awarded a degree by a university rather than a polytechnic, those with a degree in one of the sciences or engineering (SCIENG) and those living in regions with high average unemployment rates were also more likely to change careers instead of leaving the work force.

Columns 4 and 5 of Table 9.2 provide the mean for each variable for those who left teaching by reason for leaving, differentiating between voluntary exit on the one hand and involuntary exit and exit for family-related reasons on the other.[7] Compared to those leaving involuntarily or for family reasons, voluntary leavers are more likely to be male, have a science or engineering degree, have higher average degree scores, and are more likely to have a university degree rather than a degree from a polytechnic. On average, they are also more likely to have postgraduate academic qualifications, more likely to reside in the greater London area, have on average more pre-1980 work experience and more often started their first job in teaching reluctantly. On the other hand, voluntary leavers are less likely to have a bachelor's degree in education or a teaching certificate and fewer of them obtained postgraduate professional qualifications. Finally, the voluntary leavers on average had earned

Table 9.2: Sample Means of Movers by Exit Type

Variable	Movers	Exit to Nonteaching Job	Exit to Non-Employment	Voluntary Exits	Involuntary/ Family-related Exits
DURAT	31.37	38.14	29.12	34.82	29.19
SECONDARY	0.815	0.835	0.808	0.848	0.793
CERT	0.085	0.082	0.086	0.061	0.101
BED	0.368	0.318	0.384	0.326	0.394
DPGCOE	0.397	0.447	0.380	0.455	0.361
SCIENG	0.159	0.153	0.161	0.167	0.154
DEGCLASS	4.515	4.635	4.475	4.841	4.308
UNIV	0.456	0.518	0.435	0.523	0.413
ACA	0.076	0.082	0.075	0.144	0.034
NACA	0.076	0.071	0.078	0.068	0.082
MALE	0.232	0.376	0.184	0.409	0.120
UNBJ1	3.053	3.212	3.000	2.977	3.101
SCHTYPE	0.094	0.106	0.090	0.098	0.091
RELC	0.132	0.141	0.129	0.144	0.125
SCLASS	4.668	4.600	4.690	4.621	4.697
LONDON	0.135	0.153	0.129	0.159	0.120
PRE80EXP	0.725	1.300	0.533	1.216	0.413
UNEM(1)	8.314	9.055	8.067	9.005	7.876
SWAGE	2438	2481	2424	2503	2397
SNWAGE[1]	---	2428	---	2630	1577
NUMBER OF OBS.	340	85	255	132	208

[1] Calculated for nonmissing wage observations only. All wages are deflated into 1976 pounds.

higher starting salaries in teaching than those who left teaching for other reasons, and those who left voluntarily for a nonteaching job on average earned a starting salary in the nonteaching sector (SNWAGE) that was much higher than that of those who had switched to a nonteaching job involuntarily.

The average length of time former teachers spend away from the profession (DURAT2) as well as other variable means for the total sample of 340 teachers who left teaching before the 1987 survey date are reported in the first column of Table 9.3. Of the 340 spells or periods of absence from teaching, 146 (43 percent) ended in a return to teaching with all other spells right censored (CENSOR2) at the time of the 1987 survey.

Means of the variables for those who return and those who do not within the period of observation are given in columns 2 and 3. Teachers who left teaching voluntarily and not for family reasons (VOLUNTARY), and those who left for a nonteaching job (NONTEACH) rather than nonemployment, were far less likely to return to teaching than other former teachers. In fact, of the 43 percent of former teachers who returned, only 8 percent returned from a nonteaching job, while all others returned from a temporary departure from the labor force. Similarly, of those who returned only 25 percent had left teaching voluntarily rather than involuntarily or because of family and health related reasons.

Also less likely to return are former secondary school teachers, teachers with a postgraduate certificate of education, those with a science or engineering degree, and those with higher degree scores. Male teachers, teachers with a university degree and with professional postgraduate qualifications also have lower rates of return. Former teachers living in regions with relatively low unemployment rates at the time of leaving teaching (UNEMLV) are more likely to return to the teaching profession and of the teachers who had left teaching for a nonteaching job those with higher starting wages in that sector were much less likely to return. It is noteworthy that the average real starting salary of returning teachers (SWAGRT) in this sample was in fact lower than the average real starting wage they earned in their first teaching job (SWAGE).

The usefulness of this comparison of returning and nonreturning teachers for studying teacher re-entry behavior is somewhat limited by our sample design. Given the fixed length of the observation period (1980-87), the observed differences may reflect not only differences in the rate of reentry among teachers but also differences in the exit rate from teaching. Generally, for those teachers who left teaching early in the observation period the probability of observing a re-entrance before the end of the observation period, i.e., before the survey date in 1987, was much larger than for those who left towards the end of the observation period. As shown in Table 9.3, the average duration of the first teaching spell for those who returned to teaching was much shorter than that of those who did not. The differences in average characteristics between those who

Table 9.3: Sample Means of Former Teachers by Re-Entry Type

		All Former Teachers		Left before 1984	
Variable	Total Sample	Return to teaching	Do not Return	Return to teaching	Do not Return
DURAT2	23.05	13.53	30.22	15.13	51.53
CENSOR2	0.571	0.000	1.000	0.000	1.000
NONTEACH	0.250	0.082	0.376	0.062	0.300
VOLUNTARY	0.388	0.253	0.490	0.196	0.514
DURAT	31.37	24.64	36.44	15.65	16.63
SECONDARY	0.815	0.774	0.845	0.732	0.957
CERT	0.085	0.116	0.062	0.134	0.043
BED	0.368	0.425	0.325	0.412	0.329
DPGCOE	0.397	0.356	0.428	0.330	0.371
SCIENG	0.159	0.116	0.191	0.134	0.214
DEGCLASS	4.515	4.130	4.804	3.928	5.014
UNIV	0.456	0.377	0.515	0.371	0.543
ACA	0.076	0.089	0.067	0.082	0.086
NACA	0.076	0.055	0.093	0.082	0.143
MALE	0.232	0.144	0.299	0.134	0.414
UNBJ1	3.053	3.260	2.897	2.794	3.014
SCHTYPE	0.094	0.089	0.098	0.103	0.114
RELC	0.132	0.116	0.144	0.134	0.157
SCLASS	4.668	4.733	4.619	4.722	4.629
LONDON	0.135	0.137	0.134	0.134	0.143
PRE80EXP	0.725	0.675	0.763	0.593	0.871
UNEMLV	9.371	8.704	9.873	8.386	9.930
SWAGE	2438	2455	2425	2457	2385
SNWAGE[1]	2428	1865	2517	1488	2756
SWAGRT[1]	---	2114	---	2114	---
NUMBER OF OBS	340	146	194	97	70

[1] Calculated for nonmissing wage observations only. All wages are deflated into 1976 pounds.

returned to teaching compared to those who did not may therefore reflect to some extent the difference in average characteristics of early versus late leavers. In order to adjust partly for the latter differences and to focus solely on the differences between those who return and those who do not, we also present in Table 9.3 the mean values for only those teachers who had entered and left teaching during the first three years of observation, i.e., during the 1980-83 period. The means for those who subsequently returned are given in column 4 and for those who did not in column 5. The differences between the two groups are almost exactly the same as before, while in this comparison the average completed duration in teaching (DURAT) for both groups is now about the same, implying that the differences in characteristics observed earlier can be correctly interpreted as reflecting differences in average re-entry rates, and not differences in exit rates.

In the next section hazard models are specified relating the rate of exit from teaching at each level of teaching experience to a set of individual characteristics, including a teacher's current salary and a measure of his or her expected earnings in the nonteaching sector. Similarly, in our analysis of teacher re-entry decisions, the re-entry rate into teaching will be related to a set of individual characteristics that include the actual or predicted earnings in the nonteaching sector, and the salary expected when returning to teaching. Because our data set contains only partial information on these different wage measures, several estimation procedures were adopted to construct these measures using the available earnings data.

As mentioned earlier, the survey includes information about wages at several points in each individual's career. First, we know for each teacher in our sample his or her starting salary. Further, for teachers who have not left the profession by 1987, the "stayers", we observe the salary earned in 1987 (FWAGE in Table 9.1). With wage information at two points in time, we first estimated an earnings-growth function, that is, a relationship between rate of earnings growth and other pertinent variables, for teachers. Estimates of this function were then used to predict each teacher's salary at each level of teaching experience, conditional on his or her actual starting wage as well as other individual characteristics. Similarly, data on starting salaries of former teachers who had opted for a nonteaching job and data on the starting wages of graduates whose first full-time job was outside the teaching sector were employed to estimate a nonteaching starting wage equation. This equation relates starting wages in the nonteaching sector to a set of individual characteristics, including the number of months of previous teaching experience. Estimates of this equation were subsequently used to predict for each teacher his or her expected starting salary in the nonteaching sector at each level of teaching experience.[8] These imputed individual specific wage figures, measured at each number of months of teaching experience, were used in the estimation of the hazard models discussed in the next section.

Having discussed the different variables and some aggregate patterns in the data, in the next section we describe the empirical models employed in our multivariate statistical analysis of teacher attrition and re-entry patterns.

IV.   AN EMPIRICAL MODEL OF TEACHER EXIT AND RE-ENTRY DECISIONS

The theoretical considerations discussed in Section II imply that teacher salaries, expected opportunity wages and education background play an important role in teacher turnover decisions. In this section we discuss the econometric models of teacher exit and re-entry decisions that we constructed and estimated to evaluate empirically the importance of these variables as well as that of other characteristics for our sample of beginning teachers.

The perhaps most logical approach to model the relationship between the observed duration of the first spell in teaching (or the duration of the first spell of absence from teaching) and the economic and socio-economic characteristics of teachers would be to specify a regression model with the analyzed duration as dependent variable and the characteristics as explanatory variables. However, two practical aspects of the duration data discussed in the previous section make a simple regression analysis inappropriate: the right-censoring of durations at the end of the period of data collection, and the inclusion of time-varying explanatory variables.

The right-censoring problem refers to the fact that we observe incomplete spells in teaching for those teachers who had not left teaching by the end of the observation period in 1987. The calculated duration in teaching for someone who entered teaching in January 1982 and who is still teaching in June 1987 (the date of the survey) would be 65 months. This is not the actual completed duration in teaching, which is not known to us as we have no information about the length of stay in teaching beyond the survey date. In our sample 63 percent of the first teaching spells were incomplete or "censored" in this way and 57 percent of the spells of absence from teaching were so censored. For these current and former teachers we do not know the actual completed duration, but we do know that it is at least as large as the length of the observed incomplete spell.

One possible way to deal with this problem of partially missing data on completed durations would be to simply ignore these observations from our analysis and focus only on the teachers with completed durations. However, it is quite clear that our results would in this case no longer provide a representative description of the behavior of all teachers. Data on the "stayers" (those with right-censored durations) provide us much information about the propensity of teachers to leave teaching and any comprehensive analysis of teacher attrition should therefore include these observations. Similarly, data on censored absence spells give us valuable information about re-entry rates into teaching and ignoring this information will lead to a misrepresentation of the actual duration distribution and will therefore affect the general validity of our results.

The second complication concerns the problem of how to include explanatory variables that vary with calendar time and/or the duration of the teaching spell into a statistical model relating the observed duration in teaching to such variables. We expect attrition and re-entry behavior to be sensitive to changes in labor market conditions. Both teacher salaries and wage offers from other professions generally depend on the accumulated experience in teaching. Accordingly, the (imputed) wage measures that we intend to include as explanatory variables will vary with the number of months of teaching experience. In addition, the local unemployment rate, which varies with calendar time, will be included as a measure of local labor market conditions.

A convenient approach which deals with both complications is to examine the hazard rate or hazard function rather than the distribution of complete and incomplete durations. The hazard rate represents the conditional probability of an exit from a state at a given date given that the individual has occupied the state up to that date.[9] In the case of teacher attrition we can think of the hazard rate as the rate of exit (or the proportion of teachers exiting) from teaching of all teachers with a given number of months of work experience. Thus rather than modelling the length of stay in teaching, we model the risk or hazard rate of leaving teaching. Similarly in our study of re-entry behavior we will model the rate of re-entry or the hazard function of returning to teaching.

In much the same way in which explanatory variables are included in regression models, it is possible to include such variables in a hazard model to capture the differences in the hazard rate at each duration among teachers with different characteristics. Furthermore, it is possible to include explanatory variables that themselves change over time. The hazard rate of leaving teaching at a given date will depend on local market conditions at that date; on the salary currently earned as teacher, which depends on the current tenure in teaching, and on expected earnings in other professions, which may also depend on the attained work experience as teacher as well as current market conditions.

In the most popular specification of the hazard model, the proportional hazard model (Cox, 1972), the hazard or exit rate $h(t)$ at duration t is related to a set of explanatory variables in the form $h(t) = \underline{h}(t) \, exp[X(t)'\beta]$, where $\underline{h}(t)$ is the baseline hazard at duration t, $X(t)$ represents a set of time dependent and stationary explanatory variables at time t (not including a constant) and β is a vector of unknown parameters. In our case $X(t)$ includes the individual's predicted earnings in the teaching and nonteaching sectors and other individual characteristics influencing exit or re-entry decisions. The corresponding coefficients β represent the impact of a change in each of the variables on the conditional probability of an exit. Thus in a hazard model of teacher attrition, a negative coefficient for the current salary variable implies a lower attrition rate for (otherwise identical) teachers earning higher than average teacher salaries. Similarly, a positive coefficient for the expected teacher salary variable in the hazard model of returning to teaching implies that teachers who expect to earn more when returning to teaching will, all other things equal, have a higher rate of re-entry into teaching.

The baseline hazard $\underline{h}(t)$ captures the average exit rate across individuals at each duration. It therefore describes the trend in the average hazard rate over time and will indicate at which tenure levels the risk of leaving or returning to teaching will be greatest and smallest.

Instead of specifying some particular parametric form for the baseline hazard, we chose to leave it unspecified and adopted a semi-parametric estimation procedure similar to that used by Moffitt (1985), Meyer (1990) and Han and Hausman (1990), to simultaneously estimate $\underline{h}(t)$ and β. Details and a discussion of the advantages of this estimation method are provided in Appendix 9.A.

Given the theoretical considerations discussed earlier, we have no a prior reasons to believe that wages and other explanatory variables have the same effect on the different transitions out of teaching. However, if we estimate the model described above, with one single hazard function, we are implicitly assuming that the hazard rate out of teaching does not depend on the state to which a person exits or the reason why the teacher actually left. In this case the estimated parameters will represent the average effects of included variables on the attrition rate, making interpretation of these estimates and inference difficult.

More insight can be gained if we disaggregate by destination state, between exits from teaching into the nonteaching sector and from teaching into the nonemployment state. Alternatively, we can consider the different reasons for leaving, differentiating between voluntary and involuntary exits. It is possible to explore these possibly different mechanisms that govern teacher attrition by adopting a "competing risks" framework. In this framework a separate hazard or transition rate is specified corresponding to each possible transition out of teaching. We will take these cause or destination-specific hazards also to be of the proportional hazard type, each with its own baseline hazard and own vector of coefficients. The specification and estimation of this competing risks model is briefly discussed in Appendix 9.A.

V. ESTIMATION RESULTS

Before discussing the estimates of the hazard models, it will be useful to take a look at the raw duration data for both the first spell in teaching (Figure 9.2) and the first spell of absence from teaching (Figure 9.3). In both figures monthly hazard rates, defined as the ratio of the number of exits in that month over the number of teachers still "at risk", i.e., still in (or absent from) teaching, at the beginning of the month, have been averaged to obtain yearly average hazard rates. Figure 9.2 shows that the average teacher attrition rate is the highest during the first year in teaching and then declines somewhat in the following two

Figure 9.2: Yearly Average Exit Rates out of Teaching

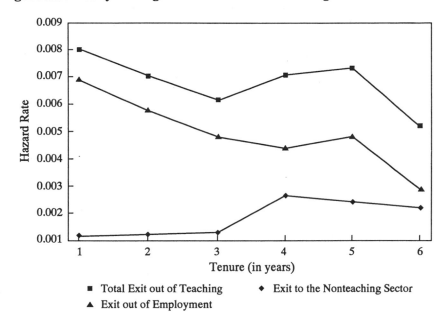

Figure 9.3: Yearly Average Re-entry Rates into Teaching

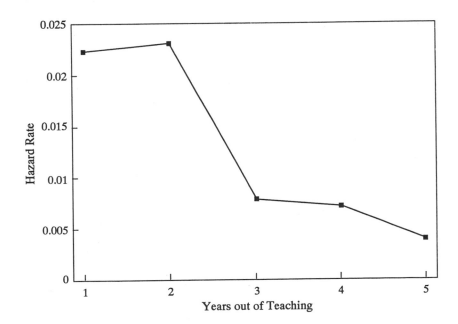

years. Interestingly, the average hazard rate increases again in the fourth and fifth year of teaching. As shown in the same figure, this nonmonotonicity is caused by the sharp increase after the third year in the propensity of teachers to leave for nonteaching jobs. The average hazard rate corresponding to exits to the nonemployment sector, on the other hand, appears to decrease steadily (except for a small increase in the fifth year).

Similar average hazard rates for the first spell of absence from teaching are shown in Figure 9.3. Average re-entry rates are particularly high during the first two years since leaving teaching, but then fall steadily thereafter. This pattern implies that most returning young teachers return to teaching after a relatively brief period of absence.

Estimates of Hazard Models of Teacher Attrition[10]

We first report the estimates of the single risk model. The results confirm that increased earnings do effectively discourage exit and offer, though somewhat weaker, support for the view that the availability of high earnings elsewhere serves to lure teachers away. As shown in Table 9.4, teacher earnings have a negative and significant effect on the exit rate. Potential earnings in the nonteaching sector on the other hand have a positive but insignificant effect. The estimates imply that an equal increase in both types of (log) earnings[11] has almost no effect on the exit rate. This implies that as a response to a given percentage increase in salaries in the nonteaching sector, educational agencies must increase teacher salaries by the same percentage in order to avoid losing more teachers.

Teachers with a bachelor's of education degree have, all else equal, a significantly lower exit rate at each level of teaching experience or tenure as teacher than those with a postgraduate certificate of education or those qualified teachers without a bachelor's degree. Compared to all other teachers, those with a BED are probably the most specialized in teaching and have the most occupation specific education. Those with postgraduate professional or secretarial qualifications have a much greater attrition rate than those who do not, even after controlling for associated differences in both predicted earnings levels. Such qualifications may either indicate that the individual has some preference for or interest in a professional nonteaching career, or better job opportunities in the nonteaching sector.

Teachers who did attend an independent secondary school have a greater than average exit rate and so do teachers with a higher social class background. As is to be expected, graduates who started their first teaching job rather reluctantly, mainly because they could not find anything better or more suitable at the time, are much more inclined to leave teaching than others. Finally, the region's unemployment rate has a negative significant effect on the hazard rate of leaving teaching. A higher unemployment rate may imply that there are fewer

Table 9.4: Estimates of Teacher Attrition Models

Variable	Single Risk Model	Competing Risks			
		Nonteach Sector	Nonempl State	Voluntary Exits	Involuntary/ Family Exits
TWAGE	-1.480*	-2.475	-1.221*	-1.498	-1.458*
	(0.502)	(1.481)	(0.585)	(1.074)	(0.641)
NTWAGE	1.458	5.117*	-0.145	3.882*	-0.999
	(1.000)	(2.178)	(1.348)	(1.580)	(1.686)
MALE	-0.182	0.121	-0.315	0.535	-0.865*
	(0.216)	(0.468)	(0.289)	(0.351)	(0.360)
CERT	-0.247	-0.808	-0.040	-0.911	0.167
	(0.290)	(0.777)	(0.354)	(0.600)	(0.391)
BED	-0.593*	-1.199*	-0.383	-1.079*	-0.262
	(0.229)	(0.605)	(0.274)	(0.423)	(0.322)
DPGCOE	0.042	0.276	-0.044	0.230	-0.103
	(0.176)	(0.443)	(0.212)	(0.340)	(0.242)
ACA	0.307	0.327	0.325	1.033*	-0.514
	(0.200)	(0.607)	(0.237)	(0.308)	(0.400)
NACA	1.332*	1.950*	1.116*	1.625*	1.090*
	(0.236)	(0.655	(0.287)	(0.444)	(0.334)
UNBJ1	0.016	0.044	0.004	0.028	0.001
	(0.012)	(0.030)	(0.015)	(0.020)	(0.017)
SCHTYPE	0.527*	0.599	0.516*	0.453	0.599*
	(0.202)	(0.505)	(0.241)	(0.374)	(0.269)
RELC	0.426*	0.357	0.449*	0.355	0.507*
	(0.167)	(0.421)	(0.201)	(0.317)	(0.226)
SCLASS	0.177*	0.179	0.180*	0.211	0.164*
	(0.061)	(0.162)	(0.071)	(0.122)	(0.085)
SECONDARY	0.017	-0.045	0.050	-0.031	0.072
	(0.161)	(0.513)	(0.186)	(0.351)	(0.211)
LONDON	-0.106	-0.317	0.020	-0.244	0.101
	(0.198)	(0.499)	(0.258)	(0.340)	(0.327)
SCIENG	-0.120	-0.784	0.146	-0.521	0.227
	(0.210)	(0.558)	(0.264)	(0.414)	(0.300)
UNEM	-0.050*	-0.045	-0.050	-0.075	-0.026
	(0.025)	(0.061)	(0.030)	(0.041)	(0.036)
Number of exits	340	85	255	132	208
Log Likelihood	-1870.91	-2004.77		-2013.99	

Number of Spells: 923. Standard errors in parentheses.

outside job opportunities. This effect appears to dominate the likely positive effect on the exit rate caused by an increased risk of layoff.

The estimate of the baseline hazard function is shown in Figure 9.4. The baseline hazard estimate reveals that the exit rate is especially high at twelve months intervals at tenure levels corresponding to the end of each academic year. Clearly this is the result of fixed-term contracts. However, the figure also shows that the risk of leaving teaching at other tenure levels is often quite considerable. In fact in our sample, approximately 61 percent of all exits did not occur at the two peak exit months in each year. Typically there are two smaller spikes between the bigger yearly spikes, suggesting that many teachers may also leave at the end of each school term.

We next estimated a competing risks model that distinguished between exits into the nonteaching sector and exits to the nonemployment state (either unemployment or out of the labor force). Estimates of the propensity to leave for a nonteaching job are shown in column 2 of Table 9.4. The main differences from the single risk model estimates are related to the two wage effects. The negative effect of higher teacher salaries is now much larger, although it is no longer statistically significant at the 5 percent level. Further, the positive effect of higher expected earnings in other occupations is now large and significant.

Teachers with a postgraduate professional degree are estimated to be more likely to leave teaching for an alternative career than those without such a degree. Graduates with a science or engineering degree are, holding potential wages and other characteristics constant, estimated to be *less* likely to exit from the teaching profession for another career. When both effects are considered jointly, having a SCIENG degree rather than another degree has a small negative effect on the probability of a career switch. Given that shortages of teachers have been reported in these areas, the estimates here seem to indicate that the problem may be more one of recruitment than retention.

Estimates of the hazard rate of leaving to the nonemployment state are shown in column 3 of Table 9.4. Teacher salaries reduce the propensity to leave teaching for the nonemployment state. Starting salaries in the nonteaching sector have virtually no effect on this exit probability. These estimates together with those in column 2, clearly indicate that both wage levels play an important but different role in the decision to change careers and in the decision to leave the labor force.

Female teachers have a higher propensity to leave, become unemployed or leave the labor force than men, suggesting that there is a greater demand for their time at home. Having a BED degree still has a negative, but somewhat less pronounced effect on the hazard rate and those with a postgraduate professional degree are more likely to leave the work force than others, possibly representing a temporary exit to unemployment.

When we compare the baseline hazard estimates for both exit types in Figures 9.5 and 9.6, the baseline hazard for exits into the nonteaching sector appears to have no clear time trend, although that for exit to the nonemployment

Figure 9.4: Baseline Hazard Estimate (Single Risk Model)

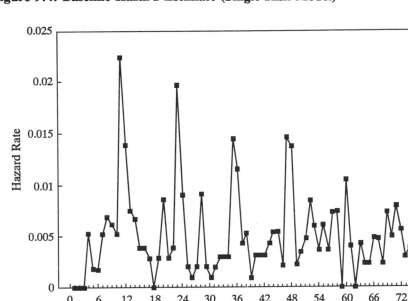

state seems to increase with length of tenure on the job.[12] Another interesting aspect of both graphs is that the peaks present at tenure dates corresponding to the end of an academic year are much less pronounced in the baseline hazard for exit to nonteaching jobs than for exit to any other destination state, suggesting that many teachers who switch careers are more prone than others to quit their teaching jobs at miscellaneous dates during the academic year.

Additional insight into the patterns of teacher attrition can be obtained by distinguishing exits by reason for leaving rather than by destination state. Columns 4 and 5 of Table 9.4 give the parameter estimates for transition rates corresponding to two mutually exclusive reasons for leaving the teaching job: involuntary departures and exits for family or health reasons on the one hand and voluntary exits (for reasons other than family or health) on the other. The latter category includes exits about which the respondent stated that he or she had left the job to obtain a better job or because of other career motives. The first includes those who were dismissed from their job, those who left because a contract had ended and those who left for family, domestic or health reasons.

The results are striking, but are those that could have been expected. While a higher salary earned as a teacher in the two cases has an almost equal effect discouraging teacher attrition, the wages available in nonteaching occupations only have a strong effect on the exit rate in the case of voluntary exit. Female teachers are more likely to leave for family reasons and those who

Figure 9.5: Baseline Hazard – Exit to Nonteaching Sector

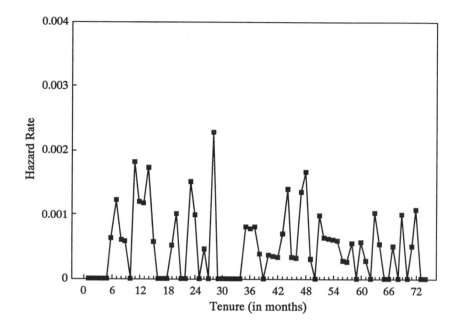

Figure 9.6: Baseline Hazard – Exit to Nonemployment State

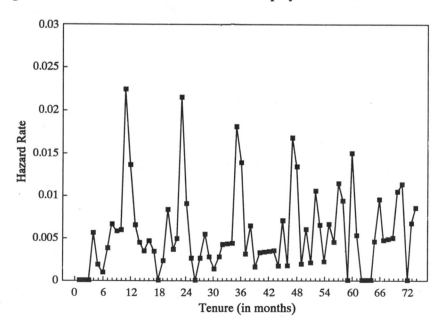

Figure 9.7: Baseline Hazard – Voluntary Exits

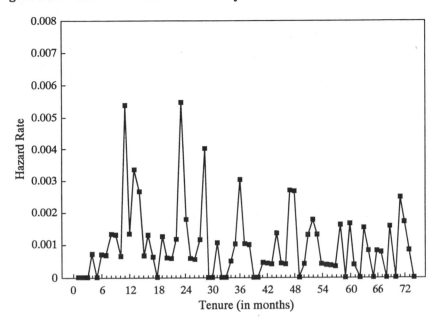

Figure 9.8: Baseline Hazard – Involuntary/Family Related Exits

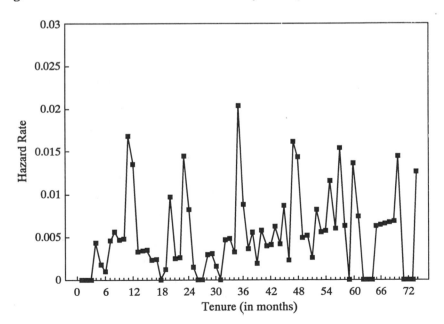

started their first job reluctantly are both more likely to leave voluntarily and to be dismissed or to leave for family or health reasons. Those with academic postgraduate qualifications are more likely to leave voluntarily, but less likely to leave for other reasons. A higher regional unemployment rate has a stronger negative effect on the voluntary exit rate than on the involuntary/family related exit rates. When we compare the baseline hazard estimates for both exit types in Figures 9.7 and 9.8, the baseline hazard for voluntary exit appears to be much less affected by length of tenure in teaching than is true of the hazard of exits for involuntary reasons, which appears to increase with tenure.

Estimate of Hazard Model of Re-entry Decisions

Estimates of the return-to-teaching hazard model are reported in Table 9.5. TWAGELV represents the teacher's estimated salary at the time he or she left teaching and has a (almost significant) positive effect on the re-entry rate, implying that those teachers who left better paying teaching jobs are more likely to return relatively soon to the profession than those who left lower paying teaching jobs. The variable NTWAGEST represents the actual starting salary in the nonteaching sector for those former teachers who had left teaching for a nonteaching job, and it represents the individual's predicted earnings in the nonteaching sector for all other leavers. The effects upon reentry into teaching can, clearly, differ among different types of leavers. However, the estimated negative and significant effect of (predicted) nonteaching earnings upon return to teaching was found to be essentially the same for those who switched careers and those who left employment (NONEMPLOY) altogether. Both estimates show former teachers to be very sensitive to potential earnings both in teaching and elsewhere.

Both the reason for leaving teaching and the state exited to are likely to be important determinants of re-entry behavior. Accordingly we also included indicator variables for exits to the nonteaching sector (NONTEACH) and for involuntary exits and exits for family or health reasons (INVOL). Unfortunately, because of the relatively small sample size it was not feasible to estimate the model for both groups separately. As is to be expected, the re-entry rate among those who changed occupation is much smaller than for those who stopped working. Further, those who left voluntarily are somewhat less likely to return to teaching than those who left involuntarily.

Turning to the other former teachers' characteristics, we find graduates with a bachelor's of education degree or a certificate of education to be somewhat more likely to return and secondary school teachers and those who had started their first teaching job reluctantly to be less likely to return, on average. In addition, the estimate of the coefficient of DURAT, representing the completed duration or accumulated teaching experience, implied that those who left with more teaching experience return less rapidly to teaching. It may be that jobs appropriate for higher experience levels are scarcer than jobs for less experienced teachers.

Finally, the estimated baseline hazard for the likelihood or propensity of returning to teaching, corresponding to the estimates in Table 9.5, is shown in Figure 9.9. It is interesting to note that, unlike the teacher attrition hazard, the monthly teacher return rate does not exhibit any clear systematic pattern of peaks. The re-entry rates are particularly high during the first two years in teaching, but fall quite quickly thereafter.

VI. CONCLUSION

This chapter relating to teaching in the U.K. has drawn attention to two relatively neglected determinants of teacher demand and teacher supply: teacher attrition and re-entry behavior. Time series data indicate the growing importance of the leaving rate in teaching and of the role of recruitment of ex-teachers back to the profession.

We studied both teachers' decisions to leave and decisions to re-enter using cohort data. The method of analysis was the estimation of proportional hazard models. The consistent finding in both the leaving decision and the decision to return to teaching is the importance of remuneration that the individual can obtain by teaching relative to the income offered outside of teaching. The results suggest at the most simplistic level that the lower the wage on offer to teachers and the higher the earnings offered in nonteaching occupations, the more likely they are to leave and not return to teaching.

The importance of relative wages in teacher exit and re-entry rates is illustrated in Table 9.6. The first part of the table shows the estimated percentage of teachers in the sample remaining in the profession after a tenure of one to five years in teaching. For example, the percentage of teachers still in teaching after five years is about 66 percent. An uniform increase in teacher salaries of 10 percent is predicted to increase this percentage to 69 percent, while an increase in expected nonteacher earnings by 10 percent is predicted to decrease it to 62 percent. In our simulations, the estimated decrease in the attrition rate caused by an increase in teacher salaries was the result of approximately equal reductions in the percentages of teachers predicted to leave for a nonteaching career and for a nonemployment alternative. The negative effect on the retention rate of an increase in wages offered in nonteaching professions, on the other hand, was almost entirely due to the increase in the percentage of teachers leaving for nonteaching positions.

The second part of Table 9.6 reports the results of similar simulation exercises to evaluate the effect of wage changes on decisions to return to teaching. The table shows the percentage of former teachers who are predicted to have returned to teaching after an absence of one to four years. A uniform 10 percent increase in teacher salary each reentrant is expected to earn reduces the proportion of former teachers who do not return to teaching within the first four years from 41 percent to 37 percent, a reduction of 10 percent. On the other hand, an increase in the earnings in the nonteaching sector increases this probability to 44 percent.

It is clear that these findings have important policy implications for the retention of teachers and the return of former teachers to the profession -- a phenomenon of growing importance.

Table 9.5: Estimates for Teacher Re-Entry Model

Variable	Estimate	Standard Error
TWAGELV	1.536	0.861
NTWAGEST · NONEMPLOY	-1.124*	0.380
NTWAGEST · NONTEACH	-1.075*	0.404
NONTEACH	-1.749	1.042
INVOL	0.325	0.244
DURAT	-0.013	0.008
MALE	-0.166	0.346
CERT	0.469	0.435
BED	0.514	0.366
DPGCOE	0.182	0.346
ACA	0.486	0.411
NACA	0.419	0.432
UNBJ1	0.019	0.017
SCHTYPE	-0.266	0.389
RELC	-0.418	0.287
SCLASS	0.047	0.096
SECONDARY	-0.345	0.244
LONDON	-0.111	0.293
SCIENG	-0.338	0.351
UNEM	-0.037	0.042
Log Likelihood	-590.43	

Number of Spells: 340 Number of exits: 146

Figure 9.9: Baseline Estimate Re-Entry Hazard

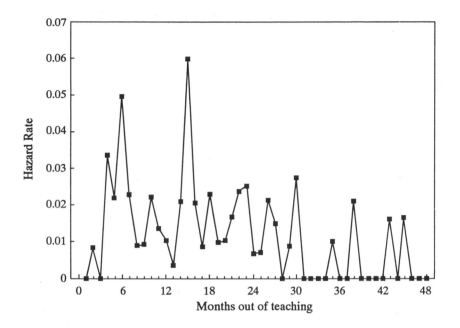

Table 9.6: Predicted Wage Effects on Teacher Attrition and Re-Entry Rates

A. Predicted Percentage of Teachers Remaining in the Profession

Years in Teaching	1	2	3	4	5
Baseline Percentage	0.916	0.835	0.777	0.712	0.657
Teacher Wages +10%	0.926	0.854	0.802	0.743	0.692
Nonteacher Wages +10%	0.904	0.814	0.750	0.679	0.620

B. Predicted Percentage of Former Teachers Not Returned to Teaching

Years out of Teaching	1	2	3	4
Baseline Percentage	0.757	0.549	0.461	0.410
Teacher Wages +10%	0.727	0.508	0.419	0.368
Nonteacher Wages +10%	0.777	0.579	0.492	0.442

Appendix 9.A: The Method of Maximum Likelihood Estimation

In this appendix we discuss in more detail the specification and estimation of the econometric models described in Section IV. As explained in that section our analysis focusses on the hazard function, rather than the density or distribution function of the duration variable. In particular, we adopt a proportional hazard form for the hazard function, $h(t)$, corresponding to the duration variable T (Cox, 1972) with

$$h_i(t) = \underline{h}(t)\ exp[X_i(t)'\ \beta]$$

where $\underline{h}(t)$ is the baseline hazard at time or duration t, $X_i(t)$ is a vector of time dependent and stationary explanatory variables for individual i at time t (not including a constant) and β is a vector of unknown parameters.

Instead of choosing some arbitrary parametric form for the baseline hazard, we left it unspecified and adopted a semiparametric estimation procedure similar to that used by Moffitt (1985), Meyer (1990) and Han and Hausman (1990), to estimate $\underline{h}(t)$ and β simultaneously. This semiparametric approach has the advantage that it prevents inconsistent estimation of the explanatory variable coefficients due to a misspecified baseline hazard and it simultaneously provides a flexible (or nonparametric) estimate of the baseline hazard.

Durations in our data are only observed in terms of whole months, implying that if an observed duration is t_i months, then the actual duration is anywhere between t_i and $t_i + 1$ months. For the proportional hazard model specified above, the probability of a spell being completed by time $t + 1$ given that it was still on going at time t (the "grouped data hazard") is given by[13]

$$Prob(t \leq T < t + 1 \mid T \geq t) = 1 - exp\ [-\ e^{X_i(t)'\beta}\gamma(t)]$$

where $\gamma(s) = \int_s^{s+1} \underline{h}(u)du$ are the integrated baseline hazard pieces. The probability of observing a completed spell of length t is then given by

$$Prob\ (t \leq T < t + 1) = Prob\ (t \leq T < t + 1 \mid T \geq t)\cdot Prob\ (T \geq t)$$

where

$$Prob\ (T \geq t) = 1 - F(t) = \prod_{s=0}^{t-1}\ [1 - Prob\ (s \leq T < s+1 \mid T \geq s)\ ]$$

is the probability of observing an incomplete spell of duration t.

For a sample of N individuals labelled $i = 1,...,N$, each with an observed duration of t_i months and a corresponding censoring indicator d_i, with $d_i=0$ if the spell is censored and $d_i=1$ if it is a completed spell, the sample likelihood (the product of the individual likelihood contributions) is given by

$$L = \prod_{i=1}^{N} [\left\{ Prob \ (t_i \leq T < t_i + 1 \mid T \geq t_i) \right\} \ di$$
$$\prod_{s=0}^{t_i-1} \left\{ 1 - Prob(s \leq T < s +1 \mid T \geq s) \right\} \ ]$$

where the conditional probabilities were defined earlier.

Maximization of the (logarithm of the) likelihood function with respect to β and the hazard pieces, i.e., the $\gamma(\ )$'s, then provides the maximum likelihood estimates reported in Section V.

The class of competing risks models, often referred to as independent competing risks models, is characterized by the presence of multiple kinds of events, where the occurrence of one type of event (for example, exit to the nonteaching sector), removes the individual from risks of other types of events (exit from teaching into the nonemployment state).In the competing risks model we specify J cause-specific transition or hazard rates corresponding to each possible exit type for individual i as $h_{ij}(t)$. Thus $h_{ij}(t)$ represents the conditional density or risk of an exit of type j for individual i at time t. Given that all exit types are mutually exclusive and exhaustive, the single or total hazard rate is then equal to $h(t) = \sum_{j=1}^{J} h_{ij}(t)$. We will take the cause-specific hazards also to be of the proportional hazard type, with its own baseline hazard and the explanatory variables entering into an index $X_i(t)' \ \beta_j$ for exits of type j.

Estimation of the competing risks model, i.e., of the cause-specific hazard functions, is similar to that for the single hazard model described above,and is discussed in detail in Narendranathan and Stewart (1990), Han and Hausman (1990), and Dolton and van der Klaauw (1994).

NOTES

1. It is possible that these dramatic changes were heavily influenced by changing maternity pay legislation in the U.K. in the late 1970s that has given women an added incentive to return to work after childbirth.

2. Full details of teacher relative salaries and their movement over time are provided in Bee and Dolton (1994).

3. In 1960, 50 percent of U.K. women graduates entered teaching on graduation. This figure declined to 32 percent in 1970 and 23 percent in 1980. The same pattern was observed for male graduates. In 1960, 21 percent of them entered teaching on graduation, by 1970 this had fallen to 12 percent and by 1980 to 6 percent.

4. This approach is usually referred to as a "reduced form" approach as opposed to a "structural" approach, in which both the direct effect of these determinants on teacher turnover decisions and their indirect effect through their influence on other life cycle decisions are separately modelled.

5. The term "right censoring" is used in duration analysis to characterize incomplete spells. For teachers who were still employed at the end of the data collection period, we do not know how long they remained in teaching after the survey date. We only know that their total spell length was at least as long as their tenure as teacher in 1987.

6. SCLASS is measured by the parents' occupation, ranked one to six with six representing professional occupations and one representing unskilled occupations.

7. A cross-tabulation of the two exit-type distinctions is presented below.

	Reason for Leaving		
Destination State	Voluntary	Invol./Fam	Total
Nonteaching Sector	66	19	85
Nonemployment State	66	189	255
Total	132	208	340

8. Details of both procedures as well as estimates of both equations can be found in Dolton and van der Klaauw (1993).

9. More formally, if the random variable T represents the duration of a spell, with probability density function $f(t)$ and corresponding distribution function $F(t)$, then the hazard function is defined as $h(t) = f(t)/(1-F(t))$.

10. This section summarizes results from a more extensive empirical analysis reported fully in Dolton and van der Klaauw (1994). In that analysis, we also allowed for the presence of unobserved heterogeneity, but its incorporation had no effect on the estimates reported here.

11. TWAGE and NTWAGE in Table 9.4 represent the (predicted) log earnings in the teaching and nonteaching sectors, respectively, and both vary with tenure in teaching. Identification of the wage effects is achieved through exclusion restrictions, where an individual's degree class, pre-1980 work experience, and institution type (UNIV) are assumed to affect an individual's propensity to leave only through their effect on wages.

12. It should be pointed out, however, that length of tenure tends to raise both types of wages, thereby producing an indirect effect on the hazard of teacher exit, not incorporated in these baseline hazard estimates. They also do not incorporate any effects of time variation in unemployment rates. When we incorporated these indirect effects on the hazard of tenure, however, the hazard shapes still closely resembled those in Figures 9.5 and 9.6.

13. A more detailed derivation of the likelihood function, its estimation and asymptotic properties of the resulting estimates can be found in Meyer (1990).

REFERENCES

Bee, M. and P.J. Dolton. 1994. Teachers' salaries in the UK: An economic examination of time series and cross section evidence. The Manchester School, (forthcoming).

Blackstone, T. and A. Crispin. 1982. How many teachers: Issues of policy, planning and demography. Bedford Way Papers 10. London: Heinneman.

Cox, D. 1972. Regression models and life tables. *Journal of the Royal Statistical Society* B,34: 187-220.

Dolton, P.J. 1990. The economics of UK teacher supply: The graduate's decision. *The Economic Journal* 100: 91-104.

Dolton, P.J. and G. Makepeace. 1992. The early careers of 1980 graduates: Work histories, job tenure, career mobility, and occupational choice. Department of Employment Research Paper 79.

Dolton, P.J. and G. Makepeace. 1993. Female labour force participation and the choice of occupation: The supply of teachers. *European Economic Review* 37: 1393-1411.

Dolton, P.J. and K. Mavromaras. 1994. Intergenerational occupational choice comparisons: The case of teachers in the UK. *The Economic Journal* (forthcoming).

Dolton, P.J. and W. van der Klaauw. 1994. The turnover of UK teachers: A competing risks analysis. Economic Research Report 94-21, C.V. Starr Center for Applied Economics: New York University.

Han, A. and J. Hausman. 1990. Flexible parametric estimation of duration and competing risk models. *Journal of Applied Econometrics* 5: 1-28.

Manski, C. F. 1987. Academic ability, earnings, and the decision to become a teacher: Evidence from the national longitudinal study of the high school class of 1972, *Public sector payrolls*. (ed.) D.A. Wise: The University of Chicago Press.

Meyer, B. 1990. Unemployment insurance and unemployment spells. *Econometrica* 58: 757-782.

Moffitt, R. 1985. Unemployment insurance and the distribution of unemployment spells. *Journal of Econometrics* 28: 85-101.

Murnane, R. and R. Olsen. 1989. The effects of salaries and opportunity costs on duration in teaching: Evidence from Michigan. *Review of Economics and Statistics* 71 (2): 347-352.

Murnane, R, and R. Olsen. 1990. The effects of salaries and opportunity costs on length of stay in teaching: Evidence from North Carolina. *Journal of Human Resources* 25 (1): 106-124.

Murnane, R., J. Singer and J. Willet. 1989. The influences of salaries and "opportunity cost" on teachers' career choices: Evidence from North Carolina. *Harvard Education Review* 59(3): 325-346.

Narendranathan, S.W., and M. Stewart. 1990. An examination of the robustness of models of the probability of finding a job for the unemployed. *Panel data and labor market studies* (eds.) J. Hartog, G. Ridder and J. Theeuwes, North-Holland, Amsterdam.

Thomas, B. and D. Deaton. 1977. *Labour shortage and economic analysis: A study of occupational labour markets*. Oxford: Basil Blackwell.

Van der Klaauw, W. 1993. Female labor supply and marital status decisions: A life cycle model. Economic Research Report 93-23, C.V. Starr Center for Applied Economics: New York University.

Zabalza, A. 1979. The determination of teacher supply. *Review of Economic Studies* 46(1): 131-47.

Zabalza, A., P. Turnbull and G. Williams. 1979. *The economics of teacher supply.* Cambridge: Cambridge University Press.

Zarkin, G. A. 1985. Occupational choice: An application to the market of public school teachers. *Quarterly Journal of Economics* 94: 409-446.

ABOUT THE EDITORS

William J. Baumol is director of the C.V. Starr Center at New York University. He was professor of economics at Princeton University for over forty years until his retirement and since 1970 he held a joint appointment with New York University. He has been president of four professional societies, including the American Economic Association. He is also a member of the Board of Trustees of the National Council on Economic Education and a member of the National Academy of Sciences.

Professor Baumol has published over five hundred articles in all of the leading scholarly journals in economics, including the *American Economic Review,* the *Journal of Political Economy*, and the *Economic Journal* to name but a few. He has also written or edited 30 books that have been translated into a dozen languages. Of particular interest to educators reading this book may be the sixth edition of his textbook *Economics Principles and Policy* (Harcourt Brace Jovanovich, 1994), which he coauthored with Alan Blinder, vice-chairman of the Federal Reserve Board.

Will Baumol was born and raised in New York City. He received his undergraduate degree in economics from the City University of New York and his Ph.D. in economics from the London School of Economics. He is married and has two children and two grandchildren.

William E. Becker is a professor of economics at Indiana University, Bloomington. He is editor of the *Journal of Economic Education* and also serves on the editorial board of the *Economics of Education Review.* Before joining the faculty of Indiana University in 1979, he was a tenured faculty member at the University of Minnesota, where he returned for the academic year of 1988 to serve as acting director of the Management Information Division.

Professor Becker's sixty plus research articles appear in the *American Economic Review, American Statistician, American Journal of Agricultural Economics, Econometric Theory, Economic Inquiry, Journal of Finance, Journal of Human Resources, Journal of Risk and Insurance, Monthly Labor Review, Review of Economics and Statistics,* and other similar scholarly outlets. He has also written or edited seven books. Many of the techniques discussed in this book are presented in more detail in his textbook *Statistics for Business and Economics* (South-Western Publishing, 1995).

Bill Becker is from Racine, Wisconsin. He earned a bachelor's degree in mathematics from the College of St. Thomas, a master's degree from the University of Wisconsin, and a Ph.D. in economics from the University of Pittsburgh. He is married and has three daughters.

CONTRIBUTORS

Masato Aoki
Simmons College

William J. Baumol
New York University and *Princeton University*

William E. Becker
Indiana University

John H. Bishop
Cornell University

David Card
Princeton University

Elchanan Cohn
University of South Carolina

Peter Dolton
University of Newcastle

Rendigs Fels
Vanderbilt University

Susan F. Feiner
College of William and Mary

Frederick Flyer
New York University

Alan B. Krueger
Princeton University

Charles R. Link
University of Delaware

James G. Mulligan
University of Delaware

Sherwin Rosen
University of Chicago

Wilbert van der Klaauw
New York University

INDEX